D1478915

RELIGIOUS RADICALS IN
TUDOR ENGLAND

¶ The ninth booke containyng the

Actes and thynges done in the reigne of kyng
Edvvard the 6.
(*ₓ*)

Woodcut added by John Foxe to the 1570 edition of his *Actes and Monuments*
(p. 1483), setting forth the special virtues of the Edwardian Church of England:
its emphasis on the Bible and on preaching; its reduction of the sacraments to
baptism and communion administered from a table in the body of the church; its
resolute purging of 'images' and other material symbols of 'popery'.

RELIGIOUS RADICALS IN TUDOR ENGLAND

J.W. MARTIN

PREFACE BY
A.G. DICKENS

THE HAMBLEDON PRESS
LONDON AND RONCEVERTE

Published by The Hambledon Press, 1989

102 Gloucester Avenue, London NW1 8HX (U.K.)

309 Greenbrier Avenue, Ronceverte WV 24970 (U.S.A.)

ISBN 1 85285 006 X

British Library Cataloguing in Publication Data

Martin, J.W. (Joseph William)
   Religious radicals in Tudor England.
   1. England Established Church Dissent, 1500-1600
   I Title
   322'. 1'0942

Library of Congress Cataloging-in-Publication Data

Martin, J.W. (Joseph W.), 1913-
   Religious radicals in Tudor England.

   Includes index.
   1. Separatists – England – History – 16th century
   2. England – Church history – 16th century
   3. Radicals – England – History – 16th century
   I. Title
   BR377.M36 1989 280'.4   88-34788

Printed and bound in Great Britain by
The Camelot Press, Southampton

Contents

List of Illustrations

Acknowledgements

All but two of the chapters in this book were, in whole or in part, previously published elsewhere and are reprinted here by kind permission of the original publishers. In most of the reprinted articles some duplicative passages have been condensed or removed, and in several of them substantial new material has been added.

3. *Archive for Reformation History*, vol. 77 (1986), pp. 281–313.
4. *Sixteenth Century Journal*, vol. 7, no. 2 (October 1976), pp. 55–74.
5. *Renaissance Quarterly*, vol. 34 (1981), pp. 359–83.
6. *Huntington Library Quarterly*, vol. 44 (1981), 231–47.
7. *Journal of Ecclesiastical History*, vol. 35 (1984), pp. 519–38.
9. *Bulletin of the Institute of Historical Research*, vol. 58 (1985), pp. 248–51.
10. *Journal of British Studies*, vol. 20, no. 1 (1980), pp. 53–73.
11. *Sixteenth Century Journal*, vol. 10, no. 2 (1979), pp. 15–22.
12. *Baptist Quarterly*, vol. 29, no. 6 (April 1982), pp. 267–81.

Acknowledgement is made also to the Huntington Library (San Marino, California) for permission to reproduce the illustration used in Chapter 5, and to the Folger Library (Washington) for permission to reproduce those appearing in Chapters 2, 7, 8 and 10 and the frontispiece.

To the Folger Library I am indebted in additional ways – directly for the unfailing help of its staff (as in a number of other libraries also) and indirectly for varied assistance from scholars brought there by its formal programs or its research facilities. Of those who have kindly given a critical look at a draft of mine or otherwise applied their expertise to my problems, most have been fellow readers at the Folger. Such debts are more extensive than I can well record here, but in addition to those indicated in particular footnotes, I wish to acknowledge now the varied assistance received over the past decade or so from E.J. Baskerville, Patrick Collinson, John Fines, Christopher Hill, Joel Hurstfield, Jennifer Loach, Jean Dietz Moss, Lois G. Schwoerer, Robert Tittler, Dewey D. Wallace, Jr., Irving and Marion Wechsler. My gratitude to A.G. Dickens is in a special category. He first launched me on the ordered investigation of Tudor religious and social history, has provided many fresh insights since, and has never been too busy to respond to new queries.

Preface

I first met Dr Joseph Martin in 1972 as a member of a seminar I was conducting in Washington at the Folger Library, that refined haven of humane study and scholarly companionship, somewhat oddly placed on Capitol Hill. He had recently retired from over a quarter-century of service, mainly as a political analyst, in the U.S. Government's intelligence community, and I was initially puzzled by his degree of sophistication in sixteenth-century English social history. Later on the mystery cleared when I learned that he had previously pursued a lively academic career.

Born in Philadelphia and a graduate of nearby Haverford College, he had taken a second B.A. at Oxford (St. Catherine's) in English language and literature and had taught in that field for several years at Black Mountain College, North Carolina, and then more briefly at Barnard College (Columbia) and the City University of New York. He looks back on the Black Mountain years as unusually stimulating, partly because Black Mountain was in its time (it closed in 1956) an innovative institution, attempting tasks in the 1930s which universities generally confronted twenty years later, and partly because of the interesting visitors its activities attracted. Its placing art and music in the centre of a liberal arts curriculum, for example, brought several former members of the Bauhaus to its staff and Walter Gropius to visit the place, while John Dewey, a member of the college's Advisory Council, would spend an informal spring week or two there, on one occasion bringing with him Albert Barnes, the idiosyncratic art collector and critic.[1] The latter part of Martin's formal graduate study at Columbia University introduced him to the general subject of religious radicalism. His doctoral dissertation, written under the supervision of the distinguished William Haller, was called *The English Revolution and the Rise of Quakerism, 1650-1660*. It left him, he has since remarked, not only with a detailed knowledge of one seventeenth-century sect, but also with a conviction that the roots of religious radicalism in the Tudor period needed further investigation.

Since 1972 Joe Martin has frequently consulted me on mid-sixteenth-

---

[1] Martin Duberman, *Black Mountain College: an Exploration in Community* (London 1974); Mary Emma Harris, *The Arts at Black Mountain College* (Cambridge, Mass. 1987).

century problems, but he has probably taught me as much as I have taught him. For example, largely through the effects of this friendship I am now greatly enlarging my hitherto perfunctory passages on the sects, as I struggle to rewrite my book, *The English Reformation*. In Martin's present book it will be apparent even from the Table of Contents that in discussing Tudor religious radicals he has not narrowly confined his attention to Protestant separatists but has also investigated anti-separatist Protestants and even a Roman Catholic or two, in all cases seeking to place them in their social context. This extension of scope forms a strong feature of the volume, not least because the frontiers dividing the sects from the major struggle between Roman Catholics and Prayer Book Protestants remain so untidy. The Catholics strove to combat the growth of orthodox Protestantism by pointing to sectarian chaos as the inevitable outcome of all specifically Protestant belief. On the other hand, there arose under the hammer of the Marian persecution a 'natural' kinship between the Prayer Book Protestants and the more moderate of the separatists. John Bradford and others sought to shepherd such moderates back into the orthodox Protestant fold. Among the interesting group known as Freewillers (chap. 3) this process had already been exemplified before Mary's accession by the return to orthodoxy of the better-educated members, such as the two clerics Robert and Thomas Cole. Likewise within the body of persecuted orthodox Protestants, largely severed both from gentry and from the upper hierarchy, the main leadership devolved upon laymen and a few humble priests, who (chap. 7) had no choice but to create underground congregations with something resembling a sectarian ethos.

This problem of ill-defined boundaries as between orthodox Protestants and separatists survived to haunt the martyrologist John Foxe, no mere detached historian but a major protagonist in a mortal struggle. How could anyone in his position avoid becoming in some measure a propagandist? He stood divided between this compulsion and the converse need for accurate coverage, since when in 1563 he produced his first full edition, most of the witnesses remained alive. In the event, as Martin shows (chap. 9), he softened or even concealed the unorthodoxy of several people now known from other evidence to have been separatists. While this situation did not obliterate his prevalent regard for the truth of his enormous and (for its time) admirably researched account, there still remain hereabouts some vulnerable areas with which we must learn to reckon.

These are by no means the only broad contextual issues treated in this present collection. The author also contributes valuably in at least two items (chaps. 5 and 6) to our modern controversies regarding the potential of the Marian Reaction. The pathetic shortness of its opportunity to re-catholicise England had always been apparent. Again, not long ago Dr Pogson described the chronic financial stringency which hampered the efforts of Cardinal Pole.[2] The key to this situation was doubtless the Queen herself, and her case calls for something more than a merely personal compassion. As we may now see, the cards were more heavily stacked against her than far more intelligent observers could have perceived in 1553. Her resolute but emotional attempt to shift nationalist England into the Habsburg orbit showed an obtuse insensitivity toward English nationalism, yet at first she could not have guessed that Spain was on a collision course with the Papacy, or that the power of Philip II to control northern Europe from the Netherlands would prove distinctly limited. All the same, even Mary might conceivably have realised that, whatever safeguards might be imposed, the introduction of a Spanish King of England must gravely complicate the religious struggle, and even that the English had in recent times failed to evince any signs of affection for Rome. Above all, Mary and her Spanish advisers never grasped that a tough Protestantism had struck deep roots into the politically significant areas of England: London, East Anglia, Essex and Kent. In addition the new beliefs had already made strong forays into East Sussex, the Thames Valley, Gloucestershire and parts of the West Midlands. This situation had occurred quite rapidly and in large part between 1547 and 1553. It has been minimised on what seems to me merely negative evidence by some revisionist historians; but was not the strength and tenacity of south-eastern Protestantism triumphantly demonstrated amid the harsh trials of 1554–1558?

Given a longer reign would not Mary have developed the intelligence to set the process in reverse? An affirmative answer would seem to represent a sublime optimism. Her Spanish loyalties, her very piety and sincerity, committed her to her Spanish advisers, experts on the crushing of heresy by the antiquated, legalist mechanisms: visitation, detection, trial and burning. As the Jesuits realised – though Reginald Pole and the Marian hierarchy did not – the battle against ideas had to be fought with ideas, and fought not only in the pulpit but through the press. On this all-important theme Dr Martin presents (chap. 6) some lively examples and conclusions.

This book would seem opportune, since the middle decades of the sixteenth century still need just the sort of prodding and gap-filling which it exemplifies. Even the literary attacks by the foes of both orthodox Protestants and separatists are here made to disgorge genuine information. So often shunned by medievalists and Elizabethans alike, this period from the forties to the sixties must now appear – though in senses somewhat different from those of the old-style ecclesiastical history – one of the more dramatic watersheds in the history of the nation. I hope that Martin's readers will conclude that it demands

[2] R.H. Pogson, 'Revival and reform in Mary Tudor's Church, a question of money', *J.E.H.*, xxv (1974), pp. 249–65.

attention both as sequel and as prelude, yet also in its own creative right. Transcending politics, it turned even persecution to profit, giving birth to numerous ancestors, including those of Anglicanism and Puritanism, the Baptists and the Society of Friends. And even more remarkably, through Mary's failure, it saw the birth-pangs of a nobler Catholicism in England.

A.G. DICKENS

Abbreviations

A. & M.	John Foxe, *Actes and Monuments*, J. Pratt, ed., 8 vols. (London 1870–77).
A.P.C.	*Acts of the Privy Council, new series*, J.R. Dasent, ed., 32 vols. (London 1890-1907).
Bradford	John Bradford, *Writings*, A. Townsend, ed., 2 vols. (Cambridge 1848-53).
B.I.H.R.	*Bulletin of the Institute of Historical Research.*
Burrage	Champlin Burrage, *The Early English Dissenters, 1500–1641*, 2 vols. (Cambridge 1912).
DNB	*Dictionary of National Biography.*
Eccl. Mem.	John Strype, *Ecclesiastical Memorials of the Church of England under Henry VIII, Edward VI and Mary*, 3 vols. (Oxford 1822).
J.E.H.	*Journal of Ecclesiastical History.*
L. & P.	*Letters and Papers of Henry VIII*, J.S. Brewer, James Gairdner, R.H. Brodie, eds., 2 vols. plus 2 addenda (London 1864–1932)
Original Letters	*Original Letters Relative to the English Reformation, 1537–1558*, H. Robinson, ed. (Cambridge 1846–47).
STC	*Short-Title Catalogue of Books Printed in England, 1475–1640.* (London 1926; revised 1976 & 1985).
Tudor Procl.	*Tudor Royal Proclamations*, P.L. Hughes, J.F. Larkin, eds., 3 vols. (New Haven 1964–69).

To the Memory of my Father

Chapter 1

Introduction

This volume was written on the assumption that the history of a society is not complete without an examination of figures who in some significant respect were dissatisfied with that society. Those treated here were radicals not in the sense of having fundamental critiques of Tudor institutions or greatly different patterns to propose, but merely in their following lines of activity that were incompatible with one or more of the basic premises of their society.

They varied greatly from each other. Henry Hart and his associates belonged to the mid-century separatist group known to historians as the Freewillers. Christopher Vitel and his fellow members of the Elizabethan Family of Love were followers of the North German mystic, Hendrik Niclas, who founded the sect on the continent around 1540. Miles Hogarde, the most effective of the Roman Catholic writers in the pamphlet war against the Protestants in Mary's reign, nevertheless chafed at his church's ban on lay preaching. Robert Crowley had no use either for Roman Catholics or for Protestant separatists, but he was ready to defy Archbishop Parker to his face on a point of conscience. John Foxe inclined to Crowley's non-conforming position on ecclesiastical vestments and held other views unusual in his time, but managed to avoid such confrontations throughout his long and honoured life.

All of them enlarge our knowledge of everyday life in the Tudor world and all made that world in some degree different from what it would have been without them. Their importance for the historian, however, lies more in the light they cast on their society than on any change they immediately effected in it. Only Foxe may be said to have directly influenced the course of English history; the modern dissenting churches look back to figures later than Tudor separatists as their founders. Yet even the most obscure of the radicals indicate aspects of Tudor society which troubled sensitive persons and led some to risk that society's harsh penalties against dissidents. In so doing they often cast shadows taller than themselves.

The pages which follow examine Tudor radicals mainly in terms of three significant phenomena of their time. First to be considered is the evolution of the conventicle. Related to this phenomenon, and to each other, are two more: the impact of the vernacular Bible on working-class Englishmen, and the accelerating growth of print culture. In some instances of the radicals' activity a degree of influence on the future is detectable; in others, their behaviour may do no more than identify an early appearance of some shift in religious sensibility recognized only in subsequent generations.

One such shift is illustrated by the Family of Love, which so disturbed Elizabeth's government as to elicit a royal proclamation against them in 1580. A point much urged against them, and implicitly admitted by the Familists themselves, was their willingness to conform publicly to the worship of the established church while holding to their own beliefs and ceremonies privately. To an age in which many saw heresy as threatening the whole fabric of society, uncertainty about a group's real beliefs was a serious matter, and present day distinctions between public religious practice and private belief were little appreciated. Committed Protestants and Roman Catholics in mid-sixteenth-century England both saw as sinful any participation in the other church's rites. Somewhat over a century later, however, the Familist practice had become essentially that followed by the Free Masons of various European countries in conducting their own rituals in private while conforming publicly to the established church of their country, whether Protestant or Roman Catholic. It was not greatly unlike the position taken by dissenters during the Occasional Conformity controversy of Queen Anne's reign, when a Presbyterian Lord Mayor might attend services in his own Presbyterian meeting house on the same Sunday that he took communion in the parish church as a requisite for holding political office. Evidence is virtually nil for lines of descent linking Elizabethan Familists to either of these later bodies, but the Familists' proselytizing success in the England of the 1570s does suggest that even then a body of Englishmen was prepared to make a conscientious separation between public and private religion.

The conventicle, as described in the first of the chapters following, is one of the phenomena which must always be taken into account as part of the background of sixteenth-century religious developments. Just as we must assume among some Tudor Englishmen a continuing fondness for the 'images' which Protestant reformers removed from the churches, so we must assume among others a tendency to assemble, on their own initiative and without the presence of an authorized cleric, in periodic meetings for Bible-reading and discussion of religious questions. Laymen, mainly of the artisan class, ran these gatherings and apparently felt that the group had what religious authority it needed through its access to the Bible. Women are frequently mentioned as participants, though never as leaders; the occasional cleric who attended was present in no official capacity. Conventicles, as these meetings came increasingly to be called, tended to be evanescent things, with little organization or formal discipline; they were easy to start and easy to snuff out in the individual case, but collectively difficult to suppress. They seem to have been a phenomenon familiar enough to be taken for granted in most contemporary references; only in special circumstances are the nature and activity of a particular conventicle described. Descriptions are to be found, however, in depositions made by two disgruntled ex-Familists about their former 'congregation' to a Surrey magistrate in 1561 and in a letter written to the same Surrey magistrate later in that decade by an alert Guildford schoolmaster (subsequently Provost of King's College, Cambridge) who was worried about the spread of Anabaptism. The letter, incidentally, indicates no awareness of the earlier conventicle in the immediate neighbourhood.

Unlike the parish church, with its parson responsible to the bishop and other officials above him, the conventicle offered no means by which the authorities might control it or even be aware of what went on there. They naturally regarded it with suspicion. By its nature it could provide a haven for persons of widely differing views and particularly for those sharply opposed to the established church. The imprisoned Protestant leader, John Hooper, recognized this when he advised his flock in the early months of Mary's reign to counter the return of the parish churches to the Roman rite by holding their own private meetings for religious discussion and spiritual support. As described in another of the chapters which follow,[1] these particular conventicles of Mary's reign in most cases sought to replicate the services of Edwardian parish churches and thought of themselves as orthodox Protestant churches forced by circumstances to worship in secret. In the eyes of the Marian church, however, they were mere conventicles and, in fact, the scarcity of ordained Protestant clerics in Marian England compelled all but a few of these lay-run gatherings to be conducted in much the same manner as more radical religious meetings.

Though we cannot with confidence say exactly what went on in a popular conventicle, the two fullest descriptions by participants (those by Kentish Freewillers *c*. 1551 and those by the two Surrey Familists in 1561)[2] both indicate that there was much discussion of various religious doctrines. Much of the early history of the Freewillers, indeed, reads somewhat like a lower class layman's version of the informal meetings at the White Horse Inn in the Cambridge of the 1520s, when the new doctrines coming out of Germany were discussed by young clerics who later took contrasting lines in English church history.

Discussion within the conventicle would in time foster the emergence of the figure known in the seventeenth century as a 'mechanick preacher'. Christopher Vitel of the Familists and Henry Hart of the

---

[1] See chapter 7.
[2] See chapter 3, section 3; chapter 10, sections 2, 5.

Freewillers are obvious sixteenth-century examples of the articulate artisan anxious to expound his religious views for a larger public, though (for reasons of personal safety) doing so less publicly than their seventeenth-century counterparts.[3] Nor was this strong desire by laymen to expound religious questions found only among radical Protestants. The London hosier, Miles Hogarde, a loyal Roman Catholic, shows it in a number of his works as much as any lay preacher. Recognizing that the church forbids preaching by laymen, he argues that the ban does not apply to expounding religious matters in print.[4]

A second phenomenon of Tudor England – seen especially in some of the Protestant separatists – was increased interest in the vernacular Bible, accompanied by gradually spreading literacy. Access to the Bible did not really depend on literacy (as several generations of Lollard activity bear witness) but was much facilitated by it. A new stage was reached in the years 1538-41, when Henry VIII authorized an English translation of the Bible, which had previously been a prohibited book, and ordered copies to be placed in parish churches. His subsequent attempts to restrict its readership to the landed and merchant classes were ineffective. For persons of the excluded categories like Henry Hart, the Bible proved a revolutionary document, its discovery possibly linked with the personal excitement of learning to read.[5] It was certainly linked with the religious conviction (set forth explicitly by John Champneys in *The harvest is at hand*) that, for earnest and godly laymen, possession of the Holy Scriptures made the clergy irrelevant. The Bible provided the key to salvation, innumerable points of guidance for man's daily life and, in its picture of ancient Israel, a variety of social models for contemporary England. It is not surprising that the Freewillers who gathered from various places in Bocking at Christmas 1550 should describe their purpose as 'for talke of Scriptures'. The prevalence of such discussions (as well as their varying nature) is indicated by conservative complaints about unseemly disputes on the Bible arising in alehouses.

A third significant phenomenon – the accelerating growth of print culture – finds illustration in various parts of this volume. Most obviously, of course, printing put more and more people like Hart and Champneys in direct contact with the Bible. Hart's was the relatively simple case of a one-book man, or so we may conclude from the marginal references in both his published tracts (*A godly newe short treatyse*, 1548, and *A consultorie for all christians*, 1549). Nor is it hard to imagine him holding forth orally in much the same vein – though more briefly – to a Lollard group a century or so earlier. But Hart's prolific Roman Catholic contemporary, Miles Hogarde, could scarcely have

[3] See chapter 11, also chapter 4, section 2.
[4] See chapter 5.
[5] See chapter 4.

written his works at all a century earlier, since most of his defences of Catholic doctrine for a popular audience were cast in the tradition of late medieval poetic allegories. Before Caxton brought printing to England, no London hosier would be likely to have even seen such writing. Defending the traditional church was certainly important to Hogarde, but so was self-expression and particularly the public airing of his religious views – which, as he argued, only printing enabled him, as a layman, to do.

Hogarde was not the only mid-century English Catholic to expound the faith for a popular audience. As early as the 1530s Richard Whitforde, a monk at Syon House till its dissolution and author of various works of devotion as well as a tract against the Lutherans, had published half a dozen different editions of *A werke for housholders*. This set forth in simple terms the meaning of the Creed, the Ten Commandments, the Seven Deadly Sins and the stages of Christ's life. Bishop Bonner, in Mary's reign, saw to it that *An honest godly instruction* was provided (ostensibly for children) explaining the liturgy for those who knew no Latin.

But the traditional church, on the whole, was less aware than its Protestant antagonists of the potentialities of the printing press and of the way it and rising literacy had enlarged and changed the audience to which the church needed to appeal. Both the Marian church and the secular regime made considerable use of the press, but in a conventional way, and the audience aimed at was only occasionally the English layman interested in reading about religious matters. Some publications were evidently intended to increase the prestige of church and crown abroad, others to assist English clerics in their work. The layman was to be inspirited and nurtured in the faith not by direct exposure to Scripture or printed expositions of it, but (in due time) by a better educated parish clergy, and it was for these clerics that most of the Marian religious tracts were produced. Lucid and well written as many of them were, they still had the tone of clerics writing for other clerics; the racy prose and satiric touches of Hogarde's *The displaying of the Protestantes* were very much the exception. The Marian church seems never to have really understood the strength of Engishmen's desire to read the Bible for themselves. It did give formal approval to the idea of preparing an acceptable translation, but the project's actual priority was evidently very low. When Marian Catholicism became exile Catholicism in Elizabeth's reign, it apparently found new importance in the laity and in actually publishing an English Bible – as it also became adept at clandestine pamphleteering. So long as it remained a state church, however, the controlling attitude was that expressed in John Standish's closely argued tract which set forth 50 reasons why the Bible should not be available in English 'for al men to read that wyll'.[6]

---

[6] See chapter 6.

Two decades later, the case of the Elizabethan Familists further showed what command of a printing press could do for a dissident group. Familists had been active in England at least as early as 1561, the year in which they aroused the concern of the Surrey magistrate, Sir William More. The national government's concern came only toward the end of the 1570s after the Familists had, over several years, smuggled into England a wide variety of tracts printed abroad. As their clerical opponents incidentally complained, use of the printed medium also enabled their English leader, Christopher Vitel, to keep personally out of the law's reach.[7]

Robert Crowley, a university-educated Protestant cleric, was a very different kind of radical from the Familist artisan, Christopher Vitel, but they evidently agreed on the importance of the new medium. Crowley in his early career during Edward VI's reign, was a social radical, disturbed about the condition of the poor – especially the new landless poor – and outspoken in his denunciation of the rich landholders and merchants who ignored their God-given responsibilities toward fellow Englishmen and fellow Christians. Failing of any significant response to a pamphlet addressed to Parliament on the poor's behalf, Crowley set up his own publishing enterprise in 1549 to try and reach the public conscience through a number of his own tracts written in rough doggerel verse, satirizing the greed of the new rich and calling for compassion toward the poor. He also published a number of serious works which he thought likely to advance the cause of Protestantism generally. These included Crowley's own translation of the Psalms (so printed as to provide a kind of Protestant service book), the General Prologue to the Wycliffite translation of the Bible and, most important of all, the first printed version of William Langland's *Piers Plowman*, the long fourteenth-century poem which was then widely regarded as a proto-Protestant work because of its sharp anti-clerical passages. The character of Piers had already been turned into a mouthpiece for popular anti-Catholic propaganda, but before Crowley no one had risked putting the whole poem into print. In thus invoking support from medieval Englishmen for his religious position, Crowley was providing an answer to the contemporary Roman Catholic taunt of 'Where was your church before Luther?' He was also reacting not unlike seventeenth-century Englishmen who invoked Magna Carta in support of their political positions.[8]

Throughout his life Crowley was strongly hostile to Roman Catholics (Miles Hogarde was one he wrote against) and apparently disapproved of Protestant separatists also. In Elizabeth's reign the focus of his radicalism changed, and, as part of the movement then beginning to be called

---

[7] See chapter 10.
[8] See chapter 8.

'Puritan', he devoted himself to purging the Church of England of its 'popish' remnants. It was as a leader of a group of beneficed London clergy, objecting to the surplice and other ecclesiastical vestments, that Crowley in 1566 dared the Archbishop of Canterbury to send him to prison for non-compliance with the ordinance. One of several puzzles about Crowley is why, given his apparent fondness for confrontation, he never took the separatist route, as some other Church of England clerics did. Another is why the focus of his radicalism shifted from what the twentieth century would see as the larger social concern of his Edwardian years to the narrower issue of clerical vestments two decades later. Was it something in Crowley's temperament, or was it simply a reflection of the larger changes between Edwardian and Elizabethan Protestantism?

John Foxe, the author of what is arguably the most influential book written in Tudor England, shared some of the radical views of Crowley, his friend and contemporary at Magdalen College, Oxford, as well as in the Marian exiles' congregation at Frankfurt, where both were on the radical side in the dispute which resulted in John Knox's leaving that congregation for Geneva. Foxe inclined to the same views as Crowley in the vestiarian controversy of the 1560s, though he held no London benefice requiring him to give formal assent to the ordinance. As J.F. Mozley noted years ago in *John Foxe and His Book*, he was radical for his time also in his opposition to employing physical pain as sanction against misguided religious beliefs, and he risked his standing with Queen Elizabeth by writing her a plea (which she ignored) to find some punishment other than burning alive for a group of Dutch Anabaptists whose religious views he abhorred.

The brief discussion of Foxe in this volume deals with still a different radical aspect, one closely connected with the preparation of his *Actes and Monuments*.[9] The hundreds of pages of this work, which did so much to implant in Englishmen a lasting hostility to Roman Catholicism, use a wide range of means to give the ordinary reader a sense of his Protestant identity and, to a lesser extent, his English identity. One of these means is showing, as Robert Crowley had tried to do in publishing *Piers Plowman*, that England had a long tradition of opposing Antichrist and church corruption. A second means is associating the martyred saints of the primitive church with another and specifically Protestant hagiography, one including not merely such major figures as John Wycliffe, John Hus and others who had defied the medieval papacy, but also a number of role-models who were almost the reader's own contemporaries. The great majority of the 275 persons Foxe lists as burned by Queen Mary were working-class men and women, only a score or so of them clerics. Foxe, of course, did not invent Protestant martyrology; the great work of his Huguenot counterpart, Jean Crespin, was published some nine

[9] See chapter 9.

years before the *Actes and Monuments* appeared in 1563. Foxe's innovation (as compared, say, to Crespin) lay in his greater use of well-chosen factual detail and of first-hand accounts, and in his realizing the need for the greatest possible accuracy in describing events which some of his readers may have actually witnessed. Consequently, the planned publication was delayed for several years while Foxe checked his data, going sometimes to official records and government agent reports made accessible by the change in regime. Similarly, he took care to correct factual errors in later editions. Using archival material and rechecking one's sources are techniques which twentieth-century history tends to take for granted, but in an age when chroniclers frequently just rephrased earlier chroniclers Foxe's methods had a certain radical flavour.

Seven of the later chapters[10] of this volume relate in one way or another to the popular conventicle. The institution is of special interest also because of the striking change which it apparently underwent during the last two decades of the century. For generations before the 1580s some Englishmen had persistently held religious meetings apart from the established church but, except in the special circumstances of Mary's reign, they had not professed formal separation from it. Those at the Bocking conventicle in 1550, for example, had suspended attendance at the parish church and gathered in religious meetings of their own, but apparently did not feel that they had severed all ties with the national church and, under interrogation by the Privy Council, indicated willingness to return to it. The Familists of the mid 1570s, though certainly separatists in behaviour, even published a tract proclaiming their adherence to the creed and ceremonies of the Church of England. Down through the Familists' time, contemporary evidence suggests, separatists seldom proclaimed separatism however much they practised it.

The new development in the conventicle might be described as the discovery of its potentialities by a number of university-trained clerics. Disaffected ministers of the Church of England had occasionally preached secretly to conventicles, as Miles Coverdale, Edwardian Bishop of Exeter, did in London in the early 1560s, but the initiative taken by Robert Browne was both defiant and public. When in 1582 he published *Reformation without tarrying for anie* and left his parish living for a Norfolk conventicle, his evident aim was sweeping criticism of the established church. Henry Barrow and his separatist congregation insisted on keeping severely apart from what he saw as the impure Church of England, and his collaborator, John Greenwood, denounced any use of the Book of Common Prayer, maintaining that true prayer must be entirely spontaneous. Since the conventicle for them was a way

---

[10] See chapters 2, 3, 4, 7, 10, 11, 12.

of showing the national church the way it should go, the loosely organized popular conventicle became in their hands a rather different thing – committed to specific beliefs, organized along more formal lines, and led by men with real claims to theological learning. The works of these men (along with Robert Harrison's) have been definitively edited by Leland H. Carlson, and examining this stage of Protestant separatism is beyond the concern of the present volume.

It is sufficient to note here that over the next several decades conventicles became more complicated institutions. Some of them evolved into the highly organized groups described in Murray Tolmie's *The Triumph of the Saints: the Separate Churches of London, 1616-1649.* Often led by men originally trained for the Church of England, these were no less organized than a parish church, although of course they were autonomous bodies. But conventicles could still be found in the tradition of the unformalized gatherings, well exemplified in the 'Seeker' groups which George Fox encountered in the north of England in 1652 and incorporated in the new Quaker movement. Both separatist traditions were conspicuously present during the two decades of the Interregnum.

Two of the sects which survived – the Baptists and the Quakers – were prominent at the time of the Revolution of 1688 also, and William and Mary's first Parliament, unlike Charles II's Parliaments, was anxious to conciliate them, not suppress them. A desire to ensure dissenter support for the new regime was, however, only one of the factors underlying the so-called Toleration Act of 1689, since there was strong feeling within the established church against concessions to dissenters. Some groups like the Presbyterians could have been accommodated by the policy of Comprehension – that is, making room for them and their religious practices within the Church of England – but the Quakers were too different in their modes of worship and church organization for such an arrangement to be possible.

In the event, the parliamentary supporters of the Act studiously avoided the word 'toleration' both in the text of the law and in their House of Commons speeches, and simply provided legal status for the religious activities of the dissenting groups without providing full political rights for their members. In effect, it officially recognized that England had become a pluralistic society – a recognition of course having implications eventually wider than the immediate religious one. Even this concession to the radical sects would have been impossible had not a sizable number of Englishmen changed their perceptions of Quakers as politically dangerous persons which they had held in the late 1650s. The stages a radical separatist group goes through to achieve such qualified acceptance by the larger society is a subject which still needs much research; this volume's examination of how the Elizabethan Familists were first perceived does no more than introduce the subject and suggest its magnitude.[11]

There is a certain logic in ending the present volume's consideration of religious radicals about two decades short of Queen Elizabeth's death, for their activity, at least that focused in the conventicle, does seem to have changed significantly about the middle of the 1580s. This change is nearly contemporaneous with the shift in attitude of Protestant clerics toward the popular arts which Patrick Collinson noted in his recently published Stenton Lecture. Adducing a wealth of supporting detail, he showed how the Protestantism of John Bale's time had embraced the drama, ballad and other popular art forms as vehicles of religious propaganda, while official Protestantism, from about 1575 on, viewed the popular arts with growing hostility.

In the character and conduct of the conventicle at this time, as in this attitude toward the arts, there seems to be a certain hardening of the lines and a distrust of unguided popular activity, although just what caused the change in attitude would be hard to say. Perhaps it came from a sense of being under pressure, and some preview of the process may be found in the relatively abundant data on the mid-century Freewiller group. This evidence suggests that it was not commitment to any single doctrine which originally brought that group together, but rather a conviction that by searching and discussing the Scriptures together they could find guidance on a variety of questions. At Bocking in 1550 their reported purpose was to examine modes of prayer in the light of the Scriptures. The issue of predestination is not mentioned at all in reports of that gathering, and even in the depositions about subsequent meetings of Freewillers in Kent it appears as only one of a number of matters discussed. One may speculate that it was mainly the conditions of life in the King's Bench prison in Mary's reign which produced a closer identification of group with particular doctrine. It was there that the Freewiller leader, Henry Hart, debated at some length on predestination with the orthodox cleric, John Bradford, and that confessions of belief circulated among Protestants of different persuasions who were all facing probable death at the stake. It was there also that a part of the group under John Trew's leadership drew up and signed a confession which formally defined their theological position. In the less stressful atmosphere of Edward's reign they had apparently felt no need for such a statement of identity.

Looking back on these Tudor radicals as a whole, one is struck again by the way they indicate other currents of thought and feeling flowing differently from the familiar currents on the surface. Miles Hogarde and Richard Whitforde were both committed Roman Catholics but each took positions which, with other names attached, the historian would label Protestant. The anti-Catholic Crowley, no less than his antagonist

[11] See chapter 12.

Hogarde, looks back to earlier generations for patterns of social justice and social stability. Even more striking is the light shed on the often-heard association between religious separatism and social or political radicalism. The separatists of the mid-seventeenth century often did take radical stands on social and political issues, but Tudor separatists generally concerned themselves only with the religious problems of the individual believer: what the Bible required of him in his daily life and what promises it held for his salvation. Such were the themes which preoccupied Henry Hart; those Marian underground congregations which we know of had nothing to do with efforts to overthrow Mary; the Familist groups centred entirely on their own religious life. The radical social pronouncements came from such national church figures as Hugh Latimer or John Hooper, and especially from the anti-separatist Robert Crowley. Perhaps the radicals' only united message is a reminder that Tudor society was more complex than we sometimes think.

Chapter 2

Tudor Popular Religion: the Rise of the Conventicle

1

The pages that follow will examine the nature and argue the importance of one element in Tudor popular religion: the conventicle. 'Conventicle', a word used in varying senses in early modern England, in the present volume means the periodic gathering for religious purposes of self-selected persons – predominantly laymen, with any clerics attending doing so in no authorized capacity. 'Popular religion' cannot be precisely defined, since no firm line divided it from the country's official religion, which coexisted with it, and strove with varying degrees of intensity to impose itself upon the entire population. The actual religious practices of the illiterate and minimally literate mass of Englishmen reflected in many ways those of the established church, but the reflection was always something less than accurate and the relative emphases were often very different. Official religion, directed by a clerical elite, sought order, coherence and continuity; popular religion, dominated by laymen, was more fluid, more focused on the immediate worries of the believer, much more concerned with religious practice than with codified doctrine.

Detailed information about popular religion has always been limited – not merely by the illiteracy of its practitioners, but also by the way the church frequently regarded them with disfavour and preserved only a hostile picture of them. Such evidence as we have about Tudor popular religion suggests that it contained varied and apparently contradictory strains – in a historical sense, looking both forward and back. Some strains or tendencies look forward to the highly organized sectarian groups of seventeenth-century England or to new concepts of sainthood; others look back to the early Middle Ages' veneration of relics and reliance on charms and spells. The present discussion, limited to this one element in Tudor popular religion, seeks primarily to describe the conventicle as fully as the contemporary evidence permits. What went on in a Tudor conventicle? What part did it play in the lives of its members? How was it regarded by others?

Since those most involved in Tudor conventicles were usually more interested in concealing than in publicizing their activities, information about them has survived only in fragments and often by accident. For Lollards our picture is a mosaic of statements made incidentally in a large number of forced confessions; for the mid-sixteenth-century conventicle there are fewer but reasonably well documented instances, one of them described at some length by two participants. It is argued that these gatherings, though differing from each other individually, amount to a developing popular institution – one not involving many people directly but sufficiently prevalent and well known to be something that Tudor Englishmen would turn to when they felt a strong enough need. This mode of popular behaviour, moreover, had implications for more than the history of religious separatism.

2

The examination starts with the Lollards. When Henry VII came to the throne in 1485, John Wycliffe had been dead for just over a century and Lollardy had changed considerably in that time. It had lost its earlier political dimension, its membership had become predominantly artisans, farmers and small traders; the doctrines they held were much simplified versions of Wycliffe's sophisticated thought, and, even so, varied markedly from group to group. But, judged by the increase in legal actions against it, Lollardy was an expanding movement in the early decades of Tudor rule. Over a dozen major prosecutions between 1486 and 1522 have left a mass of records about the movement in bishops' registers and court books, some of them still surviving in archival form, others preserved only in John Foxe's *Actes and Monuments* and additional documents printed in John Strype's *Ecclesiastical Memorials*.[1]

The group meeting had long been of special importance to Lollards.[2] The grounds for this were both theological and practical. The need for Christians to know and understand the Bible first-hand was central to Lollard doctrine; other Lollard tenets, such as the wrongfulness of venerating images and the denial of transubstantiation, were justified by reference to Biblical authority. Illiterate believers of course needed help in achieving access to the Bible, and group reading was the readiest

---

[1] John A.F. Thomson, *The Later Lollards, 1414-1520* (Oxford 1965), pp. 237-45 especially. See also A.G. Dickens, *Lollards and Protestants in the Diocese of York, 1509-1558* (Oxford 1959), 'Heresy and the Origins of English Protestantism', *Reformation Studies* (London 1982), pp. 363-82; Margaret Aston, *Lollards and Reformers: Images and Literacy in Late Medieval Religion* (London 1984); Anne Hudson, *Selections from English Wycliffite Writings* (Cambridge 1978), Introduction especially; also *Lollards and their Books* (London 1985); John Fines, 'Heresy Trials in the Diocese of Coventry and Lichfield, 1511-12', *Journal of Ecclesiastical History* XIV (1963), pp. 160-74; John Foxe, *Actes and Monuments*, J. Pratt, ed., 8 vols. (London 1870-77), IV, p. 241, remarks on the great increase of Lollard activity in the first two decades of the sixteenth century.

[2] *A. & M.*, III, p. 585, records one such meeting in 1424.

(though not the only) means available for this purpose. Learning to read thus had a religious sanction behind it and the word 'taught', which appears so frequently in Lollard confessions to the authorities, is sometimes to be taken in more than one sense. The conventicle must certainly be seen at times in the aspect of a school. In any case, as Margaret Aston has argued with a wealth of illustrations, reading by persons of that era and social status was usually something done aloud in a group, not silently and alone.[3]

Just how Lollards conducted their conventicles is hard to say. Such information as we have must be pieced together from their individual forced confessions to ecclesiastical officials; cummulatively, however, this fragmentary data is not inconsiderable. There are over 25 instances of Lollard gatherings (in four or five different counties) where we are told at least one thing done at the meeting and the surnames of three or more participants. These cases, plus incidental information in other confessions, suggest that there was no single pattern for a Lollard conventicle, though all presumably had the underlying element of religious fellowship and mutual emotional support.

Hearing a passage of Scripture was probably the most important part, though not necessarily featured on all occasions. One example is found in the account of a well attended session in the Buckinghamshire village of Chesham, sometime before 1521, that speaks of 'reading two hours together in a certain book of the Acts of the Apostles in English'.[4] (The phraseology could refer also to a commentary on the New Testament book, since listening to Lollard writings was another common item at these meetings.) Another man's statement that 'he read divers tymes in the New Testament in English' to a gathering in Colchester is typical of other sessions.[5] On several occasions, however, passages from the Bible are reported as recited to conventicles rather than read. Some of the women reciting certain passages of Scripture may well have been unable to read them,[6] but the London Lollard who was heard to recite the Epistle of James 'perfectly without book' was probably literate enough, since he was a goldsmith by occupation and his wife had lent the informant a copy of the Gospel of Matthew.[7] It seems likely that recited Scripture was considered superior to read Scripture for conventicle use, much as an

---

[3] Aston, *op. cit.*, Chap. 6.

[4] *A. & M.*, IV, p. 230.

[5] John Strype, *Ecclesiastical Memorials* (Oxford 1822), I, ii, pp. 64–65. See also *A. & M.*, IV, p. 226 and *Letters and Papers of Henry VIII*, 21 vols, plus 2 Addenda, J.S. Brewer, James Gairdner, R.H. Brodie eds. (London 1864–1932), IV, i, no. 4029.

[6] *E.g.*, Alice Colins of Burford who would customarily recite to conventicles there 'the Ten Commandments and the Epistles of Peter and James'; her daughter Joan recited similarly, *A. & M.*, IV, p. 238. See also IV, pp. 224–25 giving the passages Agnes Ashford of Chesham taught James Morden to recite.

[7] *A. & M.*, IV, p. 228; see also *Eccl. Mem.* I, ii, p. 53.

original sermon would be considered superior to an official homily read from the pulpit.

Expounding the Bible, or otherwise presenting Lollard religious views, was apparently as frequent an event in Lollard conventicles as presenting the Biblical text itself. The conventicles of a Lollard centre such as Amersham (Buckinghamshire) or Colchester or London provided natural forums for such itinerant Lollard preachers as Thomas Man or John Hacker.[8] Lollards also circulated written sermons: the conventicle in the Berkshire village of Speen, near Newbury, is recorded in 1530 as listening to a read 'lecture . . . of the passion of Christ [for] the space of two hours'.[9] A conventicle in the Coventry area was reported in the 1511-12 heresy trials as having had Lollard books read to it, and part of the anti-transubstantiation tract, *Wickliffe's Wicket*, was read in 1527 to an Essex conventicle at Boxted.[10]

Conventicles were also places for impromptu religious discussion. In some cases a reading from a work of Wycliffite commentary evidently led directly to discussion – as at Burford about 1521 and at Boxted in 1527 – and 'conferrings' is coupled with 'readings' in the interrogation of a Lollard woman at Amersham in 1521.[11] In the last instance, as in some others, the main role in the discussion seems to have been taken by leaders of the movement, possibly in connection with a preaching tour,[12] but other instances show the ordinary Lollard also much inclined to religious discussion. The most striking case concerns at least a half-dozen named persons who were reported in 1521 to 'keep their conventicle' in the house of one of them in Amersham 'after church on holydays', presumably to discuss what they had seen and heard there.[13]

There are only sketchy indications that Lollard conventicles developed any ceremonies of their own. One is found in an unusual gathering, conducted by William Sweeting, a man who had had to change his locale many times in a long Lollard career, and James Brewster, an illiterate carpenter coming originally from Colchester. They met with a few other persons in what were then the open fields of Chelsea, where Sweeting, a man of some education, was then supporting himself by looking after the village animals. As reported at their trials in 1511, the group engaged in religious discussion of varied sorts, but at some unspecified point Brewster would say, 'Now the Son of the living God help us', and

---

[8] At the time of Man's burning in 1518 he was said to have preached in eight named towns, besides London and unspecified places in Suffolk and Norfolk; his accusation charged him and his wife with having 'turned' 600 or 700 people, *A. & M.*, IV, pp. 213, 211. On Hacker see *L. & P.*, IV, i, no. 4029 and 4030.

[9] *A. & M.*, IV, pp. 583-84.

[10] Fines, *op. cit.*, p. 166; *Eccl. Mem.*, I, ii, pp. 54-55.

[11] *A. & M.*, IV, p. 236; *Eccl. Mem.*, I, ii, pp. 53-54; *A. & M.*, IV, p. 223.

[12] *A. & M.*, IV, p. 228; *L. & P.*, IV, i, no. 4175.

[13] *A. & M.*, IV, p. 224.

Sweeting would reply, 'Now Almighty God do so'.[14] There are also hints that a marriage among sixteenth-century Lollards could occasion some formal group attention. One evidently large meeting, marked by the reading 'of a certain epistle of St. Paul' (Ephesians 5 ? Colossians 3 ?), is reported held in a barn at Staines on the Thames after the marriage of a prominent Lollard's daughter. In the same year, 1521, a tailor in Burford was charged, among other things, with 'reading in an English book after a marriage'.[15] Finally, there is the puzzling statement, unexplained in the record, which a Lollard on trial at Coventry in 1511 admitted having made at a meeting: 'May we all drink of cuppe and, at the departing, god kepe you and god blesse you.'[16]

The picture of a Lollard conventicle which emerges from these scattered examples is of a fairly vigorous institution still in a very fluid state. Arising probably from gatherings of like-minded neighbours or from extended household worship (and of course continuing to meet in private houses), it existed in small units, a number of these groups apparently flourishing at the same time in Amersham or London. These cells of 'known men' (as Lollards were called) were also linked in some sort of loose network which might provide a visiting preacher, help in procuring a New Testament, or refuge when a man like William Sweeting needed to flee to another part of the country. There is no hint of formally designated officers, but the leadership of certain persons seems clearly recognized. For example, John Tyball of Steeple Bumstead in Essex went to London in company with Thomas Hilles, an associate from the Witham conventicle some 20 air-miles distant, on the practical mission of obtaining a New Testament; earlier, he had been one of several involved in an effort to convert the parish priest of Steeple Bumstead to Lollard views.[17] John Foxe, referring to the main Lollard conventicle in Amersham, names its four 'principal readers or instructors' (one was the itinerant preacher Thomas Man) and claims that

[14] *A. & M.*, IV, pp. 214-16. I am grateful to Andrew Hope for first calling my attention to William Sweeting.

[15] *A. & M.*, IV, 228, 235. One of the things on which Lollard attitudes varied was marriage ceremonies. The implication in both these instances is that a marriage ceremony had already occurred, presumably at the parish church, but a markedly different Lollard attitude toward marriage ceremonies is evident in the Norwich heresy trials of 1428-31. There, in a number of cases, one of the beliefs abjured by the accused was that marriage required 'only consent of love betuxe man and woman withoute contract of wordes and withoute solemnizacion in churche', *Heresy Trials in the Diocese of Norwich, 1428-31*, Norman P. Tanner, ed. (London 1977), p. 179; see also pp. 147, 153, 160, 165, 170, 177, 183, 185, 189, 196, 199, 205.

[16] Fines, *op. cit.*, p. 166. That it is a festive, not a sacerdotal, cup referred to here is suggested by the bowl (and its inscription) owned by the church of St. Margaret Pattens, London, as described by Susan Brigden, 'Religious and Social Obligation in Early Sixteenth Century London', *Past and Present*, No. 103 (May 1984), p. 72.

[17] *Eccl. Mem.*, I, ii, pp. 50-56.

this 'congregation' lasted from about 1490 to 1521.[18]

Most other individual conventicles appear to have had a rather short lifetime, but starting a new one required only a forceful leader or two and access by one means or another to a few of Lollardy's treasured books. Of local leadership there seems to have been no lack. The movement was handicapped by never having controlled a printing press of its own, but the trial records are full of references to books they did possess and more than 235 manuscripts of parts of the Wycliffe Bible are now known, though by no means all of these were originally in Lollard hands.[19]

The attitude of the authorities toward Lollard conventicles is of some interest. The extensive record of interrogations and forced confessions shows great concern about a number of the Lollards' heretical views – on transubstantiation, on the saints, on pilgrimages and on images – and also about their possession of vernacular Bibles and books of Lollard propaganda. Relatively little attention is given to the conventicle *per se*, though the authorities were evidently aware of it and used the word 'conventicle' from time to time. The preamble to the royal proclamation of March 6, 1529, does speak of 'malicious and wicked sets of heretics and Lollards' as sowing 'sedition',[20] but none of the extensive interrogations of individual Lollards (conducted, of course, by churchmen) suggests that they were seen as politically, economically or socially radical. A modern observer might note that they seem especially fond of the Epistle of James with its rather egalitarian sentiments, but this apparently produced no comment at the time. The Lollards themselves seem interested only in immediate religious questions (hardly anything is said about papal authority, for instance) and one thinks at times that many of them would have been quite happy merely to set up their own supplementary version of the parish church, while still resorting to the established church for marriage or burial ceremonies. As a movement the Lollards were 'popular' not in the sense of attracting the majority of the population, but in being lay-run and entirely autonomous.

3

The picture of the conventicle becomes more complicated during those years – roughly the latter half of Henry VIII's reign – when the authorities' concern was shifting from Lollards to Lutherans, Anabaptists and Sacramentaries. The word 'Lollard', or a variant thereof, continued to be used interchangeably with 'heretic' through the 1530s (the long royal proclamation of 1529 against heresy uses it four

---

[18] *A. & M.*, IV, pp. 213-14.

[19] Hudson, *Lollards and their Books*, pp. 182-3.

[20] *Tudor Royal Proclamations*, P.L. Hughes and J.F. Larkin, eds., 3 vols. (New Haven 1964-69), I, pp. 181-82.

times and 'Luther' only twice) and as late as 1555 a man was prosecuted for 'Lollardy' in York.[21] In a few recorded instances we can identify in a particular Lollard conventicle some aspect of the new Lutheran influence from overseas. The most dramatic of these was the 1527 visit of the two Essex Lollards, John Tyball and Thomas Hilles, to the well known Robert Barnes, who was then under a kind of lax house arrest at the London establishment of the Austin Friars. Tyball has left the fuller of the two accounts of the meeting but that of Hilles agrees with it in all but a few details. Both the Lollards accept Barnes's breezy assertion that his printed New Testament (of which they purchase copies at about three shillings each) is superior to their old Lollard version, while he undertakes on his part to write a letter to the parish priest of Steeple Bumstead to further the conversion which they say they have initiated and hope to complete.[22] Here, as at a conventicle meeting in 1530 at Hughenden in Buckinghamshire, the Lollards welcomed additional support for their position but evidently saw in this no reason for changing their religious allegiance.

The Hughendon conventicle heard the Scriptures read and expounded by one Nicholas Field from London, who also spoke against pilgrimages and images and, citing his own experience 'beyond the seas in Almany' [Germany], said it was necessary to fast only on the twelve 'ember days' of each year. In the same year one of the members of the Speen conventicle confessed to having been originally 'instructed' by a priest 'who had been with Luther two years'.[23] In general, however, direct Lutheran influence on Lollard conventicles seems slight – whether because of Luther's own poor opinion of the Epistle of St. James and the Lollards' fondness for it, or (more likely) because Lutheranism came to England through other channels, such as the clerical discussions in the White Horse Inn at Cambridge in the 1520s, or the printed books whose importation the Christian Brethren were organized to encourage.

The radical groups most troubling the government during the 1530s and 1540s were the 'Anabaptists' (frequently a cover-all term applied to radicals generally) and the 'Sacramentaries' (those denying the Real

---

[21] *E.g.*, *L. & P.*, *Addenda*, I, i, no. 753 (1531), *L. & P.*, IX, no. 84 (1535), XIII, ii, no. 715 (1538); Dickens, *Lollards and Protestants*, pp. 230–31, quoting 1555 court records. The mixing of radical religious influences from varied sources is extensively described in John F. Davis, *Heresy and Reformation in the South East of England, 1520-1559* (London 1983).

[22] Tyball's statement to the Bishop of London on April 28, 1528, printed in *Eccl. Mem.*, I, ii. pp. 50-56, gives a less plausible date for his interview with Barnes, who by September 1526 would have been only just released from imprisonment in the Fleet to custody of the Austin Friars (*A. & M.*, V, p. 419), whereas both accounts portray Barnes as much at ease and almost holding court there. 'About Whitsuntide' 1527 is the date given by Hilles in *L. & P.*, IV, i, no. 4850, where a wealth of corroborating detail indicates that he is the unnamed heretic being examined on October 15, 1528.

[23] *A. & M.*, IV, pp. 583-84.

Presence in the Eucharist) as seen in various recorded prosecutions of individuals. But with one exception, there is no record of these heresies being associated with lay-run organizations like those of the Lollards. In the case of the 'Sacramentaries of Calais', for instance, the activity centred in a parish church there, focused on doctrine rather than religious practice, and had as its leading figure the well-educated Adam Damlip, who, before his conversion, had been chaplain to Bishop John Fisher.[24]
. Government records do survive of a 1532 conventicle of Anabaptists meeting in the London home of one John Raulinges. Eight other members are named (some Englishmen, some Flemings and most of them artisans) and they are said to have 'divers tymes assembled' there; two of them are said to hold that no exposition of Scripture is to be believed, but only the text of the Bible itself. The government's interest is clearly in finding and seizing all 300 copies of *The Anabaptist's Confession*, an imported book now lost, but whether book-smuggling was actually the main interest of the conventicle it is now impossible to say.[15] This Anabaptist conventicle was unusual also in containing both Englishmen and foreigners. Anabaptists are generally referred to, both in royal proclamations and in chroniclers' accounts of trials and punishments for heresy, as immigrants from the continent. For example, the Anabaptist conventicle of 1575, which caused such a furor after it was discovered on Easter morning, is described as entirely Dutch in membership and those who recanted as turned over to the Dutch church in London for future invigilation.[26]

Though information on particular conventicles is scanty, there are incidental references to their continuing existence.[27] More important, perhaps, are the indications that the forces which earlier found expression in the Lollard gatherings were still active and even gaining in strength. The most powerful of these was probably the growing interest in the vernacular Bible among the laity – in the early 1530s against the determined opposition of conservative churchmen and later in the decade with their reluctant cooperation.

One aspect of this growing interest is colourfully illustrated by the case of John Harrydaunce, a London bricklayer who held forth publicly

[24] *A. & M.*, V, pp. 498-525.
[25] *L. & P., Addenda*, I, i, no. 809; for a somewhat fuller transcription of the document see I.B. Horst, *The Radical Brethren: Anabaptism and the English Reformation to 1558* (Nieuwkoop 1972), Appendix A, pp. 183-84.
[26] John Stow, *Chronicles of England*, 1580 (STC 23333), pp. 1180-82; see also pp. 1014-15 for 1538 incidents and *Tudor Procl.*, I, pp. 227-28 (1535), pp. 270-6 (1538), pp. 278-80 (1539), II, 148-49 (1560).
[27] *E.g.*, the polemically phrased question among the papers connected with the 1543 'prebendaries' plot' against Cranmer: 'Whether a tailor in Canterbury do read and expound the Bible in his own house, to which the Commissary knowingly permits open resort,' *L. & P.*, XVIII, ii, No. 546 (p. 291). See also the activities recorded in 1543 of John Toftes and other members of his family, *L. & P.*, XVIII, ii, No. 546 (pp. 307, 312).

on the Bible on various occasions from August 1537 through August 1539.[28] His expounding of Scripture took place from his evidently sizable house in Whitechapel parish and attracted such widespread attention that he was formally investigated by two successive Lord Mayors of London. In 1537 he told the Mayor that he could neither read nor write but had been trying to learn Scripture for 30 years – a statement which indicates that he must have first encountered the Bible in a Lollard version. The chronicler Wriothesley, presumably reflecting popular attitudes to some extent, records that, despite this lack of education, 'he declared Scripture as well as he had studyed at the Universities'. Only stray sentences have survived from these discourses, but it seems likely that they largely followed the Lollard pattern of reciting memorized passages of the Bible. As with more than one lay preacher since, however, Harrydaunce evidently strung these quotations together in his own order with short interpolated comments. On July 22, 1539, for example, he is reported saying, 'No marvel if the world doth persecute holy men and setters forth of light, for Christ said, They shall come after me which shall persecute the tellers of truth.'

The concern of the authorities was mainly about the threat to public order, especially that arising from the 'tumult' occasioned by his discourse on a July Sunday evening in 1539 from a window of Harrydaunce's house which overlooked the main street of Whitechapel. The Archbishop of Canterbury reportedly could discover nothing more serious in his interrogation of Harrydaunce than preaching without a license, but he was eventually silenced by making him bear a faggot at St. Paul's in December 1539. Harrydaunce's own account to the Mayor in 1539 played down the size of the July 'tumult' but admitted that he had 'declared the word of God' on about twenty occasions before groups of half a dozen or so 'neighbours' in his own garden. His reputation as a firm Protestant, however, apparently helped the numbers of his auditors to grow considerably in legend.[29]

Harrydaunce is to be seen more as an individual lay preacher than as leader of a conventicle, for his audiences seem to have lacked stable membership and continuity of religious interest. The picture emerging from the two Lord Mayors' investigations is of a well known and generally tolerated eccentric, but this in itself is insufficient to explain the

---

[28] *L. & P.*, XII, ii, No. 594, No. 624, XIV, ii, No. 42, *Wriothesley's Chronicle*, W.D. Hamilton, ed., 2 vols. (London 1875), II, pp. 82–83, 93.

[29] In 1554 the Protestant courtier, Edward Underhill, trusted him to help conceal Underhill's then dangerous Protestant books, but in his reminiscences later, Underhill spoke of Harrydaunce's preaching 'the gospelle in his garden every halydaye, where I have sene a thowsande people,' *Narratives of the Reformation*, J.G. Nichols, ed. (London 1857), p. 171. John Strype, writing well over a century later, used the same statement to make Harrydaunce one of the leaders of the Protestant underground congregations of Mary's reign, *Memorials of Archbishop Cranmer* (Oxford 1840), p. 526.

relatively lenient treatment Harrydaunce received from the authorities –
markedly more so than that received earlier in the century by various
Lollards who were also well regarded in their local communities. The
new factor was that by August 1539 a royal proclamation had given
approval to the English Bible, and the reformers of the Church of
England were evincing some desire to encourage Bible reading on the
popular level. In April of the previous year, for instance, Cranmer had
written Thomas Cromwell asking him to intervene with justices at
Canterbury who had indicted for 'unlawful assembly' six named
Kentishmen merely because (Cranmer was informed) they were among
those 'which favour God's word'.[30] One of the six, Henry Hart of
Pluckley, was to reappear in Queen Mary's reign as leader of the sect of
'Freewillers' and antagonist of the orthodox Protestant, John Bradford,
in the debate over predestination in the King's Bench prison.

The legalization of the vernacular Bible had another striking effect
among the illiterate laity. A number of them would gather at times by an
English Bible, which had been placed in a parish church for public
reading, and listen while a better educated layman read passages aloud –
often (as opponents of the 'Godspellers' maintained) with the primary
intent of confuting the parish priest or interrupting services of which
they disapproved. One such case involved a man named John Porter and
the English Bibles in St. Paul's Cathedral. As Foxe relates it, so long as
Cromwell remained in power, Bishop Bonner allowed these readings
(which presumably included some Biblical exposition also) to continue,
but after Cromwell's fall he contrived Porter's commitment to prison,
where Porter died of ill treatment.[31] It is easy to see how such Bible-
reading sessions could prove the germ of a conventicle, particularly after
the public reading had been banned, though no specific instance of this
has been recorded.

Another area where discussion of religious matters was evidently on
the rise, and where the germs of a conventicle might be nurtured, was the
casual gathering in a local alehouse. In a 1546 case, one Thomas Skygges
evidently regarded alehouses near Brentwood in Essex as a promising
place for propagating his views on the Eucharist, and a local report
complained that he 'hath confedered himself with divers young men and
hath been a common talker of Scripture'. The Privy Council, asked
about the disposition of a number of persons convicted of heresy, ruled
that two were to be allowed penance but that Skygges and two others
were to be burned as publicly as possible.[32]

---

[30] Thomas Cranmer, *Works*, J.E. Cox, ed., 2 vols. (Cambridge 1846), II, p. 367.
[31] *A. & M.*, V, pp. 451-52.
[32] *L. & P.*, XXI, ii, No. 836, No. 845; *Acts of the Privy Council, new series*, J.R. Dasent,
ed., 32 vols. (London 1890-1907), I, p. 412.

4

Edward VI's reign, which saw the national church take a strongly Protestant direction, also witnessed developments in the conventicle. These were related to the marked increase in the open discussion of religious questions that is seen particularly in the years 1548-50. A sharp rise in publishing over Henry VIII's last years is evident from the listing in *The Short-Title Catalogue of Books Printed in English, 1475-1640*, and manifestations of religious radicalism met with a somewhat more tolerant attitude. 'Anabaptist' questioners apparently had no hesitation in interrupting the divinity lectures of the Protestant leader, John Hooper, at St. Paul's in June 1549, and the ecclesiastical authorities tried for a year to avoid carrying out the sentence of execution against Joan Bocher for denying that Christ took flesh from the Virgin Mary.[33] In both instances there is further evidence that the radicals concerned had followers active in other parts of England also. A year later, Hooper was sent on a preaching tour against Anabaptists in Essex and Kent and a high level commission was appointed to deal with the problem in those two counties. Joan Bocher is reported by a Roman Catholic writer to have boasted at her execution 'that there were a thousand in London of her sect'.[34]

The most important case of an Edwardian conventicle, however, was that which provoked extensive attention from the Privy Council by its gathering at Christmas time 1550 in the Essex village of Bocking. The arrest and subsequent interrogation by the Privy Council of over a dozen participants, along with depositions collected about some of them in the months following, provide more detailed information than any available earlier of what went on in a conventicle meeting. The group acquired the name of 'Freewillers' from later historians, apparently because its senior leader, Henry Hart, took this side of the predestination issue in the celebrated debate with the orthodox Protestant, John Bradford, in late 1554 when both were confined to the King's Bench prison by Queen Mary's government.[35] The contemporary record, however, suggests

[33] Hooper to Henry Bullinger, *Original Letters Relative to the English Reformation*, H. Robinson, ed., (Cambridge 1846-47), pp. 65-66.

[34] *Ibid.*, pp. 86-87; *Eccl. Mem.*, II, i, p. 385; Miles Hogarde, *Displaying of the Protestantes*, 1556 (STC 13558), fol. 47.

[35] *A.P.C.*, III, pp. 198-99, 206-07; British Library Harleian MS 421, fol. 133-34, printed in Champlin Burrage, *The Early English Dissenters*, 2 vols., (Cambridge 1912), II, pp. 1-4; John Bradford, *Writings*, A. Townsend, ed., 2 vols. (Cambridge 1853-58), I, pp. 307-30, II, pp. 170-71, 180, 215-16; John Trew, 'The cause of contention in the King's Bench as concerning sects in religion,' *Authentic Documents Relative to the Predestinarian Controversy*, Richard Laurence, ed. (Oxford 1819), pp. 37-70; Henry Hart, *A godly newe short treatyse*, 1548, *A consultorie for all Christians*, 1549; see also chapter 3 below.

that the group's primary commitment was not to any particular doctrine but to discussing among themselves various questions then agitating their part of the religious scene. The issue of free will became so topical in the mid-century years as almost to compel discussion by such a group, but it figures very little in two previously published tracts of Henry Hart, is not mentioned at all in the reported proceedings at Bocking, and is only one of a number of subjects which subsequent depositions describe members talking over among themselves. The Bocking session, as reported to the Privy Council by a participant, concerned itself with

> thinges of the Scripture, speciallie wheather it were necessarie to stande or kneele, barehedde or covered, at prayer; which at length was concluded not to be material, but the hartes before God was it that imported and no thing else.

The depositions taken later about statements in other meetings of the Freewillers do indeed contain some strong affirmations of belief in free will, but the numbering of the 'articles' to which the depositions respond indicates that we have only a selection of those originally made. What is perhaps more significant is the wording of these attributed statements; most of them by their phrasing suggest an animated debate. Henry Hart, for example, is quoted by one deponent as saying that 'Saincte Paule might have dampned himselfe if he listed' and by another as saying that 'his faithe was not growndid opon Lernyd men, for all errors were broughte in by Lernyd men'; another man asserts that 'to playe at annye game for money it is Synne'.

Those engaging in these discussions included not only artisans and farmers but a few men who were to achieve some standing in Elizabethan Protestantism; the latter, however, seem to have had no special status within the conventicle.[36] Though lacking any formally designated officers, the Freewillers did have arrangements for collecting funds and, like the Lollards, evidently joined their various cells in a loose network. Kentish members went back and forth freely between such centres as Maidstone, Faversham and Ashford, for one deponent (from the village of Lenham) quotes a statement he had heard made by a man from Ashford 'in Coles's house at Faversham'. The Bocking gathering, evidently planned in advance, included men from various locations in both counties. Nothing is known about set procedures followed in the meetings; there are no references to formal scripture readings or group prayers, and they may well have continued to rely for these on the parish church. A number of the participants at Bocking admitted to having refused communion for 'upwards of two years', but their statements about prayer, as shown above, indicate a willingness to join in other parts

---

[36] *E.g.*, Robert Cole, Thomas Cole, John Ledley; see Biographical Register of Freewillers, chapter 3, appendix below.

of the orthodox Protestant service. Later on, the Freewiller group imprisoned in the King's Bench prison were most of them ready to join with the orthodox prisoners in a common Christmas communion service if a compromise formulation on doctrine could be agreed on first.

5

The conventicle received a different kind of stimulus during the five years of Queen Mary's government, when any gathering for Protestant worship became legally a mere conventicle. Orthodox Protestants were thus confronted with the choice of either returning to Roman Catholic worship or of behaving like the radical religious groups and surreptitiously organizing their own – as Bishop Hooper urged in a letter written from prison early in Mary's reign. Their best course, he said, was to 'have assemblies together' for prayer, religious discussion and fellowship. The best known of these groups was the main London underground congregation which managed to meet periodically (in numbers of 30 or 40 upwards and at various locations, including a ship in the Thames) throughout the whole of Mary's reign, always presided over by an ordained minister. The scarcity of Protestant clerics within England, however, made this an exceptional case. Most of the known Marian conventicles – orthodox as well as the less numerous radical groups – were run by laymen who, like the members generally, were predominantly working class. Just how many of these lay-run congregations there were it is impossible to say; John Foxe, like their other contemporaries, refers to them as a familiar phenomenon not worthy of special note, and reserves his statistics for the martyrs. Hooper does not phrase his recommendation to form such groups as if he were advising anything unusual.[37]

What went on in these Marian conventicles is somewhat better documented than in the case of the earlier Lollard gatherings. Of the main London congregation, for example, a government agent who had attended it wrote that 'commonly the usage is to have all the English service without any diminishing, wholly as it was in the time of King Edward the Sixth.' In the more numerous lay-run congregations, of course, the sacrament was not administered, but the Edwardian Prayer Book still seems to have provided the basic structure for worship, sometimes supplemented by the reading of longer Bible passages. The phrase 'the meditation of God's holy word', occuring in the description of a well-documented group in 1558, could refer to religious discussion

---

[37] *A. & M.*, VI, pp. 663; VIII, 558-59. Foxe's chief interest is in the clerically-run London congregations but he is still the best source on the underground congregations generally. See also pp. 126-9, 132, 134, 136-8 below.

also.[38] One vivid description of religious discussion survives: a theological debate between orthodox and radical Protestants at a Colchester inn in September 1555. Such discussions were apparently common in this strongly Protestant town, for the orthodox Protestant, who describes the occasion in a letter over 20 years later, remarks that he had gone there from his home in Cambridgeshire in search of spiritual sustenance. He was dismayed, however, to find the orthodox champion worsted in the debate.[39]

The main London congregation was a highly organized group, with a lay officer called 'deacon' who kept two rollbooks of the membership, one of them listing those who were in arrears in their financial assessments. The congregation was also in correspondence with the Protestant exiles abroad and on one occasion solicited through them a ruling from the Swiss divine, Henry Bullinger, on a case of conscience troubling one of its members.[40] On at least one occasion the leader of a lay-run congregation is known to have given pastoral advice. Lay-led groups seem to have been too short-lived to develop any organizational structure or any enduring relationships with other conventicles. An information network of some sort evidently existed, for the layman Jeffrey Hurst was able from time to time to bring ordained ministers on secret visits to his group in the remote Lancashire village of Shakerly.[41]

Most orthodox Protestants were apparently happy enough to go back to their parish churches after Elizabeth's accession and regard the underground congregations as a mere interlude. But the Marian years did leave an influence on the development of the conventicle. For one thing, the area of its activities – at least for those congregations served by an ordained cleric – had then expanded to include all the religious, though not the secular, functions of the parish church. This had not been true of Lollard conventicles. Furthermore, in the Marian conventicles generally more people, and people of more varied views, had had a taste of running religious affairs for themselves. Even the main London congregation, nearest of any of them to being externally controlled, had enjoyed an autonomy known to few Edwardian or Elizabethan religious bodies – an autonomy which was cited later as a precedent. One striking instance occurred early in Elizabeth's reign when a number of Londoners, who had been haled before Bishop Grindal for an illegal religious gathering in Plumbers' Hall, justified their action by explicit reference to the Marian congregations. 'When our preachers were displaced by your laws,' their spokesman asserted, 'and we were

---

[38] *A. & M.*, VIII, pp. 458; 468.
[39] William Wilkinson, *A Confutation of certaine articles*, 1579 (STC 25665), prefatory historical material.
[40] *A. & M.*, VIII, pp. 454, 458–60; letter printed in *Eccl. Mem.*, III, ii, pp. 133–35.
[41] *A. & M.*, VIII, pp. 412, 562.

commanded to your courts from day to day for not coming to our parish churches, then we bethought us what were best to do and we remembered that there was a congregation of us in this city in Queen Mary's days.'[42]

6

Elizabeth's government addressed itself in its early years to reorganizing the national church, and in doing seems to have also occasioned – at least in London – additional conventicle activity. The chronicler John Stow writes of a number of 'Anabaptist' groups gathering in some half-dozen London locations which he specifies – apparently meaning by 'Anabaptists' religious radicals generally.[43] The new factors seem to have been the scale of such activity and the cooperation which these conventicles received from clerics within the Church of England who were indignant that so many 'popish' elements (as they saw them) still survived in a supposedly reformed church. An important centre of this latter activity was the parish church of the Minories outside Aldgate, which for some years remained exempt from the Bishop of London's control. Even so respected a figure as Miles Coverdale, who had been Edwardian Bishop of Exeter, would on occasion preach secretly to one of these radical conventicles.[44] On into the 1570s, however, the aim of most of these dissident elements continued to be reforming the national church, not leaving it. Robert Crowley, for example, was ready in the mid-1560s to lead a protest by over 30 beneficed London ministers on the vestments issue and defy Archbishop Parker to imprison him – but not to take himself out of the church entirely.[45] Even the spokesman for the Plumbers' Hall congregation quoted above was threatening formal separation, not declaring it.

A conventicle meeting at about the same time in rural Surrey similarly shows its members feeling that the parish church did not fully meet their religious needs, but at the same time being unwilling to break completely with the established ecclesiastical order. This group is described in unusual detail in a document which internal evidence makes it possible to date between 1566 and mid-1570 and attribute mainly to Roger Goad, then schoolmaster at Guildford and later Provost of King's College, Cambridge.[46] Seeing the group as possibly Anabaptist in nature, he

[42] Edmund Grindal, *Remains*, W. Nicholson, ed. (Cambridge 1843), p. 203.

[43] Stow, *Three Fifteenth Century Chronicles with Historical Memoranda by John Stow*, James Gairdner, ed. (London 1880), pp. 143–44.

[44] H. Gareth Owen, 'A Nursery of Elizabethan Nonconformity,' *J.E.H.*, XVII (1966), pp. 65–76.

[45] Matthew Parker, *Correspondence*, J. Bruce and J.T. Perowne, eds. (Cambridge 1853), pp. 267–79.

[46] Folger Library Loseley MS. L. b. 99, printed as appendix to this chapter.

recounts how John Water, a Guildford artisan, holds meetings in his house several times a month on market days and there reads from 'the Bible or some other booke' and expounds it for 'the space of one houre at every meeting'. Questioned repeatedly and in detail by the writer about the group, Water strenuously denies holding any of the specified Anabaptist belifes and 'shewed hym selfe well contented to lyke all thinges in the churche set forth nowe by publike authoritie'. Discussing with the vicar of the neighbouring parish of Wonersh the problem of 'close and secret suspected Anabaptists', the writer learns that some Wonersh parishioners are also regular attendants at Water's Guildford conventicle, but both clerics agree that they 'can fynde no cause to accuse them' of Anabaptism after talking with them. The suspicion nevertheless remains in the writer's mind, and he adds that the brother of a recent mayor of Guildford (and a friend of Water) 'hathe ben suspected to holde that sect of a long tyme' and 'has lodged a dosen of that sect in his house at Guildeforde'. Also mentioned are another brother of the mayor 'dwelling in the west country who is an earnest fellowe that way', as well as a clothier who is suspected partly because he resisted the assessments made on him for poor relief and kept in his house for half a year 'a suspected fellowe' who was also a clothier but did practically no work.

The document as a whole suggests a broader picture of Tudor popular religion. The parishioners here are interested mainly in reading the Bible for themselves and looking after those with like interests, but content to leave specific points of doctrine to higher authority. The clergy here are much concerned about doctrine and not at all sure what their parishioners really believe.

Another document, also relating to the Guildford area and to the same decade, describes a markedly different kind of Tudor conventicle and this through the eyes of two actual participants. It is a deposition in over 60 individually attested paragraphs (one deponent signing only by his mark) made before a Surrey magistrate in 1561 by two disgruntled members of the Family of Love, or Familists, the name usually given to followers of the continental mystic, Hendrik Niclas.[47] The Familists aroused much concern in Elizabeth's government around 1580 (when they were the target of a suppressive royal proclamation) because of their secret meetings, their extensive use of printed propaganda smuggled in from abroad, and their readiness to deny their true beliefs even on oath before magistrates.[48]

Though professing themselves loyal members of the Church of England, they circulated in print a number of clashing beliefs, set up their own 'congregations' (the deposition of 1561 locates these in half a dozen

---

[47] Folger MS. L. b, 98, printed in Jean D. Moss, *'Godded with God:' Hendrik Niclaes and His Family of Love* (Philadelphia 1981), Appendix 1, pp. 70-74.

[48] *Tudor Procl.*, II, pp. 474-75; see also chapter 10 below.

English counties) presided over by an elaborate hierarchy of bishops, elders and deacons. They proclaimed a strict discipline over their members extending even to their choice of marriage partners. The group the deponents describe in Surrey is one of about 30 persons – 'all unlearned save that some of them can read English' – who meet secretly in a member's dwelling at night, finance themselves by collections at each session, and are not admitted to full membership till they reach the age of 30. The more interesting picture is that conveyed indirectly of the content of the meetings, which evidently included Bible-reading and some ceremonies such as admitting new members with a kiss. Though discussion of Familist beliefs was supposedly limited to closed sessions of the more seasoned members, the varied points of doctrine reported by the neophyte deponents suggest that much doctrinal discussion was conducted in everyone's hearing and was one of the features attracting members to attend. The statements they record generally stress the perfectibility of believers and add up to no coherent theological system, but do include such titillating items as 'there was a world before Adam's time as there is now'. The deponents remark in the early paragraphs that 'The bishop or elder doth always tell his congregation that he hath more to teach them so that he doth continually feed them with expectation of new matters.'

Some partial corroboration of this account of a Familist gathering, particularly as to its emphasis on Bible-reading and fellowship, is to be found in a 'confession' dated December 13, 1574 made by six persons at Balsham, Cambridgeshire. John Strype, who prints the three-page document, records it as successful in dispelling the accusations that they were Familists – as in fact they probably were, since only six months later their leader, Robert Sharp, made an explicit recantation of Familism at Paul's Cross, abduring the works of Hendrik Niclas by name. The Balsham confession takes up a number of the specific beliefs Familists were generally credited with entertaining and denies them categorically, one after the other. But evidently the charge of holding 'private conventicles' cannot be plausibly denied. There the reply is that they have indeed held 'meetings upon the holydays, after supper, at sundry times, in our private houses,' but only 'for the reading of Scripture . . . for our own instruction and our several families.' They promise to restrict such gatherings to no more than family worship in the future.[49]

In the Elizabethan Familists we find a conventicle as well provided with designated officers and organizational structure as many of the separatist churches of the mid-seventeenth century, but still denying that it was separatist and by no means refusing all contact with the national church as unscriptural and corrupt. In this respect the Familists foreshadow the later masonic orders which professed themselves

[49] Strype, *Life of Archbishop Parker* (Oxford, 1821), II, pp. 382-85.

conforming members of whatever was the established church of their country.[50]

One more element – seen in a document which has been read as England's first congregational compact – was added to the Tudor conventicle by Richard Fitz's 'Privy Church', a body about which little information has survived. In the surviving document, however, some two dozen Londoners (some of them previously involved in the Plumbers' Hall gathering) jointly promise abstinence from religious services using 'popish garments' and administering the sacraments impurely.[51]

The conventicle as surveyed thus far may be characterized as implicitly separatist but not explicitly so. Small though significant numbers of Englishmen had for generations past felt a need for religious practices not authorized – indeed disapproved – by the established church and had proceeded to engage in these practices. Except during Mary's brief revival of Roman Catholicism, however, they seem to have had no notion that in so doing they were putting themselves entirely outside the established church or setting up a complete rival church of their own. Sometime after 1580 a new stage was reached: the potentialities of the popular conventicle came to be exploited in one direction for explicit and even aggressive separatism and in the other direction for indoctrinating parishioners more fully into the religious life of the Elizabethan church. These new influences on the conventicle came largely from university men interested in changing certain forms of the church as well as in the religious instruction of laymen.

More preaching in the parish church services had, indeed, been a main objective of the more ardent Protestant clerics from Henry VIII's reign on, and from the beginning of Elizabeth's reign various institutional devices had been developed to provide public preaching and religious instruction in other contexts also. 'Prophesyings', or weekday sermons by a number of ministers speaking on the same text, were banned by the Queen in 1577 but continued in many places as single sermons under the name of 'exercises'. Other localities arranged rosters for the clergy of the area to preach market-day sermons in rotation ('lectures by combination'), and a growing number of endowed lectureships were established to provide supplementary sermons both on Sundays and weekdays. Most, but by no means all, of these supplementary sermons

---

[50] The 1561 deponents report that it had been group policy in Mary's reign to attend Roman Catholic services, and Familists on the continent generally professed themselves conforming Catholics. On the Freemasons see Margaret C. Jacob, *The Radical Enlightenment* (London 1981), Chap. 4.

[51] Burrage II, pp. 15-18; see also Collinson, *Elizabethan Puritan Movement* (London 1967), pp. 90-91.

came from clergy of pronounced Puritan tendencies.[52]

At all these lectures and 'exercises', however, the layman's role was that of a listener only, and the more 'forward' Puritan clerics sought means of involving laymen more actively. One such means was that sometimes called 'sermons by repetition' – that is, the practice of going over the main points of a Sunday morning sermon in a private household session either that evening or on one following.[53] Sometimes, as in the case of the energetic George Gifford of Maldon, the preacher himself would be present. Such a gathering, if seen as either catechizing or as household worship, was not in itself illegal, but it could be readily made so by the presence of outside visitors or the undertaking of additional religious activities not permissible for laymen. It is not surprising, for example, that Bishop Aylmer applied the term 'night conventicles' to such gatherings attended by the cleric John Huckle whom he had placed under suspension.[54] Because of the danger of getting tarred by the 'conventicle' brush, a cleric seeking to involve laymen in any but the most conventional religious activities could not normally count on the support of his superiors.

In one instance we have a detailed record of a Puritan cleric's organizing a picked group of his parishioners to participate with him in a joint effort to improve the quality of their spiritual lives. This was Richard Rogers in the Essex village of Wethersfield, where he held an endowed lectureship (apparently performing a curate's duties as well) and was an active member of the small Braintree conference of ministers. The lay group consisted of 'well nigh twenty' Wethersfield people of strong religious interests and seems to have met weekly from the fall of 1587 to some time in 1588, as recorded both in the 'Fifth Treatise' of Roger's lengthy published work, *Seven Treatises*, and in a few references in the diary he kept for over three years in the 1580s.[55] In his published account of the meetings Rogers takes pains to emphasize that he ('the preacher') was in charge at all times, that the laymen were 'no Brownists' but 'diligent and ordinaire frequenters of publicke assemblies with the people of God' and in no sense formed a 'conventicle'. They 'did convenant' to examine their spiritual lives together and authorized 'the

---

[52] Collinson, *op. cit.*, pp. 168-76; *Godly People* (London 1983), pp. 468-98; Paul S. Seaver, *The Puritan Lectureships, 1560-1662* (Palo Alto, Calif. 1970).

[53] Collinson, *Elizabethan Puritan Movement*, pp. 375-77.

[54] Strype, *Life of John Aylmer* (Oxford 1821), p. 171; Collinson, *Godly People*, pp. 10-11, citing various meetings. See also F.G. Emmison, *Elizabethan Life: Morals and the Church Courts* (Chelmsford 1973), pp. 97-99, for a number of individual cases illustrating how difficult it was to draw a hard line between legal and illegal gatherings, and suggesting the prevalence of both kinds.

[55] *Seven Treatises*, 1603 (STC 21215), pp. 477 ff. *Two Elizabethan Puritan Diaries*, M.M. Knappen, ed. (Chicago 1933), pp. 53-86. References in the *Diary* are often uncertain and the dating is sometimes clearly in error.

Preacher to set down the summe of their conference and communication together' for the instruction of others.[56] There follow some 20 folio pages of fairly typical Puritan analysis of the problems of keeping to the knife-edge line of right living – of being 'merie without lightnese, sad without unfruitfull dumpinesse, beleeving God without presuming . . .'

What is noteworthy about this laymen's meditation group is that Rogers apparently found in it much the same stimulation and fellowship as he found in the fasts and meditation sessions with his colleagues of the Braintree ministerial conference; he refers to both sets of meditation sessions as sharpening ('whetting') the sensibilities of the participants.[57] Rogers' diary records him as much disturbed by the existence of separatists and he was presumably aware that the close fellowship which they offered was part of their religious attraction. His parish meditation group, which he urged his fellow ministers to imitate,[58] did, among other things, turn the kind of fellowship offered by the popular conventicle to the strengthening of the national church. As he rather proudly asserted in print, those who had joined the parish's 'godly conference' were stimulated 'to enjoy its publicke ministrie more chearfully and fruitfully afterwards'.[59]

Rogers' was a minority position on this point, however; it was mainly separatist clerics who exploited the potentialities of the popular conventicle. The best known of these was Robert Browne, who in 1582 published his dramatically titled tract, *Reformation without tarying for anie*, and left the Church of England for a Norfolk conventicle. Browne himself had made his peace with the establishment before the decade was over, but Henry Barrow took an even sharper stand, proclaiming to Lord Burghley and Archbishop Whitgift in open court the four insuperable reasons why he saw his separatist congregation, and not the Church of England, as scripturally the true church. The stories of Browne and Barrow (and of their respective collaborators, Robert Harrison and John Greenwood) are too extensive – and too well covered elsewhere[60] – to be rehearsed here. It is worth remembering, however, that Browne's reforming effort depended in part on an underlying confidence that he would have a conventicle to turn to and to reshape subsequently as a model of the true church.[61] From Barrow and

---

[56] *Seven Treatises*, pp. 477–78.
[57] *Diary*, p. 64; *Seven Treatises*, p. 478.
[58] *Diary*, pp. 76, 67–68.
[59] *Seven Treatises*, p. 478.
[60] Robert Harrison and Robert Browne, *Writings*, Albert Peel and Leland H. Carlson, eds. (London 1953); Henry Barrow, *Writings, 1587-90*, Carlson, ed. (London 1962); John Greenwood, *Writings, 1587-90*, Carlson, ed. (London 1962); Henry Barrow, *Writings, 1590-91*, Carlson, ed. (London 1966); Henry Barrow and John Greenwood, *Writings 1591-93*, Carlson, ed. (London 1970).
[61] See Browne's remark in his autobiographical 'True and short declaration,' *Writings, op. cit.*, p. 405.

Greenwood on (though by no means following the exact course they plotted) the conventicle's development looks forward to such highly organized bodies as the separatist churches of the 1630s and 1640s.[62]

These separatist churches, of course, represent only one line of the conventicle's development, and much the better documented line, since they tended increasingly to keep records of their own. But the less formalized and entirely lay-run conventicles evidently continued also, as seen by their emergence in large numbers after the suppressive controls broke down in the 1640s. The Seeker groups, for example, which George Fox evangelized so extensively for the Quakers, are obscure in their origins but one component, surely, is an established practice of ordinary laymen running religious gatherings for themselves.

7

Looking back at the sixteenth-century conventicle as a whole, one has a twentieth-century question or two to raise about it. The first of these relates to the role of women in the Tudor conventicle, a subject difficult to draw firm conclusions on, because available information comes through persons whose primary interest was neither in the conventicle itself nor in women's participation in religious affairs. Women must be presumed among those present at conventicle meetings, since these were mostly held in the home of a member; like the male participants, the women came mainly from the artisan level of society. It is only in times of special persecution, however, that the record shows women playing any prominent role.

Thus, during the drives against Lollards in the early decades of the century women are reported as reciting passages of Scripture at Lollard meetings and 'instructing' others in the faith individually, and female names appear frequently in the lists of those interrogated.[63] Queen Mary's effort to restore Roman Catholicism in 1553-58 provides a similar picture. London's main underground Protestant congregation had a fishmonger's wife as one of its collectors of funds for prison relief, and one Margaret Mearing was an active recruiter of new members – so incautiously so that the congregation's pastor finally expelled her on security grounds. Out of 22 named persons arrested at a Protestant meeting in Colchester and sent up to London together for trial, eight were women, while in the nearby village of Great Bentley the underground congregation was kept going for much of its life by one William Mount and his wife Alice and step-daughter Rose Allin.[64] The

---

[62] E.g., as described in Murray Tolmie, *The Triumph of the Saints: the Separate Churches of London, 1616-1649* (Cambridge 1977).

[63] *A. & M.*, IV, pp. 238, 225, 228; see also pp. 223-24, 229-37.

[64] *A. & M.*, VIII, pp. 459, 450-51, 303-07, 382-84.

The Picture of xxij . godly and faithfull Christians, apprehended about Colchester, prisoned together in one bande, and so with three leaders at the most, brought vpto London.

The maner how these xxij. prisoners were brought vp from Colchester to London by thꝛee keepers.

You shall be led before Princes and rulers for my names sake. *Math.* 10.

Woodcut of the celebrated incident in Mary's reign when twenty-two conventicle members were arrested in Colchester and marched roped together to London for trial. Foxe's accompanying roll-call of the conventicle lists eight of the twenty-two as women. (*A. & M.*, 1570 ed., p. 2138.)

history of one of the radical separatist groups, the Freewillers, presents a contrast which is perhaps only coincidental but is nonetheless interesting. In the record of its brushes with the authorities during the less stressful days of Edward VI, no woman appears among the two dozen or so named as important members, but in 1555, when some of the group confined in the King's Bench prison drew up a confession of faith, one of the twelve signers was a woman.[65]

Examining the way the conventicle developed over the century, one is struck not merely by its general growth but by how much it was changing toward the end of this period. Previous groups seem to have been generally content with an undeclared separatism in those aspects of the religious life which especially concerned them, leaving some other aspects to the established church. Barrow, however, insisted that his congregation's separation must be explicit and complete. The earlier conventicles had been mostly informal affairs, lay-run, lacking designated officers and indeed any sharp line between those theologically educated and those not. Membership was restricted mainly by physical risks strong enough to deter anyone not himself strongly committed; explicit moral and doctrinal criteria appear to have been rather rare.[66]

The popular conventicle's meetings tended to be for its own members, not a platform for public preaching. Both the personal backgrounds and the wider reforming aims of the new university-educated conventicle leaders, however, tended to put more emphasis on public preaching and on more formal structure within the conventicle. It may be noted also that these changes in the nature of the conventicle occurred at roughly the same time as English Protestantism was becoming less 'popular' in other respects also – ceasing to see the drama (as John Bale had done) and the popular ballad as suitable vehicles for its propaganda, and forsaking Bale's earthy language for the dignified diction found in the classic editions of John Foxe's *Book of Martyrs*.[67]

Throughout the Tudor period, it has been argued, the conventicle was a significant part of popular religious life because it met what a portion of the lay population evidently felt to be basic religious needs. One of these was the emotional security and fellowship provided by group worship. A second was more detailed knowledge than could be found in the

---

[65] *A.P.C.*, III, pp. 198-99, 206-07 and Burrage II, pp. 1-4, contrasting with Trew, *op. cit.*, pp. 69-70.

[66] But see *A. & M.*, VIII, p. 384, for a Marian government agent's report that Henry Hart imposed a 13-point set of regulations on Freewillers at the time they were contending with orthodox Protestant prisoners in the King's Bench.

[67] Collinson, *From Iconoclasm to Iconophobia: the Cultural Impact of the Second English Reformation* (1985 Stenton Lecture, University of Reading, 1986); also his 'Truth and Legend: the Veracity of John Foxes's Book of Martyrs,' in *Clio's Mirror: Historiography in Britain and the Netherlands*, A.C. Duke and C.A. Tamse, eds. (Zutphen 1985), pp. 36, ff. 49, 50.

traditional services of the parish church about the nature of their faith and its implications for their daily life. A third was the opportunity to participate themselves in discussing these matters. The importance of the first two needs found recognition by the authorities in legislation decreeing church attendance, in the varied institutional devices for providing more sermons, and in a growing effort to explain doctrine through more effective catechizing.[68] But however much the established church might do to meet the first two needs, the layman wanting to talk about religion in a group larger than his own household generally had no recourse but the conventicle or the alehouse.

Men came to the popular conventicle, the best-documented Tudor instances suggest, very largely because they had questions – questions about daily conduct or eternal salvation to which the formal answers of the national church seemed unsatisfactory or at least unstirring. At a session of the Freewillers they could inquire about the requisites for true prayer or the implications of original sin, and do so on a basis closer to equality than was to be found elsewhere in a sixteenth-century world. Even in the formally stratified Familist group at Guildford the leaders seem to have appealed to an interest in questioning. Under the new university-educated leadership, the emphasis tended to shift to answers – that is, to doctrinal formulations by which a trained cleric could defend his position, a position which tended to become that of the group also. This, of course, was a new stage in the institution of the conventicle, giving it coherence at the cost of an earlier spontaneity.

Another long-range question concerns the implications for secular history of an institution that consisted of unauthorized popular gatherings about matters beyond the boundaries of everyday life. How ideas persist and are transmitted along the lower borders of literacy is a murky subject, but it has long been clear that certain areas of England such as Essex and Buckinghamshire (not to mention London) produced radical activity of various kinds from the fifteenth century through the seventeenth. An established practice of gathering in conventicles could go far to explain why.

Tudor popular conventicles, often termed 'seditious' by the government, actually centred their attention on their members' personal religious concerns, displaying virtually no interest in who held power at Westminster or even in secular questions much nearer home, but the conventicle was by its nature well suited to be a vehicle for views of many kinds. In the middle two decades of the seventeenth century, indeed, it repeatedly showed its potential for expressing and influencing public opinion at the grass roots. Individual conventicles, as has been seen,

[68] Ian Green, '"For Children in Yeeres and Children in Understanding:" the Emergence of the English Catechism under Elizabeth and the Early Stuarts,' *J.E.H.*, XXXVII, No. 3 (July 1986), pp. 397-425.

could be readily suppressed by a few well directed arrests, but as an institution it was remarkably resilient, requiring little to start a new group beyond a felt need, a vigorous impromptu leader and perhaps a vivid memory or two. It is not surprising that the authorities in church and state generally regarded the conventicle with suspicion.

Appendix: Folger Library, MS. L.b. 99[69]

Endorsement: charges of suspicion of being Anabaptists at Guildford

We are very doughtfull (yf yt may please you) of a certen heresy of Annabaptistry which we very muche feare that some of our neighbors do holde. Not that we are able to accuse them particularly of any article touching the same secte. But by cause some of them hathe bin suspected thereof along tyme, and also by cause some other suspected in lyke case dothe frequent and use one anothers company styll.

Suche suspected causes as we have gathered touching this matter we have sett down as foloweth.

It was reported to me at my first coming to dwell at Guildford that John Water, joyner, had on the market dayes great resort come to his house of suche suspected persons which dwelt abought Wonershe, Bramley and other places therabout, and when they were come together the said Water had them all into a chamber in his house, and having them all together in the chamber he toke the Bible or some other booke and did reade therin to them and after wards he did interpret and expounde yt unto them and so continued together by the space on one houre at every meting, and then departed. Which meting was not past twise in amoneth or three tymes at the most. So that one simple servant of his (being not very wise) did report this of her maister and further she said that her

---

[69] Folger MS L. b. 99, an unsigned document printed in full below. The dating is conjectured from the references to 'Mr. Goade' as an accomplished preacher and to 'Mr. Thomas Baker' as the 'late mayor' of Guildford (see notes below).

maister coulde preche as well as Mr Goade.[70]

Afterwards yt happened that one tolde Water all this tale in my presentes, whereat he semed to be very much greved; then said I unto Water There is a company not farre of (as I heare say) that holde very strange opinions and are of the sect of the Annabaptistes. Then he would knowe of me what strange opinions they holde. I said they deny the baptism of infants, the lawfull aucthorite of the magistrate, the lawfull use of swering etc. He answered that they were of better countenans then they that did holde those opinions and could defend them, but denied that he helde any suche. Yet me think (sayd I) you speake very suspiciously in the liking of them that holde these opinions, and so by occasion we brake of at that tyme.

Very shortly after by occasion I talked with hym agayne of the same matter, at which tyme (I beinge very earnest with hym uppon the report aforesaid), but he utterly denied to holde any opinion agaynst the worde of godd and shewed hym selfe very well contented to lyke all thinges in the churche set forthe nowe by publike authorite. Sithens which tyme I have not had muche talke with hym about any suche matters. But when I talke with the vicare of Wonershe some tyme, I aske hym how he dothe with his close and secret suspected Annabaptists in his parishe. Then he saithe to me that the chieffest of them dwellethe in my parishe and namethe to me Water. I saye then to hym that I have proved hym that way as muche as I may, and can fynde no suche matter in hym. Even (saithe he) so have I talked with my parishioners and can fynde no cause to accuse them thereof, and yet we have great suspicion that ther is suche matter among them, for ther be certen of Wonershe and therabout that dothe frequent Water house once aweke or once in fourtene dayes, and as I am informed the said Water hathe recourse unto them at certen tymes.

Also ther is one George Baker. He is nowe abidinge (and hathe ben this halfe year) with his brother Mr Thomas Baker[71] late mayor of G. This George hathe ben suspected to holde that sect of a longe tyme, and he is

[70] Probably Roger Goad, provost of King's College, Cambridge, who was Master of the Free Grammar School at Guildford between 1565 and mid-1570, and in 1572 Lady Margaret Preacher at Cambridge and also a preacher at court. The document as a whole seems to be of multiple authorship with the third, fourth and fifth paragraphs written by someone who had come from elsewhere to live in Guildford. This fact, plus the author's ready knowledge of Anabaptist heresies, his being on confidential terms with the vicar of Wonersh, and the embarrassment of John Water at being compared as a preacher to 'Mr. Goade' in the author's presence, all make Goad himself seem the likely author of these paragraphs. Since Goad is also reported to have played some part in interrogating suspected Familists in Cambridgeshire later on in 1580, the compiling of the whole report may also have been done at his initiative (DNB; O. Manning and W. Bray, *History and Antiquities of Surrey*, 3 vols. (1804–14), i. 79; Strype, *Annals of the Reformation*, 4 vols. (Oxford 1824), ii. ii. p. 41: Hist. MSS. Comm., *7th Report.*, app. p. 622.

[71] Thomas Baker served one-year terms as mayor of Guildford in 1565, 1575 and 1580 (Manning and Bray, pp. 38, 39).

agreat companion of the said Water, and is often at his house, and also walke together abroade in the fyeldes dyverse tymes. If the said Mr Thomas Baker be free from that sect (as I hope he be) I am very gladd thereof, but I dought he hathe ben somewhat bendinge that way, and hathe lodged a dosen of that sect at once in his house in Guildeforde, but it is agoode while sithens, and he hathe another brother named Harry Baker dwelling in the west country who is an earnest fellowe that way, and he commethe this way other whiles, and he had a sister that spent muche of her substance uppon that company.

Also there is one John Warner clothier whom we do somewhat suspect, althoughe he be not so close and subtile as the others are, yet we dought he smelleth of that sect, by cause he commethe seldome to churche to the communion and when he is adjudged by the ordinary to contribute monye for his faultes to the poore according to the lawe, than he said that the judge had no suche auctthorite by the lawe of god to take awaye his mony from hym, and that he might as well take his coote from his backe, and that he did wickedly so to do. And when he was advertised not so to judge of the magistrate, he answered, what I thinke of the magistrate I will kepe to my selfe. Also about ayere agone he kept a suspected fellowe in his house of that secte for the space of halfe ayere, beinge of his own occupation, but yet for the moost part he was idle. His name was John Joure.

Chapter 3

'The First that Made Separation from the Reformed Church of England'

1

The words are those of John Strype, the late-seventeenth-century ecclesiastical historian, and he is speaking of the group which he calls 'Freewillers' and which its contemporaries in Edward VI's and Mary's reigns called 'Freewill men'. Having 'gathered congregations of their own,' he evidently considered, set them apart from other religious dissidents to whom there are sundry earlier references.[1]

The Freewillers were more than a historian's 'first'; their impact on their contemporaries was at times emphatic and, to the modern historian, a little puzzling. After a meeting they held in the Essex village of Bocking at Christmas 1550, Edward's Privy Council sent out arrest orders for 18 of them, 13 of whom it subsequently interrogated in some detail.[2] Later on, in the King's Bench prison during Mary's reign, they conducted an extensive argument on predestination with John Bradford, the future martyr, and he wrote to Cranmer and Ridley about them, saying that unless their doctrinal influence were countered, 'more hurt will come by them than ever came by the papists'.[3] Yet one of those arrested by the Privy Council in January 1551 preached before Cranmer at Maidstone in February 1553 and eleven years later (then as Archdeacon of Essex) before Queen Elizabeth; another was ordained and given church livings by Elizabeth's first Bishop of London; prayers and meditations by a third were a continuing publisher's item in England during the rest of the sixteenth century.

The Freewillers, however, have an interest that goes beyond merely offering such paradoxes for resolution; they are important simply because they are separatists. As groups of self-selected persons meeting periodically for religious purposes without an authorized cleric,

---

[1] John Strype, *Ecclesiastical Memorials*, 3 vols. (Oxford 1822), II, i, p. 369. Regarding earlier dissidents see *Tudor Royal Proclamations*, P.L. Hughes and J.F. Larkin, eds., 3 vols. (New Haven 1964-69), I, pp. 227-28, 270-76, 280.

[2] *Acts of the Privy Council, new series*, J.R. Dasent, ed., 32 vols. (London 1890-1907), III, pp. 198-99, 206-07.

[3] John Bradford, *Writings*, A. Townsend, ed., 2 vols. (Cambridge 1848-53), II, pp. 170-71.

separatists were outside the framework and controls of the national church and aroused strong disapproval on both ecclesiastical and civil grounds. Down to the end of the sixteenth century, the recalcitrant separatist stood in danger of being hanged or even burned alive, whereas the nonconforming cleric within the new Church of England faced no more than loss of his living or imprisonment.[4] The persistence of separatists in the face of such disapproval suggests that their society failed in some significant way to meet their intellectual or emotional needs. To examine different groups of separatists in their varied aspects – not just their relationships to the theological tradition which they affronted – can shed light from a new direction on that society.

It is first necessary, however, to expand considerably our present knowledge of specific separatist groups (which differed from each other rather more than is apparently recognized by some who have theorized confidently about them) and we need especially to know how they behaved as well as what they professed. Detailed information is admittedly scarce, even though separatists and conventicles (as their unauthorized gatherings came increasingly to be called) were by no means a rare phenomenon in England from Lollard times on. Most of what information we have, moreover, comes through their opponents. Solid factual data, such as has permitted such valuable research on the ordinary clergy in recent years, is rare indeed. In these circumstances, it is tempting to extrapolate backwards from the familiar and relatively well-organized sects of the late Elizabethan and Stuart eras. What is sought here, of course, is a view of mid-century separatism from strictly contemporary evidence.

As early separatist groups go, the Freewillers offer a promising start for detailed examination. Contemporary information on them is – comparatively – extensive, not only in volume but in variety of sources. We have their own account of the controversy in the King's Bench as well as that of John Bradford and other orthodox Protestants. We have two published tracts by one of their leaders, a recantation sermon by a former member, and published prayers by two others. There are government records on them from the contrasting regimes of Edward and Mary, as well as miscellaneous references from several points of view. And (as recorded in the Appendix) over 40 onetime members or sympathizers can be identified by name.

The Freewillers have not been entirely neglected by modern historians, but they have almost always been looked at in only a single

---

[4] Doctrinal grounds might account for the case of Francis Ket, burned primarily for Arianism in 1589, but John Greenwood, hanged in 1593, was, like the Archbishop who sentenced him, theologically a follower of John Calvin.

aspect, relating to some larger matter.[5] The present discussion takes the group as a subject in itself and examines it in as much detail as contemporary information permits. It will proceed in roughly chronological order, starting with some attention to the environment of radical religious disputation in which the group first appears. It will then discuss the Bocking conventicle, and the apparent consequences in Edward's reign, and from there go to the controversies in the King's Bench during Mary's reign and what is known of the activities of onetime Freewillers thereafter. It seeks particularly to discover what kind of men and women became Freewillers, what brought them together in the group or groups so named, and how these groups operated. The biographical appendix summarizes what is known about Freewillers individually.

2

The name 'Free-will men', as one of Bishop Bonner's agents remarks in reporting on the group's activities, was applied to them, by 'the Predestinators'.[6] They do not apply the name to themselves: John Trew, in his long account of 'The cause of contention in the King's Bench as concerning sects in religion', uses only the pronoun 'we' to refer to his group.[7] Nor does the term appear at any point in the fairly extensive

---

[5] R.W. Dixon, *History of the Church of England from the Abolition of the Roman Jurisdiction*, 6 vols. (London 1884–1910), III, pp. 300–24, treats them mainly as an unfortunate consequence of the government's policy of licensing preachers; A.G. Dickens, *The English Reformation* (London 1964), p. 238, sees them as an example of the government's concern about radical sectaries; O.T. Hargrave, 'The Freewillers in the English Reformation', *Church History*, XXXVII (1968), pp. 271–80, and *The Doctrine of Predestination in the English Reformation*, unpublished doctoral dissertation, Vanderbilt University, 1966, pp. 124–30, focuses almost entirely on the dispute over predestination in the King's Bench prison; Dewey D. Wallace, Jr., *Puritanism and Predestination in English Protestant Theology, 1525–1695* (Chapel Hill, N.C. 1982), pp. 202–03, puts this aspect of the Freewillers in a more considered historical perspective; I.B. Horst, *The Radical Brethren: Anabaptism and the English Reformation to 1558* (Nieuwkoop 1972), pp. 122–36, seeks to associate the Freewillers with the continental Anabaptists, a line followed also by George H. Williams, *The Radical Reformation* (London 1962), pp. 790–91; M.M. Knappen, *Tudor Puritanism* (Chicago 1965), pp. 149–51, sees the Freewillers as 'primitive Arminians' with a surprising ascetic strain; B.R. White, *The English Separatist Tradition from the Marian Martyrs to the Pilgrim Fathers* (Oxford 1971), p. 162, dismisses them as having little to do with the separatist tradition; J.W. Martin, 'English Protestant Separatism at its Beginnings: Henry Hart and the Free-will Men', *The Sixteenth Century Journal*, VII, No. 2 (Oct. 1976), pp. 55–74, focuses mainly on the Freewillers' senior leader. See also below Chapter 4.

[6] John Foxe, *Actes and Monuments*, J. Pratt, ed., 8 vols. (London 1870–77), VIII, p. 384.

[7] John Trew, 'The cause of the contention in the King's Bench as concerning sects in religion', printed from Bodleian MS 53 in Richard Laurence, ed., *Authentic Documents Relative to the Predestinarian Controversy* (Oxford 1819), pp. 37–70.

entries in the Privy Council register noting actions taken about the Bocking conventicle early in 1551, or even in the depositions recorded some months later about the Kentish group's practices and the varied beliefs of its members.[8] As the cases of the Lollards and the Quakers illustrate, religious groups have often acquired a generally current name from some relatively incidental characteristic. The term 'Free-will men', as will be shown later, was in the mid-century years also used as an epithet of wider applicability. This is possibly why John Strype, when referring to this particular group, normally uses 'Freewillers' in his own text, though retaining 'Free-will men' in contemporary documents which he prints. I follow Strype's usage and refer to the group as 'Freewillers', though recognizing that this is not strictly a mid-sixteenth century term.[9]

Strype mentions the Freewillers as only one of a variety of religious dissidents in Edward's reign, and they, of course, need to be seen against this background. It is easy to forget the diverse nature of the elements which the Edwardian church contended against under the names of Arians, sacramentaries and Anabaptists, and to forget also the amorphous and shifting character of these dissident elements as they disputed with each other. The first two terms were used with some consistency to mean those who denied, respectively, the Christian Trinity and the Real Presence in the communion service, but 'Anabaptists' could include not merely those insisting on believers' baptism but also (as John Hooper complained to Henry Bullinger in June 1549) antinomians and even some proponents of a special kind of predestination.[10] One must beware of envisaging such mid-Tudor dissidents in terms of the organized groups which professed similar doctrines in subsequent generations.

The early years of Edward VI's reign saw an outburst of religious disputation, as Henry's anti-heresy statutes became dead letters along with his efforts to decree just who might read the English Bible. The presses became much more active. Recorded publishing totals for the five full years of Edward are nearly double those for his father's last five

[8] Champlin Burrage, *The Early English Dissenters*, 2 vols. (Cambridge 1912), II, p. 1–4, printing British Library Harleian MS 421, fol. 133–34ᵛ. The date '*c.* 1550', added in a later hand at the top of the manuscript, cannot be precise, since 'going to Essex' is mentioned in two depositions.

[9] Horst, *op. cit.*, pp. 135–36, no. 147. My research fully supports Horst's finding on this point (but not his remark that outsiders generally called the group 'Anabaptists'). The earliest use of 'Freewiller' I have encountered is on the title page of a tract published by Thomas Helwys in 1611, 'An advertisement or admonition unto the congregation which men call the New Fryelers [Freewillers] in the lowe countries, written in Dutch', printed in Burrage, I, p. 252.

[10] *Original Letters Relative to the English Reformation*, H. Robinson, ed. (Cambridge 1846), p. 65.

full years, markedly higher than those for the five full years of his sister Mary's reign and higher also than those for the first five full years of Elizabeth.[11] It was not freedom of the press in any twentieth-century sense which obtained under Protector Somerset, but the area of permissible discussion did widen appreciably, and there is reason to believe that even more radical views were being debated orally. A rather disorganized tract by John Champneys in 1548, *The harvest is at hand wherein that tares shall be bound and cast into the fire and brent* (STC 4956), has an air of revolutionary expectation in its title and two other striking themes in its text. One of these is the view, expressed several times in varied wording, that the vernacular Bible now meets all a Christian's religious needs because 'the Apostles lefte nothynge unwritten which was profitable to our fayth but have declared the whole counsell of God beying nedefull for us to know.'[12] Another and even more persistent theme is Champneys' feelings that the layman, reading the Bible in a reverent spirit, will be more hindered than helped by the traditional clergy, who tend to set up 'man's imaginings' against the word of God. 'For neither reason nor learning can declare the true religion in Christ,' Champneys asserts, and later he proposes a contest, like Elijah's with the priests of Baal, in which he promises that, as an unlearned layman, he will show the true meaning of Scripture 'by God's assistance and only by the Spirite of Christ.'[13] The detailed public recantation obtained from Champneys shortly after this publication included a promise to recall 'as many of his books' as he could, suggesting that he may have had other titles in print also, but this is his only surviving Edwardian publication.[14]

Champneys was not alone in his discovery of the vernacular Bible and what it meant for laymen's independence of the clergy. Henry Hart, who came originally from a village in Kent. published in these years two tracts showing a similar attitude toward the English Bible and toward learned clerics.[15] On the conservative side, the Kentish clergyman, John Proctor, wrote satirically of 'such nombre of heresyes so nigh home, so many infected with them within this Ile of England: within Englande, I saye, where everye man, everye woman pretendeth to be a gospeller, everye

[11] Philip R. Rider, *A Chronological Index to the Revised Edition of Pollard and Redgrave's Short-title Catalogue* (De Kalb, Illinois 1978) supplies, for STC Vol. II only, a computer printout basis for the following count of five-year period, 1542–46, 194; 1548–52, 355; 1554–58, 307; 1559–63, 233. If one remembers that these figures apply to roughly half the STC-recorded items for those years, they are compatible with the earlier calculations in John N. King: 'Freedom of the Press, Protestant Propaganda and Protector Somerset', *Huntingdon Library Quarterly*, XL, No. 1 (1976), pp. 1–9.

[12] *Harvest at hand*, sig. E 6^v; cf. also D 4^v, E 2, E 4.

[13] *Ibid.*, sig. B 4^v, D 8.

[14] John Strype, *Memorials of Thomas Cranmer* (Oxford 1840), pp. 254–57.

[15] *A godly newe short treatyse*, 1548 (STC 12887), sig. A 7^v, A 8, B 1^v; *A consultorie for all Christians*, 1549 (STC 12564), A 4.

boye, eche gyrle trayned & exercised in readynge the holy Scripture of Jesus Christ'.[16]

Kent and Essex, the two counties of the Freewillers' principal activity, were (along with London) the main areas of religious radicalism, being not only those most accessible to Anabaptist and other religious influences from the continent, but also regions of Lollard activity for generations past. The most conspicuous single radical of Edward's reign, Joan Bocher (or Joan of Kent) has recently been the subject of an essay describing in detail the mingling in her of the new Anabaptist and the old Lollard strains.[17] Her vocal defiance of the Protestant cleric preaching at her burning in 1550 was reported by a Roman Catholic writer to include the claim 'that there were a thousand in London of her sect' – an assertion indicating an order of magnitude which seemed credible to her and probably to others also.[18] The boast was taken seriously enough for the Protestant cleric, Edmund Becke, to respond with a verse tract aimed at the heresy she was burned for, *A brefe confutation of this most detestable and anabaptistical opinion that Christ did not take his flesh of the blessed Vyrgyn Mary* (STC 1709) and ridiculing Joan in its second stanza as 'the wayward Virago, that wold not repent, The devils Eldest daughter, which lately was brent.'

Further indications of orthodox concern over the religous radicals are of varied sorts. Hooper, writing again to Bullinger in June 1550, describes himself as about to leave London, 'by the King's command,' for Essex and Kent where he hopes to combat 'the frenzy of the Anabaptists.'[19] In the following January, a royal commission was formally appointed to deal with religious radicalism in these two counties, its 31 members including such prominent laymen as Sir John Cheke and Sir Thomas Smith, as well as some half-dozen strongly Protestant bishops.[20] Other orthodox Protestants, notably the refugee Frenchman, Jean Veron, undertook to translate attacks on the continental Anabapists by Calvin and Bullinger, usually adding prefaces about the pertinence of these authoritative writings to the English scene.[21]

[16] *The fal of the late Arrian*, 1549 (STC 20406), A 84ᵛ.

[17] John F. Davis, 'Joan of Kent, Lollardy and the English Reformtion', *J.E.H.*, XXXIII, No. 2 (April 1982), pp. 225-33; see also his more extensive *Heresy and Reformation in the South East of England, 1520-1559* (London 1983).

[18] Miles Hogarde, *Displaying of the Protestantes*, 1556 (STC 13558), fol. 47ᵛ. I am indebted to John Fines for bringing the significance of this reference to my attention.

[19] *Original Letters*, pp. 86-7.

[20] *Eccl. Mem.*, II, i., p. 385; ii, p. 200.

[21] E.g., Bullinger: *An holsom antidotus against the Anabaptists*, 1548 (STC 4059), *Dialoge between the seditious libertine or rebel Anabaptist & the true obedient Christian*, 1551 (STC 4068), *Defence of the baptisme of children against the pestiferous Anabaptistes*, 1551 (STC 4069); Calvin, *Instruction agaynst the pestiferous errours of the Anabaptistes*, 1549 (STC 4463).

Predestination attracted much of the religious discussion on both learned and popular levels. The doctrine seemed especially attractive to younger and more vigorous Protestants such as John Bradford, and was often seen as a critical issue between orthodox Protestantism and both Roman Catholicism and Anabaptism. For example, Robert Crowley, in a detailed refutation of the sermon preached by the apostate Protestant, Nicholas Shaxton, at the burning of Anne Askew in 1546, uses the epithets 'free will men' and 'free will masters' to characterize some of the Roman Catholic influence on him.[22] The orthodox William Turner, in attacking Anabaptists, uses their belief in free will as one ground for his attack; Nicholas Lesse does likewise in dedicating his translation from St. Augustine to Proctor Somerset's wife.[23]

Fully orthodox Protestants also disagreed among themselves on various aspects of predestination.[24] The views of the same person, moreover, could change markedly within a relatively few years. Thus, by the time Bernardo Ochino published *The Labyrinth* in Italian (about 1560) and, from abroad, dedicated it to Queen Elizabeth, he had become disturbed by some of the intellectual difficulties posed by the doctrine, and he proceeded to qualify some of the earlier positions taken in his book of sermons published in English in 1551.[25] John Clement, an orthodox Protestant artisan who died in one of Mary's prisons in 1556, cited these sermons as support for the doctrine in its full rigour.[26] Similarly, John Champneys, who in his 1548 tract had made such implicitly predestinarian remarks as 'a gyft of the holy ghost to theym which be of the electe people of God,'[27] wrote in 1560 or 1561 a qualified defence of free will and was attacked by both Robert Crowley and Jean Veron for doing so; Veron indeed attacked him by name as 'the blynde

---

[22] *The confutation of xiii articles* [1548] (STC 6083), sigs. H 8ᵛ ff. See also the dialogue on predestination between the orthodox Protestant, John Careless, and his Roman Catholic interrogator, *A. & M.*, VIII, p. 169.

[23] *A preservative or triacle agaynst the poyson of Pelagius*, 1551 (STC 24368); *A worke of the predestination of saints . . . by S. Augustine*, 1550 (STC 920). See also John Knox's long attack on the radical Robert Cooke: 'An answer to the cavilation of an adversary respecting the doctrine of predestination,' 1560, *Works*, David Laing, ed. (Edinburgh 1875), V, pp. 7–444.

[24] John ab Ulmis writes Bullinger from Oxford in April 1550 that it is wonderful how far Hooper and Bartholomew Traheron 'disagree respecting God's predestination of men', *Original Letters*, II, p. 406. Bodleian MS 53 also preserves a controversial exchange on predestination between Latimer's disciple, Augustine Bernhere, and two orthodox Protestants, John Laurence and John Barre.

[25] Karl Benrath, *Bernardino Ochino of Siena*, trans. H. Zimmern (New York 1877), pp. 250–59; *Certayne sermons of the ryghte famous and excellente clerk, Master Bernadino Ochino* [1551], (STC 18766).

[26] Clement's confession, printed in *Eccl. Mem.*, III, ii, pp. 463ff.

[27] *Harvest at hand*, sigs. C 4ᵛ, F 7ᵛ, G 3.

guide of the free wyll men.'[28] 'Free will men' was already in use in Protestant circles as a general pejorative and continued to be so as late as the debate between John Whitgift and Walter Travers in the 1570s.[29] When Veron calls Champneys 'the blynde guide of the free wyll men' it does not necessarily associate him with any specific group.

By the 1550s the issue of predestination versus free will was certainly one of the topics in liveliest dispute in England – one that no religious group could monopolize and none, probably, could long ignore.

3

The Freewillers are first definitely noted as a group (though not under that or any other particular name) in the actions taken by the Privy Council following their Christmas gathering at Bocking in 1550. The register for 27 January records that one Upcharde of Bocking, who had been arrested a few days earlier, 'was brought before the Counsaill tooching a certein assemblie that had been made in Christmas last.' Upcharde confessed '[there] were certein Kentishmen' in the town who were to have lodged with a clothier named Robert Cooke but transferred suddenly to Upcharde's house 'bicause Cookes wief was in childebed.' About noon the next day, Upcharde continued, 'divers of the towne . . . came in and there thei fell in argument of things of the Scripture, speciallie wheather it were necessarie to stande or kneele, barehedde or covered, at prayer; which at length was concluded in ceremonie not to be materiall, but the hartes before God was it that imported and no thing els.' The Council reacted immediately, 'bicause it seemed suche an assembley, being of xl persons or moo, shulde meane some great matter,' and sent orders to the sheriffs of Essex and Kent for the arrest of 16 named persons, committing Upcharde 'and one Sympson of the same sorte' to the Marshalsea for the time being. A week later, on 3 February, 12 of the 16 were examined by the Council and reiterated 'the cause of their assemblie to be for talke of Scriptures', adding somewhat repentantly that 'they had refused the Communyon above ii yeres upon verie superstitiouse and erronyose purposes withe divers other evill oppynyons worthie of great punyshement.' The Council then committed five of them to prison and released the other seven on

---

[28] The 1560 or 1561 original of Champney's later qualified defence of free will is lost, but it survives in a reprint in J.A.: *An historical narration of the judgement of some most learned and godly English bishops, holy martyrs and others . . . concerning God's election*, 1631 (STC 4), pp. 1-66. Vernon's attack occurs in the separately paginated second part of his *A fruteful treatis of predestination . . . whereunto are added . . . a very necessary boke against the free wyll men*, 1561 (STC 24681), fol. 28ᵛ. See also Vernon's *A moste necessary treatise of free will, not only against the Papistes but also against the Anabaptistes*, [1561] (STC 24684), a tract which ends on a mainly anti-Roman Catholic note.

[29] John Whitgift, *Works*, J. Ayre, ed., 3 vols. (Cambridge 1851), I, pp. 94-95.

recognizance, 'the condicion tappere whan thei shalbe called upon, and to resorte to their Ordinarie for resolucion of their oppynyons in case thei have any doubte in religion.'[30]

The subject was then considered by the Council to be closed. Its major concern – understandably, after major uprisings in Cornwall and Norfolk in 1549 and smaller outbreaks elsewhere[31] – was evidently the simple fact of an unexpected gathering of some 60 persons (the figure reported to the Privy Council), many of them from another county. Four of the five men committed to prison were from places other than Bocking, and the conditions for release of the others were such as to deny them occasion for convening another such meeting.

These unusually detailed notes in the register also shed considerable light on the nature of the group that had met at Bocking. The gathering was not haphazard but planned with some care, apparently after smaller previous meetings elsewhere. Its location may even have been chosen in part because Bocking was not under the jurisdiction of the Bishop of London like other Essex parishes, but was a 'peculiar' of the Archbishop of Canterbury.[32] All 18 participants identified in the Privy Council register are male with English-sounding names. Of the eleven from Essex, two are listed as clothiers from Bocking and one as a cowherd from 'Stamphorde' (possibly Stanford Rivers or Stanford-le-Hope, about 15 or 25 miles southwest or south of Bocking); the other seven are listed as from places in Kent – Maidstone, Ashford, Pluckley and Lenham – and Cole from Maidstone was further identified as a schoolmaster. There is no indication of formal organization or formally designated leadership. All testimony agreed, however, on religious discussion being the purpose of their gathering – on this occasion regarding prayer but, by implication, in previous sessions on the nature of the communion service.

A wider range of topics were discussed at other times, according to depositions by nine persons, taken in Kent at some undetermined time or times after the Bocking conventicle, which two of the depositions mention.[33] Only a selection of the depositions survive and these were evidently chosen for the vivid – not to say alarming – statements which they contain. The 'articles' of inquiry are numbered as high as 46, but a mere 16 are actually mentioned and the subject of only 14 can be

---

[30] *A.P.C.*, III, pp. 196-99, 206-07.

[31] See Barrett L. Beer: *Rebellion and Riot: Popular Disorder in England during the Reign of Edward VI* (Kent, Ohio 1962), chap. 6 especially.

[32] A decade or so later, separatists in London exploited for some years the fact that the parish of the Minories was a 'peculiar' exempt from the Bishop of London's jurisdiction (H. Gareth Owen: 'A Nursery of Elizabethan Nonconformity', *J.E.H.*, 17 (1966) pp. 65-67). Bocking was still a 'peculiar' as late as the nineteenth century, Samuel Lewis, *A Topographical Dictionary of England*, 4 vols. (London 1831), I, p. 196.

[33] Burrage, II, pp. 1-4.

identified from the statements given. Nine deponents are named and the opinions of six others (plus one of the deponents) are quoted; one of the deponents is identified as 'clarke' and another as 'mr'. Two of those quoted (Thomas Cole, the schoolmaster from Maidstone, and Nicholas Yonge of Lenham) were among those examined by the Privy Council. The statements are dated to different occasions, two of them in August ('Lamas day' and 'about Bartholomewetide') and one to an occasion about a year in the past. All of the statements on doctrine have the tone of lively debate. Thus, 'Cole of Faversham' asserted 'that the doctryne of predestynation was meter for diviles then for christian men;' Henry Hart was quoted in three different versions of the propostion 'that Saincte Paule might have dampned himselfe if he listed;' 'Cole of Maidstone saide and affirmed that children were not borne in originall syne.' Most, but not all, of the doctrinal views relate to predestination; Hart is quoted also as saying that 'his faithe was not growndid opon Lernyd men, for all errors were broughte in by Lernyd men.'

There are, however, about as many statements quoted on daily conduct (e.g. 'to playe at annye game for money it is Synne') and on the activities of the group. Membership is clearly restricted (they are obligated 'not to Salute a Synner or a man whome they knowe not'). Financial contributions are referred to, and members are evidently accustomed to travelling from one town to another for meetings. In one instance, a deponent from the village of Lenham quotes a statement he had heard made 'in Cole's house at Faversham' by a member from the town of Ashford. Nothing is said about formal organization or officers, but Henry Hart seems to be regarded as senior leader, since his views are quoted several times and no one else's more than once. Hart does not appear in the Privy Council record on Bocking, but mention was made earlier of his two published tracts, neither of which pays much attention to the question of predestination.

It seems likely that these depositions about Freewillers found a use as the 'boke of examinations' which the Privy Council sent to Cranmer on 27 September, 1552, to help him in his mission of dealing with a 'sect newly sprung in Kent,' for a few months later Cranmer was to be found listening to a recantation sermon by the same 'Cole of Maidstone' who is quoted in one of the depositions. The new sect, however, is given no name in the Privy Council register, nor is it identified with the group meeting at Bocking in 1550.[34]

[34] *A.P.C.*, IV, p. 131. It has been suggested that this group may have been an early Familist congregation, but Freewillers were specially associated with Kent and Familists were not. In the depositions of 1561 by two ex-Familists in Surrey – the earliest firm evidence about Familists in England – Familist congregations were said to exist in half a dozen other English counties, but Kent was not one of these, Folger Library Losely MS L.b. 98, printed in Jean D. Moss: *'Godded with God': Hendrik Niclaes and his Family of Love* (Philadelphia 1981), p. 74.

4

The controversy among Protestants in the King's Bench prison was not a matter of one formal argument, or even two, between a Freewiller group and orthodox Protestants but rather one of continued disputation – as the enforced leisure of prison life invited – on a number of questions besides predestination. It was predestination, however, which provided the main topic of dispute – in part, perhaps, because the doctrine held a special importance for John Bradford, who had been one of the leading younger clerics of the Edwardian church and was easily the dominant figure among all the prisoners in the King's Bench. His 'Defence of Election' was written in late 1554, partly in response to a paper of Henry Hart's on the 'enormities' of predestination, and ten of his prison letters involve, in one way or another, past or present Freewillers. It is clear from these letters and other sources that some of the seven persons, appearing both in the King's Bench disputes and in the Edwardian documents cited previously, had been converted to orthodox Protestantism before Bradford wrote. Thus, Robert Cole of Faversham, quoted in the depositions as thinking predestination a doctrine suitable for devils, appears in John Bradford's prison letters as a trusted ally in the predestination controversy, and is reported by a government agent as based in an inn in the City of London and to 'resort much unto the King's Bench, unto the prisoners.'[35] One of Cole's colleagues at the inn was John Ledley whom the Privy Council had ordered arrested for participation in the Bocking conventicle. Nicholas Shetterton, another of those similarly ordered arrested in 1551, is also addressed as an ally in Bradford's letters, and may have been the author of the long anonymous letter (printed by Strype) to his former comrades among the Freewillers, recounting how he has found the truth among the orthodox Protestants, along with such former friends as 'our brethren Ledley and Cole.'[36]

Hart, who challenged Bradford on the doctrine of predestination, was generally considered the leading figure on the free will side and appears in his writings as a man capable of piercing insights. He goes to the heart of current iconoclastic feeling, for instance, in a marginal note in his first published tract, 'An ydol is that which hathe the love of the harte and is placed in the roume of God'.[37] In his two published tracts he has little directly to say about predestination, but is much concerned about the Bible as a guide to right conduct and evidently disturbed by the possibility that men might take its promises of salvation to be

[35] *A. & M.*, VIII, p. 384.
[36] *Eccl. Mem.*, III, ii, pp. 325-34. Shetterton's prison letters to members of his family show him as quite capable of writing it, *A. & M.*, VII, pp. 313-18.
[37] *A godly newe short treatyse*, sig. B 1ᵛ.

unconditional: 'Thinkest thou that they shall be preserved and defended of God that continue and delite in sinne and wickednes?'[38] His contentions against Bradford we know only through the latter's assurance in the second part of the 'Defence of Election' that he has quoted Hart in detail, 'not leaving out one tittle of every word as he hath put it abroad.'[39] Hart rejects the doctrine, it would seem from the six 'enormities' he sets forth, primarily because it conflicts with the concept of God which he has derived from his own reading of Scripture. The God predestination reveals to him is incompatible with a God of mercy; it undercuts the redeeming power of Christ; it makes God responsible for a man's good or evil actions and not the man himself, and so 'colourably denieth excommunication to be had and used in the congregation of Christ.' Hart cites biblical passages in support of his points, but not very extensively, and Bradford, as a trained theologian, has little difficulty in showing that Hart has not examined all the relevant texts or explored the full implications of his statements.

Bradford himself, after his letter to Cranmer and Ridley expressing alarm about the Freewillers, seems to have decided that there were considerations involved more important than purity of doctrine. In a kind of farewell letter in mid-February 1555 addressed to some 13 persons who had been on all sides of the dispute, he made a plea for avoiding controversy on the issue, and he reiterated this plea in separate letters to John Philpot, former archdeacon of Winchester, and to two Freewillers who maintained their position.[40] To the former Freewiller, Robert Cole, he wrote, 'If we cannot agree on all points, either the points perchance be not so necessary, or else by love we shall hereafter be brought to see that which yet is hid.'[41]

Animosity toward the Freewillers continued, however, among other Protestant prisoners. The orthodox layman, John Careless, after being baited by his Roman Catholic interrogator about Hart as a fellow heretic, denounced Hart for having 'shamefully seduced' others 'with his foul Pelagian opinions, both in the days of that good King Edward and since his departure.' Hart, Careless said, had written his own 'confession' on the back of one Careless had written and circulated among the prisoners for signatures.[42] A similar view of Freewillers is taken in a long confession, dated 1 April 1556, by the Protestant prisoner John Clements, a wheelwright.[43]

[38] *A consultorie for all Christians*, sig. E 2.
[39] Bradford, I, p. 309; pp. 318-29 for Hart's paragraphs.
[40] Bradford, II, pp. 194-98; 180.
[41] *Ibid.*, pp. 215-16.
[42] *A. & M.*, VII, 164-65. A copy of Hart's confession survives (along with the signatures of orthodox prisoners denouncing it as 'blasphemous') in Emmanuel College MS 260, fol. 67, dateable as 21 April, 1556.
[43] *Eccl. Mem.*, III, ii, pp. 446-67.

Controversy in the King's Bench, however, focused also on topics unrelated to predestination. Careless's interrogator jabbed him about Arians and Anabaptists (mentioning two particular prisoners in the former category),[44] and the hot-tempered John Philpot, wrote an 'Apology for Spitting upon an Arian' which devotes two or three of its pages to denouncing the Freewiller prisoners as well.[45] The Freewiller John Trew, in his 'Cause of the contention in the King's Bench,' describes his group's confrontation with the orthodox as first arising over gambling, which a Freewiller deposition made in Edward's reign declared to be a sin, but which their present fellow prisoners saw as a religiously harmless way of passing the time. The Freewillers, concerned as so often about personal conduct, urged that they 'redeem the time' with prayer and Bible-reading, while the orthodox cited Scripture to 'affirm play and pastimes to be clean to Christians.' The sectaries, of course, countered with opposing texts.[46] There was, perhaps, a touch of class antagonism at one or two points: the Freewillers saw the others as holding that 'none but great learned men could have the true understanding of the word of God,' complained that their share of prison relief funds (which evidently came through orthodox channels) was withheld from them, and that the orthodox 'would neither eat nor drink with us, nor yet bid us God speed.'[47] Inevitably, disputes over predestination entered into their relations also, Trew citing a score or so of 'enormities' they found in it.

Trew also describes a number of reconciliations, apparently reached by agreeing to keep quiet about points on which the two groups sharply differed, but these truces kept breaking down. One such break came from the Freewillers' refusal to recognize as valid (as orthodox Protestants at this time generally did) baptisms performed years earlier by priests in communion with Rome. In the heat of another dispute, Trew says, the orthodox 'threatened us that we were like to die for it if the Gospel should reign again.'[48]

Trew relates two mediation efforts in some detail. One was headed by Sympson and Upcharde, the first men to be arrested at the time of the Bocking conventicle. Though they were now warmly regarded by the orthodox,[49] both they and Trew's associates were evidently still

[44] *A. & M.*, VII, pp. 165, 169.
[45] *Examinations and Writings*, R. Eden, ed. (Cambridge 1842), pp. 306-08.
[46] Trew, pp. 37-39.
[47] *Ibid.*, p. 47. Bradford, in a conciliatory letter to Trew and his group denied that prison relief funds had been withheld from the Freewiller group, Bradford II, p. 180.
[48] Trew, pp. 54, 57.
[49] One of Bradford's letters on the predestination controversy refers to 'my brother Symson' (Bradford II, p. 128), and the orthodox John Careless calls Upcharde 'my dear brother' in a long and effusive letter, printed by Foxe as to 'T.V.' (*A. & M.*, VIII, pp. 183-5), though the manuscript version gives his full name (Emmanuel College MS 260, 108, fols. 213-4).

conscious of a common bond. Sympson especially tried to bring the two prison groups together in what Trew describes as an effort to 'devise such order between us (concerning the unity) as might most redound to God's glory and the health and quietness of his church.'[50] This attempt, however, was overtaken by a second negotiation when Trew, learning that the orthodox planned a Christmas communion at which the Freewillers were invited to receive with them, undertook negotiations of his own with Careless in order to 'have the unity thoroughly established first, lest we did receive it to our damnation.' Attempts to draft a joint confession came to grief, however, and the effort ended with mutual accusations of bad faith.[51] Trew prints, over the date of 30 January 1555, the seven-article confession he had drafted for both sides to sign, appending to it twelve Freewiller signatures – one of them by his chief associate, Thomas Avington, and another by a woman prisoner. It is concessive in a number of respects, such as fully endorsing the sacraments and preaching of the Edwardian church and admitting 'that our knowledge is imperfect' on many points, but it does insist in Article 4 that, though 'all salvation . . . cometh to us wholly and solely through the mercy and favour of God,' nevertheless 'all who truly repent shall be saved and that there is no decree of God to the contrary.'[52] The signers probably represent the hard core of Freewillers in the King's Bench after an undetermined number of others had been converted to orthodox Protestantism.

The disputations and negotiations came to no conclusive end. A number of the participants went to the stake during 1555, including the clerics Bradford and Philpot and, on the Freewiller side, Shetterton, Middleton and Avington. Careless died in prison about July 1556 and Trew, according to Careless, escaped by breaking his informal parole to a jailer; Hart was reported dead in 1557; various others just disappear from sight.

The life of the Freewillers as a group is to be discerned in some of the prison events. Their collective identity was clearly of prime importance, at least to Trew's residual group, and was related to particular beliefs they held. At the same time, both they and the orthodox recognized a common religious bond between them (as seen in the desire for a joint communion service and in the sharing of prison relief funds), and the Freewillers indicated that, within limits, doctrine was negotiable in order to achieve the fellowship of a confirmed unity. Within the group there was evidently recognition of some persons, such as Hart and Trew, as having leading roles but no formal organization like that seen in the congregational compacts of later groups. The 'thirteen articles', which a

[50] Trew, p. 57.
[51] *Ibid.*, pp. 58-63.
[52] *Ibid.*, pp. 65-70.

government agent implied that Hart used as a device to control the group,[53] are not referred to by any of those actually involved in the King's Bench discussions, and Trew, speaking for his group in some of the negotiations, still felt himself bound to obtain the explicit concurrence of the other members.

5

Another aspect of the Freewillers – not directly referred to in the King's Bench controversies – is their concern with personal, 'interior' religion. They were, of course, not alone in this. Amid sixteenth-century England's extensive arguments over matters of state and matters of doctrine, there was also a persistent interest in private devotions – as evidenced in the publication of some 20 editions of all or part of *The Imitation of Christ* in English which the *Short-Title Catalogue* notes for the years 1500–80, as well as various devotional works of largely English origin. There are, for example, Catherine Parr's compilation, *Prayers stirring the mynd*, 1545 (STC 4818), compilations such as *Certayne praiers and godlye meditacions*, [1546?] (STC 2996), and *Prayers and meditacions wherein the minde is styred pacientlye to suffre all afflictions*, [1546] (STC 4820), Thomas Becon's *The pomander of prayer*, 1558 (STC 1744), and the anonymous *A godly and holsom preservatyve against disparacion*, [1559] (STC 20205). John Bradford was a major writer of such works; prayers and meditations, indeed, make up more than a fifth of the contents of the standard Parker Society edition of his works. These books of private devotion generally have no pronounced Protestant or Roman Catholic flavour; in fact, as a modern historian has shown, Bradford drew heavily for some of his meditations on the early sixteenth-century Spanish humanist, Juan Luis Vives.[54]

The Freewiller group as a whole, in discussing prayers at its 1550 gathering in Bocking, had concluded that the outer manner of prayer was of no importance and that only one's inner attitude ('the hartes before God') mattered. This interest was underlined in a small book, containing prayers by two individual members of the group, Robert Cole and John Ledley, which was published in Mary's reign under the title, *Godly meditacions verye necessarie to bee sayde of all Christen men* (STC 17776) and survives only in a single copy. This is bound with two other small books of private devotions, and internal evidence establishes that it was printed sometime between Mary's marriage to Philip II in July 1554

---

[53] *A. & M.*, VIII, p. 384.
[54] Helen C. White, *Tudor Books of Private Devotion* (Madison, Wis., 1951). Bradford also translated, and wrote a preface to, Melanchthon's *A godly treatise of prayer*, 1553 (STC 17791).

and her death in November 1558.[55]

Godly meditacions contains seven rather varied prayers, three of them signed or initialled. The first (here only initialled but signed 'Robert Cole' in a later edition) is in marked contrast to the shorter and more conventional prayers usually found in such works. Where these latter are often 'public' prayers, asking for peace and safety from the plague, or more standard personal desires such as physical safety and final salvation, Cole's prayer asks for a purer spiritual life, for 'the true judgment of spirites, that I may be neyther decyved by love nor by hate.'[56] A few pages earlier he asks: 'O Lord, graunt that I may never envi ani good mans love or womans because they eyther do love god & his people more than I or els that they be beloved of ani more than I.' There is also a taste for rhetoric evident in Cole's manner of praying: 'O Lord make me merrie in thee without lightnes, sad without mistrust, sober without dulnes, true without desperacion, trusting in thee without presumption.'[57]

Ledley's prayer is about twice the length of Cole's and in very similar vein – asking, for instance, for 'grace to walke with a good conscience before thee and towardes al men in bying and sellyng, and in all other my doynges; to cast away all lying, craft and deceit, and I be not a reader of thy holy worde and a talker onelye.' Ledley is perhaps fonder than Cole of paraphrasing Scripture in his prayers and he strikes the note of contrition somewhat more strongly. In one passage dealing with his marriage he is unusually frank: 'O Lord, make me to bee contente with this woman thou has geven me to be my wyfe, and let her love alwaies satisfie me. O Lord, give her an hart of understanding and set thy feare always before her eyes.'[58]

The expression of such private meditations was, of course, not dependent on the holding of separatist meetings, but it is easy to see how it would be encouraged by the emotional support of gatherings such as that at Bocking which discussed the manner of prayer – a gathering it is hard to imagine taking place in a mid-Tudor parish church.

That there was indeed a wider interest in these views of Cole and Ledley is indicated by the subsequent publishing history of their devotional writing, starting with their larger volume, *Certayne godly exercises, meditacions and prayers very necessary and profytable for all persons and all times* (STC 10617), issued probably in 1560. The passages quoted above are essentially retained, some of them being further elaborated rhetorically and Ledley's passage about his marriage being somewhat

[55] I am grateful to Philippa Tudor for first bringing this book – and its correct dating – to my attention.
[56] *Godly meditacion*, sig. B. 1.
[57] *Ibid.*, A 6ᵛ; A 7ᵛ.
[58] *Ibid.*, C 7ᵛ; D 3.

toned down. Cole contributes additionally some shorter and more conventional prayers for particular occasions. He also has a longer piece, *Certein exercises to meditate, very profitable to every Christen*, which consists largely of admonitions to humble one's self before God and to pray often.[59]

Ledley's long prayer in this volume repeats both a number of passages from his own prayer and from Cole's (the second passage in the Marian publication quoted above). He continues to paraphrase Scripture extensively and adds a passage or two like the following: 'Graunt me this gifte that I may be swyfte to heare, slowe to speak & slowe to wrathe, that my hart do not go after any evyll and wicked imaginations.'[60] The title of this selection approximates the subtitle of the volume, and the emphasis throughout is on a very personal religion. One can see in this a distinctive Ledley style and type of prayer – though the anonymous selection almost preceding it shows that others could write in the Ledley manner also.

A few more years into Elizabeth's reign it was evident that the term 'Ledley's prayers' had acquired a certain generic meaning, identifying somewhat stylized petitions for guidance in one's private spiritual life. In 1568, in the first of five successive editions of Henry Bull's compilation, *Christen prayers and holy meditations* (STC 4028), a separate section, accounting for over a third of the entire volume, was introduced under the heading, 'Prayers commonlye called lydleys prayers, with certaine godly additions', and the first item in this section is substantially the long prayer of Ledley's from the 1560 volume. No uniform practice was followed in the four following editions. The 'Ledley's prayers' section does not appear in the 1570 volume (STC 4029), but in that conjecturally dated as 1578 (STC 4030) the statement, 'Wherunto are added the praiers commonly called Lidleys prayers', appears on the title page. The section was probably included also in the edition of 1584 (STC 4031), though here we can only surmise.[61] The 1596 edition contains the usual separate section, though with little remaining of the actual phrases used in the signed prayers of the 1560 edition. The concerns and style of many of the prayers, however, are similar enough and it is evident that, some 40 years after the passing of the Freewillers and their group concern for private devotions, the term 'Ledley's prayers' still had meaning and appeal for a segment of the English reading public.

---

[59] *Godly exercises*, B 6ᵛ–8.

[60] *Ibid.*, F 4ᵛ.

[61] The only surviving copy is apparently defective; it is considerably shorter than the other editions and lacks the usual Table of Contents at the end, but the carry-over word, 'Prayers', on the last surviving page looks like the beginning of the subhead for the 'Ledley's prayers' section in the 1568 edition.

6

Further light on the Freewillers is cast by the career of Thomas Cole, who was the best educated and subsequently the best known of those in the group. In the arrest order after the Bocking conventicle he is described as schoolmaster of Maidstone and in the depositions taken somewhat later on Freewiller beliefs and practices he is quoted as denying the doctrine of original sin. The sermon he preached before Cranmer in Maidstone church in February 1553 was evidently designed as a general recantation and clearing of his name from all allegations of heresy.[62]

From that sermon on, his career contained nothing more heterodox than an inclination to what came to be considered the Puritan wing of the Church of England. He was in the English community at Frankfurt by September 1554 (well before the controversies in the King's Bench reached their height) and played an active role in exile affairs, generally adhering to the party of Knox and Whittingham. Returning to England, he was made rector of High Ongar and Archdeacon of Essex, and figured in rather varied ways in the life of the Elizabethan church until his death in 1571. He was widely admired for his pulpit eloquence and preached a sermon before Queen Elizabeth which was printed in 1564 (STC 5540). This, unlike the earlier sermon before Cranmer, was a fairly standard piece of work, paying tribute (with abundant biblical citations) to princes as protectors and 'nurses' of God's church, and tactfully reminding the Queen of the obligations that this entailed. Cole's career as a whole was marked by interest in varied activities and apparently by more than normal energy, but his basic attitudes seem to have been those of an establishment figure.

The sermon preached before Cranmer has its puzzling aspects, and in examining it one needs to keep in mind both the nature of the preacher and the nature of the occasion. Cole is a trained theologian, fond of learned comparisons and lawyer-like distinctions, scorning to translate from the Latin his many biblical quotations. As a reference in the sermon indicates, the church where it was preached contained in some prominent position two men bearing faggots or other symbols of recantation and penance, but mentioned by Cole as having no real connection with him. The rhetorical device he adopts for abjuring and denouncing heresy is to descibe a dozen or so particular beliefs and practices as 'poisoned flowers' with which the Devil seeks to attract and entangle men. Some of these Cole refutes by argument and scriptural quotation; others he simply denounces. At the end of the list he denies

---

[62] *A godly and frutefull sermon, made at Maydstone . . . by M. Thomas Cole, scholemayster there, against dyvers erronious opinions of the Anabaptistes and others*, 1553 (STC 5539).

that he has described them 'in the way of recantation,' asserting that 'I came hyther in the way of exhortacion'[63] and devoting the remaining dozen pages or more to an evangelistic plea for spiritual conversion and reform of conduct. 'Nowe is the tyme,' he cries, 'that oure Lorde knocketh at the doore of your conscience,' repeating the first four words in paragraph after paragraph of varied pleas and ending with specific appeals to justices, other officers, husbands, wives, servants, and so on, each to 'behave hym selfe as the mynister of God.'[64]

What is of special interest, of course, is Cole's list of particular 'poisoned flowers' followed by his categorical assertion that 'For God is my witnes, before whom I stand, I never helde or taught any of these or such lyke errours, neither do I knowe anye that doth hold or mayntayne any of them besydes these two simple men, which are here punished for their offences.'[65] Since several of these 'errours' are closely matched to views attributed to various Freewillers in the depositions taken after the Bocking conventicle, and one of them ('to deny that children be borne in original synne') is a direct quotation from Cole himself,[66] his statements have somewhat understandably been characterized as 'double-talk'.[67] Cole, however, must have known that his previous statements would have been duly reported and that absolute denial would not be credible. What he is probably doing in the passage quoted, therefore, is drawing a distinction between discussing or debating a belief and holding, maintaining or teaching it as an article of faith. This distinction is quite compatible with what we know from other sources about the group's practices. The Freewillers at Bocking discussed various aspects of prayer but concluded that nothing about it was to be held essential except the petitioner's sincerity; they were willing later on to withdraw their objections to the Edwardian church's communion service; even John Trew's hard-core group in the King's Bench showed flexibility on points of doctrine. The phrasing of the doctrinal statements by Freewillers quoted in the depositions is also significant, having the tone not of formally adopted articles of faith but, as remarked earlier, that of propositions in a lively debate.

We may, indeed, have a partial replay of a Freewiller debate in the sermon's assertion that gambling 'of itself is not deadly syn', and its subsequent discussion of the point, which runs to greater length than that on most other 'poisoned flowers'. The Freewiller William Greneland, as quoted in the depositions, had declared flatly that 'to play at annye game for money it is Synne', while Cole's sermon argues that the sinfulness

---

[63] *Ibid.*, D 3, 4.
[64] *Ibid.*, D 7, E 2.
[65] *Ibid.*, D 3ᵛ.
[66] *Ibid.*, C 8; see Burrage II, p. 3, for the deposition's version of Cole's statement.
[67] Horst, *op. cit.*, p. 124.

resides only in the things it may lead to, such as idleness, quarrels, blasphemy and the loss of a family's sustenance by its breadwinner. What Cole denounces primarily is 'a precisenes' taken to such a degree 'that at length a good man might judg everything, although it were but indifferent, to be damnable sin.'[68] On another topic, Cole denounces the view that free will by itself can enable man to 'doo all thynges pleasynge to God,' and also the belief that all men are predestined to be saved beyond the possiblity of damnation. Against this view, attributed to Humphrey Middleton in the depositions, Cole paradoxically employs some of the arguments used by Henry Hart against the predestination of the elect.[69]

Two of the sermon's 'poisoned flowers' relate directly to separatism. Addressing fellow group members as 'brother' and 'sister' – a practice found in various sects but not recorded as one followed by the Freewillers – is briefly denounced near the end of the list as divisive of Christian unity. Earlier in his list of 'errours' Cole makes a more comprehensive statement on separatism. Here he vigorously opposes 'segregation from other as from wycked and damned men not worthy to communicate the sacraments or to eate and drynke with them.' This was a point on which there was evident disagreement, or at least uncertainty, among the Freewillers – as among many other Christians before and since. Nicholas Yonge is quoted in the depositions as saying flatly 'that they wolde not communycate with Synners,' but John Trew was eager for a joint communion with the orthodox Protestant prisoners under certain conditions, and at another time took offence at their refusal to eat and drink with the Freewillers. In the sermon, Cole denounces as 'authors of sectes' all those who, 'mislyking the common order, choose ceremonies and doctrines of theyr own inventions,' but he follows immediately with an insistence that it is not 'unlawful, neyther cause of division, for any man to use in his house any private order' for the education of youth in godliness, providing 'it be consonant with the woorde of God and in no contempt of the common order.'[70]

Other beliefs and practices denounced in the sermon include antinomian doctrines, which Freewiller meetings may have discussed but without leaving any record of such discussions, and unauthorized public preaching – which is nowhere reported about them and indeed would have been quite foreign to their known pattern of activity.[71]

---

[68] *Sermon at Maydstone*, D 2.
[69] *Ibid.*, C 4; B 4.
[70] *Ibid.*, D 1ᵛ; C 5ᵛ.
[71] *Ibid.*, C 2, 3, 7.

7

Nothing further is heard of the Freewillers as a group after Mary's reign; its known lifetime is limited to a mere half-dozen years, and even those imperfectly documented. Some tentative conclusions about the group, nevertheless, seem justified.

First and most obvious, the group attracted persons of diverse backgrounds and abilities. Thomas Cole was a learned cleric, quoting extensively in Latin in his sermon before Cranmer; Henry Hart is on record (not only in the depositions but in his printed tracts) as considering learned men to be dangerous guides in matters of religion. Robert Cole, whether a university man or not, shows himself articulate, well read biblically, and spiritually sensitive – as do Ledley and Shetterton also. None of the last three seems from his prayers or letters to be greatly interested in doctrinal controversy. John Trew and his fellow signers of the 1555 confession, on the other hand, sound more like the later stereotype of the sectary – quick to take a distinctive doctrinal position and support it by a wealth of biblical citation. Socially, as far as one can judge from the few occupational designations in the record, Freewillers were mostly small-town artisans. What briefly united these diverse personalities in those uncertain times was an evident need to discuss their personal concerns about religion with others who shared them, and (as the subsequent careers of some of them showed) an unusual degree of enterprise in doing so.

Second, Freewillers were a layman's group and had no discernible hesitation in gathering as laymen to discuss any aspect of religion. The cleric Thomas Cole was present in no authorized clerical capacity. The vernacular Bible had put laymen in a position to tackle religious questions for themselves, as the 'talke of Scripture' at the Bocking conventicle illustrated. For some, at least, there was perhaps a sense of common quest in disclaiming learned guides and teaching themselves 'out of God's booke.'[72]

Third, Freewillers (despite their label) were not firmly attached to any single doctrine or set of doctrines. The most fully reported member of the group, Henry Hart, varied considerably in his religious emphases, having nothing to say about some issues as current as transubstantiation and, except in his reply to Bradford's 'Treatise on Election', less than one might expect on predestination. Thomas Cole is to be believed in his flat denial that he had 'helde or taught' any of the heretical views denounced in his sermon before Cranmer. Even the Freewillers headed by John Trew in the King's Bench showed a good deal of flexibility in what they

---

[72] See Shetterton's retrospective prison letters to his brother, *A. & M.*, VII, pp. 314-16.

would accept in the confession of 30 January 1555.

Fourth (and equally important), Freewillers nevertheless felt a strong need for discussing a number of current religious questions, including the doctrine of predestination. Their concern was with matters of personal rather than public religion; the subject of the papal allegiance, for example, seems never to have been mentioned. Their interest went instead to such matters as the nature and importance of private prayer, the meaning of the Bible for daily conduct and even to such issues as gambling. That discussing religious questions – and hearing them discussed – was a deep-rooted, complex and continuing interest for Tudor Englishmen is suggested by such developments within the Church of England as the 'prophesyings' banned by Queen Elizabeth in the 1570s and the endowed lectureships later on.

Fifth, they were a rather fluid group, and the extent of their separation from the Protestant Church of England was something the Freewillers themselves were not clear about. Their kind of religious discussion, employing such sharply worded propositions as those recorded in the depositions of Edward's reign, could be pursued effectively only among those having a degree of mutual sympathy and trust, and so demanded that they be – for this purpose, at least – a self-selected group holding themselves somewhat apart. The questions discussed were, for many, topics of such gravity as to be approachable only in a company of the like-minded. Though the group gave itself no name, it was very conscious of having an identity of its own, as the events in the King's Bench illustrate. But neither in the disputations there, nor during their interrogations following the Bocking conventicle, did Freewillers repudiate all participation in the rites of the national church or cite biblical texts about avoiding the defilement of associating with the wicked.

Finally, it is to be noted of the Freewillers that many remained attached to the group for a relatively short time. Nor was this merely the result of the Marian imprisonments and executions. Of seven identified as members in King Edward's reign who appear again in the King's Bench controversy, only Hart appears as a still convinced Freewiller, while several of the others were evidently active on the other side. Thomas Cole, of course, had returned to orthodox Protestantism even before Edward's death. Some of the dozen signers of Trew's 1555 confession may have dated back to the Bocking conventicle, but the record sheds no light on this. For a number of the group, at least, membership turned out to be less a permanent commitment than a kind of schooling process – a way not found in parish churches, or other institutions of their day of giving urgent consideration to their problems of personal religion. Their problems having been confronted, these members were apparently satisfied thereafter with orthodox Protestantism.

Later separatists were to differ in various ways. Henry Barrow's congregation in the 1590s was quite sure that separation from the established church had to be absolute. Others were to make adherence to a congregational compact or to a particular theological tenet decisive for membership. Still others were distinguished as the devoted followers of a single leader. Many were more confident than the Freewillers of just what they stood for. Some were to achieve permanence. Such groups also became much more numerous in the ensuing century or so and, because many engaged in public preaching, far more visible. The primary elements of Protestant separatism, however, are already to be found in the mid-Tudor Freewillers.

Appendix

Biographical Register of Freewillers

The 47 names listed below of persons at one time or another sympathetically associated with a Freewiller group come mainly from three firm contemporary sources: arrest orders issued by the Privy Council following the Bocking conventicle; depositions by Freewillers in Kent taken at some time after that; signatures of the confession of faith by Freewillers in the King's Bench, 30 January 1555. When at least two less decisive pieces of evidence seem to converge on a name, it also has been added, but appearance among the 13 addressees of John Bradford's farewell letter to those involved in one way or another in the predestination controversy has not, in itself, been considered sufficient to add names to the list (e.g. Roger Newman, William Porrege, Richard Prowde).

A number of the names were fairly common at the time; Thomas Broke and Richard Harman, for example, have the same names as rather active Protestants in different spheres well over a decade earlier. In four instances where a coincidence of names occurs during Mary's reign, the considerations weighing against identifying them have been set forth in footnotes. Another Freewiller identification which has been rejected concerns the 'Wodman' who joined with the ex-Freewillers, Sympson and Upcharde, in the unsuccessful effort to reconcile the Freewiller and orthodox Protestant groups in the King's Bench prison during late 1554 (Trew, p. 57). It is tempting to believe that this man was the Richard Woodman, ironmaker of Warbleton, Sussex, who was a prisoner in the King's Bench from June 1554 to mid-October 1555 and much interested in doctrinal disputation, later becoming an itinerant preacher and being burned in June 1557 (*A. & M.*, VIII, pp. 332-77); but the 'Wodman' of Trew's account is nowhere specifically categorized as a Freewiller.

Arede, Thomas: Signed confession of 30 January 1555 (Trew, pp. 69, 70).

Avington, also Abington, Abyngton, Thomas (turner, Ardingly, Sussex): Signed confession of 30 January 1555 (Trew, pp. 69, 70); appears in Bradford's letters as Trew's principal associate in hard-core Freewiller group (Bradford II, pp. 180-81, 214); burned at Lewes, June 1555 (*A. & M.*, VIII, p. 151).

Bagge also Blagge, Richard (Essex): Ordered arrested 27 January 1551, interrogated 3 February and released on recognizance (*A.P.C.*, III, pp. 199, 207).

Barret, also Barrey, John (cowherd, 'Stamphorde', Essex): Ordered arrested 27 January 1551, interrogated 3 February and 'Commytted to ----' (*A.P.C.*, III, pp. 199, 206-07).

Boughtell, (Essex): Ordered arrested 27 January 1551, interrogated 3 February and 'Commytted to ----' (*A.P.C.*, III, pp, 199, 206-07).

Brodebridge, also Brodbridge, George (Bromfield, Kent): Anti-predestinarian views reported by three deponents, *c.* 1551 (Burrage II, p. 2). Under Mary, tried 3 August 1555, giving orthodox Protestant replies; burned at Canterbury (*A. & M.*, VII, p. 383).

Broke, Thomas (referred to as 'mr', Kent): One of three deponents *c.* 1551 re Freewiller practices and beliefs (Burrage II, pp. 2, 3).

Chamberlain: Listed by Strype as a 'teacher' among Freewillers in King's Bench prison (*Cranmer*, p. 502); John Careless, orthodox Protestant prisoner, told in April 1556 by Roman Catholic interrogator that one Chamberlain, like Henry Hart, 'hath written a book against thy faith' (*A. &. M.*, VIII, p. 164).

Choderton (Ashford, Kent): Ordered arrested 27 January 1551 (*A.P.C.*, III, p. 199).

Cole, also Coles, Robert (cleric, Faversham, Kent): Reported in depositions *c.* 1551 as making strong anti-predestinarian statement, also holding Freewiller meeting in his Faversham house (Burrage II, pp. 1, 3).
In Mary's reign, he and wife 'persecuted' out of Faversham, where he apparently had a personal feud with local J.P. (*A. &. M.*, VIII, Appendix VI and p. 790, identified there as 'now minister of Bow in London'); reported by government agent as based in London inn with

John Ledley for propaganda aimed especially at prisoners in King's
Bench, also keeping in touch with exiles (*A. & M.*, VIII, p. 384).
Appears in Bradford's letters as converted to orthodox Protestantism
(Bradford II, pp. 133-35, 215-16, 243-44), likewise in letter by ex-
Freewiller (printed in Strype, *Eccl. Mem.*, III, ii, pp. 329, 334);
reported by Foxe as assisting Thomas Bentham in 1558 in pastorate of
principal London underground congregation (*A. &. M.*, VIII, pp.
559, 788); listed by Strype with some 20 'sustainers' of Protestants in
prison or exile (*Eccl. Mem.*, III, i, p. 224); contributed, with Ledley and
others, to published volume of prayers (STC 17776, dateable
internally as 1554-58).
Under Elizabeth, rector of St. Mary-le-Bow, 1559-76 and All
Hallows, Bread Street, 1569-76 (R. Newcourt: *Repertorium
Ecclesiasticum Parochiae Londinense*, London 1710-17, I, pp. 439, 219);
in dispute over vestments in 1564-66, held up by Grindal's chancellor
as model of conformity after having previously objected (Strype,
Grindal, pp. 144-45; see also *Correspondence of Archbishop Parker*, Bruce
& Perowne, eds., (Cambridge 1853), p. 278); in December 1560
referred to by Bentham, then Bishop of Coventry and Lichfield, as
one through whom he was seeking advice on proper New Year's gift
for the Queen ('The Letter Book of Thomas Bentham', R.O'Day and
J. Berlatsky, eds., *Camden Miscellany* (London 1979), p. 184).[73]

Cole, also Coole, Colle, Thomas (cleric Maidstone, Kent): Described as
Maidstone schoolmaster in arrest order of 27 January 1551,
interrogated 3 February, 'Commytted to ----' (*A.P.C.*, III, pp. 199,
206-07); quoted in depositions *c.* 1551 as denying original sin (Burrage
II, p. 3); in February 1553 preached before Cranmer in Maidstone
sermon, later printed, 'against the Anabaptists' (STC 5539).
In Mary's reign, an early exile, prominent on side of Knox and
Whittingham in dispute at Frankfurt, signing joint statement there,
September 1554, and writing about developments to friend shortly
afterwards (*Troubles begonne at Frankford*, 1846 reprint, Petheram, ed.,
pp. 20, 59-62).
Under Elizabeth, became rector of High Ongar, 1559, Archdeacon of
Essex, 1561, named Dean of Salisbury a month before his death in July
1571; D.D., Cambridge with statement 'M.A. Oxford 14 years',

[73] Possibly, as stated in C.H. Garrett, *The Marian Exiles* (Cambridge 1938), pp. 121-
22, he is the Bedfordshire Robert Cole who entered King's College from Eton in 1542,
proceeded B.A. 1546-47, M.A. 1550, and was fellow 1545-51; this identification would
make more plausible his choice to assist Bentham in the London pastorate and his two
rectorships in the Elizabethan church, but it is hard to see on what basis the Bedfordshire
Cole would have been so firmly established in Faversham, *c.* 1551. The name was
common at the time: *e.g.*, the Robert Cole who, as rector of Epsom, wrote in April 1580
(over three years after the Faversham Cole's death) to the magistrate Sir William More,
complaining about a vindictive recusant (Folger Library MS L. b. 309).

(*Alumni Cantabrigiensis*, J. Venn and J.A. Venn, eds., (Cambridge 1922), I, i, p. 368; *Zurich Letters*, second series, H. Robinson ed., (Cambridge 1846), p. 349). Acclaimed at death for pulpit eloquence (*ibid.*, pp. 319, 362), he had preached sermons at the Spital, 1560, -61 and -63 (*Machyn's Diary*, J.G. Nichols, ed. (London 1848), pp. 231, 234, 305), and before the Queen in March 1564 (*A godly sermon at Windsor*, STC 5540). Miscellaneous recorded activities include those at the Convocation of 1562, enforcing an instruction of Grindal's to prevent 'superstitious behaviour' during Rogation Week (Grindal, *Remains*, W. Nicholson, ed. (Cambridge 1843), pp. 240-41) with such vigor as apparently to require measures by the Privy Council for his protection in 1564 (*A.P.C.*, VII, p. 145); applying to Archbishop Parker for redress of what he saw as injustice in a marital case in Kent (Parker, *Correspondence* (Cambridge 1853), p. 303); presiding at a trial of witches at the Assizes (Alan Macfarlane: *Witchcraft in Tudor and Stuart England* (London 1970), p. 73).

Cooke, Robert (clothier, Bocking, Essex): Ordered arrested 27 January 1551, as the originally intended host of Kentishmen attending Bocking conventicle (*A.P.C.*, III, pp. 198-99).

Dynestake, Rycharde ('clarke', Kent): One of three deponents testifying together, *c.* 1551, about Freewiller beliefs and practices (Burrage, II, pp. 2, 3).

Eglise, also Eglins, John (clothier, Bocking, Essex): Ordered arrested 27 January 1551, interrogated 3 February, released on recognizance (*A.P.C.*, III, pp. 199, 207).

Forstall, William (Kent): One of several deponents, *c.* 1551 about Henry Hart's statements against learned men and predestination (Burrage II, p. 2).

Gibson, also Gybson: Mentioned with Hart and Kempe by the orthodox Protestant, Careless, in April 1556, as one trying to dissuade prisoners from the true faith (*A. & M.*, VIII, p. 164); mentioned by Strype as a Freewiller 'teacher' (*Cranmer*, p. 502); one of 13 addressees, as 'John Gibson' of Bradford's farewell letter of mid-February 1555 (Bradford II, pp. 194-98).[74]

Grenelande, William (Kent): One of deponents, *c.* 1551, about Freewiller practices, stating also his own belief that gambling is sin (Burrage II, p. 3).

Grey, John (Kent): Deponent, *c.* 1551, on statements of Hart and Robert Cole (Burrage II, p. 1).

[74] This Gibson is evidently a different person from the wealthy 'Master Gibson' whom Bradford mentions in a letter to John Philpot, apparently from the Compter, as a fellow prisoner whom he hopes to convert 'afore my death' (Bradford II, pp. 243-44), and who is probably the Richard Gibson burned at Smithfield in November 1557, after having been imprisoned in the Compter for debt over three years earlier (*A. & M.*, VIII, pp. 436-43.

Guelle, John: Signed confession of 30 January 1555 (Trew, pp. 67, 70).

Harman, Richard: Signed confession of 30 January 1555 (Trew, pp. 69, 70).

Hart, also Harte, Henry, also Harry (Pluckley, Kent): Mentioned in 1538 letter by Cranmer as one of several suffering legal harassment as supporters of 'the new doctrine' (Cranmer, *Works*, Cox, ed. (Cambridge 1844–46) II, p. 367); published *A godly newe short treatyse*, 1548 (STC 12887), 2nd ed. as *A godly exhortation*, 1549 (STC 12887.3), *A consultorie for all Christians*, 1549 (STC 12564). Quoted in several depositions, *c.* 1551, making statements against predestination and learned men as religious guides (Burrage II, pp. 1, 2).

In Mary's reign, reported by government agent as living in an artisan's house near London Bridge and directing the Freewiller group on basis of '13 articles' of his own drafting (*A. & M.*, VIII, p. 384); his paper on 'Enormities of Election' occasioned Part II of Bradford's 'Defence of Election', dated 11 October 1554, and various Bradford letters mention him (Bradford I, pp. 307-30; II, pp. 128, 169-71, 194-98); another Hart statement circulated in prison aroused anger from Careless and other orthodox Protestants (*A. & M.*, VIII, pp. 164-65). In 1557, ecclesiastical visitation of Pluckley reported Hart 'now dead' (*Archdeacon Harpsfield's Visitation Returns, 1557*, L.E. Whatmore, ed. (London 1950), p. 120).

Hitcherst, Matthew: Signed confession of 30 January 1555 (Trew, pp. 69, 70).

Hitcherst, Robert: Signed confession of 30 January 1555 (Trew, pp. 69, 70).

Jacksonne, John: Signed confession of 30 January 1555 (Trew, pp. 69, 70).

Kempe, John: Reported by Marian government agent as associate of Hart's, living in same London house and frequently travelling into Kent; orthodox Protestant prisoner, Careless, describes him as Hart's associate in winning prisoners away from orthodoxy (*A. & M.*, VIII, pp. 384, 164); Strype terms him a Freewiller 'teacher' (*Cranmer*, p. 502); Bradford includes him among 13 addressees of farewell letter on King's Bench controversy (Bradford II, pp. 194-98).[75]

Kinge, John (Bocking, Essex): Ordered arrested 27 January 1551, interrogated 3 Febrary, released on recognizance (*A.P.C.*, III, pp. 199, 207).

Ledley, also Lidley, Lydley, John (Ashford, Kent): Ordered arrested 27 January 1551 (*A.P.C.*, III, p. 199).

In Mary's reign, he and wife were 'persecuted' out of Ashford (*A. &*

[75] Not to be confused with 'John Kempe, then of Godstone in Surrey, now Minister in the Isle of Wight', whose extensive account of himself Foxe prints in the 3rd (1576) ed. of *A. & M.*, pp. 2975-77, 'to purge . . . his good name'.

M., VIII, Appendix, Document VI); later reported by government agent as based at a London inn with Robert Cole and wife, and another man, propagandizing prisoners in the King's Bench (*A. & M.*, VIII, p. 384), on the orthodox Protestant side, as references in letter by ex-Freewiller make clear (Strype, *Eccl. Mem.*, III, ii, pp. 329-34); listed as one of 20 'sustainers' of Protestants in prison and exile (Strype, *Eccl. Mem.*, III, i, p. 224); one of 13 addressees of Bradford's farewell letter on King's Bench controversy (Bradford II, pp. 194-98). Contributed prayers, with Robert Cole and others, to volume published in Mary's reign (STC 17776); under Elizabeth, prayers published in his name in 1560 (STC 10617), 1568 (STC 4028), 1578 (STC 4030) and 1596 (STC 4032).

Lynsey, Roger: Deponent, *c.* 1551, about Freewiller beliefs and practices (Burrage II, pp. 2, 3).

Middleton, Humphrey (Ashford, Kent): Quoted in deposition, *c.* 1551, as asserting all men are predestined to be saved (Burrage II, p. 3).
In Mary's reign, one of 13 addressees of Bradford's farewell in King's Bench controversy (Bradford II, pp. 194-98); burned at Canterbury, July 1555 (*A. & M.*, VII, p. 312).

Morres, Edmonde (Kent): Deponent, *c.* 1551, about Freewiller beliefs and practices (Burrage II, p. 1).

Myxsto, also Myxer, Thomas (Essex): Ordered arrested 27 January 1551, interrogated 3 February, released on recognizance (*A.P.C.*, III, pp. 199, 207).

Plume, John (Lenham, Kent): Deponent *c.* 1551, about Freewiller beliefs and practices (Burrage II, pp. 3, 4).

Pygrinde, also Piggerell, Thomas (Essex): Ordered arrested 27 January 1551, interrogated 3 February, released on recognizance (*A.P.C.*, III, pp. 199, 207).

Ramsaye, Laurence (Kent): Deponent, *c.* 1551 about Freewiller beliefs and practices (Burrage II, p. 1).

Russell, Margery: Signed confession of 30 January 1555 (Trew, pp. 69, 70).

Saxby, John: Signed confession of 30 January 1555 (Trew, pp. 69, 70).

Sharpe, Thomas (Pluckley, Kent): Ordered arrested 27 January 1551, interrogated 3 February, released on recognizance (*A.P.C.*, III, pp. 199, 207).

Shetterton, also Sheterden, Sheterenden, Shitterden, Nicholas (Pluckley, Kent): Ordered arrested 27 January 1551, interrogated 3 February, 'Commyted to ----' (*A.P.C.*, III, 199, 207).
One of 13 addressees of Bradford's farewell letter and addressed in another Bradford letter as one already converted to orthodoxy (Bradford II pp. 194-98, 133-34); tried for heresy, 25 June 1555, giving orthodox Protestant answers (though prison letters to his brother speak of his having taught himself out of the Bible); burned at

Canterbury 12 July 1555 (*A. & M.*, VII, pp. 306-16).

Sibley, William ('Lannams' (Lenham), Kent): Ordered arrested 27 January 1551, interrogated 3 February, 'Commytted to ——' (*A.P.C.*, III, pp. 199, 206-07).

Skelthorpe: Referred to by Bradford as recent convert from Freewillers (Bradford II, p. 243).

Stevenson, Cornelius: Signed confession of 30 January 1555 (Trew, pp. 69-70); reported converted to orthodoxy in undated letter by John Careless, who died in July 1556 (Emmanuel Coll., Cambridge, MS 260, fol. 239.5).

Sympson, also Symson (Bocking, Essex): Ordered imprisoned in the Marshalsea, 27 January 1551 as one 'of the same sort' as Upcharde, host for Kentish attenders of the Bocking conventicle (*A.P.C.*, III, p. 199).

In Mary's reign, apparently considered by Bradford to be orthodox (Bradford II, p. 128), and in late 1554 was one of several trying to reconcile Trew's Freewiller group in the King's Bench with the orthodox Protestants; Sympson evidently had sufficient credentials with both sides to be principal mediator (Trew, pp. 57, 58).[76]

Trew, John: Author of the narrative, 'The cause of the contention in the King's Bench', including the Freewiller confession of 30 January 1555

---

[76] Sympson has been identified by some with Cuthbert Symson, the deacon of the principal London underground congregation – apparently because the manuscript of John Bradford's 'Farewell to the City of London' has the same 'Cuthbert Symson' on it (Bradford I, p. 434, n. 2, citing Emmanuel College MS 1. 2.8, no. 51). This Symson would be a logical recipient for Bradford's manuscript, but it is hard to see how the Sympson of rural Essex could in four or five years have become established as a tailor in the city of London and be described by a government informer as 'a rich man' not long before he was arrested in December 1557 and burned (*A. & M.*, VIII, pp. 454-60).

M.R. Watts (*The Dissenters*, (Oxford 1978), I, p. 12) rejects this identification and inclines to one John Simpson, a husbandman from Great Wigborough, some 15 miles southeast of Bocking, who was tried by Bonner in May 1555 and burned in June (*A. & M.*, VII, pp. 86-90); Watts also notes the unsourced statement in Doris Witard: *Bibles in Barrels: a History of Essex Baptists* (Southend-on-Sea 1962), p. 21, that the will of Robert Cooke, the originally intended host for the Bocking conventicle, was witnessed by a John Simpson and a Richard Upchard. (The Sympson and Upcharde of the *A.P.C.* references appear there without Christian names.)

Further support for this identification is given by an item in Emmanuel College's 'Letters of the Martyrs' collection (MS 160.19, fols. 47, 48) in which 'John Simpson, condemned for the truth', writes on 29 Mary 1555 an epistle of 'exhortacion to the congregation dispersed in Suffolk, Norfolke, Essex, Kent and elsewhere'. This Simpson is himself the recipient of a letter of comfort and exhortation from John Denley, gentleman of Maidstone, who, along with John Newman, a pewterer of Maidstone, was arrested in Essex 'going to visit such their godly friends as they then had in the county of Essex'; both were burned in August 1555. It is tempting to see, in these facts, a continuation of the Freewiller fellowship which had brought Thomas Cole and others – possibly even Denley and Newman themselves – from Maidstone to Essex at Christmastime 1550, but nothing in the trial records as printed by Foxe makes them sound other than orthodox Protestants.

(Trew, pp. 37-70); principal addressee of two Bradford letters which see him as leader of hard-core Freewillers in the King's Bench (Bradford II, pp. 180-1); his statements were used by a Roman Catholic interrogator there to bait the orthodox John Careless; reported *c.* June 1556 by Careless to have escaped from prison by breaking parole to his keepers (*A. & M.*, VIII, pp. 166-68, 189).

Upcharde, also Upchardes, Upcher, Upchaire, Upchayre, Upcheave, Upchire (weaver, Bocking, Essex): Sent for by Privy Council 22 January 1551, examined 27 January about the 'assemblie in his howse in Christmas last' and 'committed to the Marshalsie' (*A.P.C.*, III, pp. 196, 198-99).

In Mary's reign, driven out of Bocking by persecution (*A. & M.*, VIII, Appendix Document VI); became an orthodox Protestant, as evident in letter sent him by the strongly orthodox John Careless (*A. & M.*, VIII, pp. 189-91, there addressed to 'T.V.' but full name used in the original, Emmanuel College MS 260, 108, fols. 213-4); one of several who tried unsuccessfully to reconcile Trew's Freewiller group in the King's Bench with the orthodox Protestants there (Trew, pp. 57, 58).

In exile, he and family registered among Englishmen at Frankfurt in 1557 (Huguenot Society, *Proceedings*, Vol. IV, London 1892-94, pp. 86-89); later accompanied Thomas Lever on mission to Geneva and settled in congregation at Aarau (*Troubles begonne at Frankford*, pp. 85, 86; also Archives of Aarau as printed in Garrett, *The Marian Exiles*, p. 355).

Under Elizabeth, ordained by Grindal, 25 April, 1560 (Strype, *Grindal*, pp. 58-60); was successively rector of Fordham, 1561, and St. Leonard's Colchester, resigning latter in 1582 (Newcourt, *Reportorium Ecclesiasticum Parochiae Londinense*, II, pp. 270, 173). As cleric, granted temporary dispensation by Grindal, 1560, to officiate without surplice (Grindal to Archdeacon Pullan, Corpus Christi College, Oxford, MS 319, no. 54, fol. 183); *c.* 1583, was one of 27 Essex ministers petitioning Privy Council against imposition of ex officio oath (*Seconde part of a register*, Albert Peel, ed. (Cambridge 1915), I, pp. 225-26); also, 1583, one of 12 and 15 ministers signing, respectively, two other documents of strongly Puritan tendency (printed in R.G. Usher: *The Elizabethan Presbyterian Movement*, (London 1905), pp. 88-89, 91).

Wickham, Henry: Signer of confession of 30 January 1555 (Trew, pp. 69, 70).

Wolmere, Robert (Essex): Ordered arrested 27 January 1551 (*A.P.C.*, III, p. 199).

Yonge, also Yong, Thomas, also Nicholas (Lenham, Kent): Ordered arrested 27 January 1551 and interrogated 3 February as Thomas Y., released on recognizance as Nicholas Y. (*A.P.C.*, III, pp. 199, 206-07); deponent, *c.* 1551, quotes him as saying Freewillers 'wolde not communycate with Synners' (Burrage II, p. 4).

Chapter 4

Henry Hart and the Impact of the Vernacular Bible

1

Though the Protestant Reformers in all countries put new emphasis on the Bible and encouraged the people to read it, access to the vernacular Bible nowhere became so sharp a Reformation issue as it was in England. The difference is attributable in large part to the preceding generations of conflict between the late medieval church and the Lollards. Lollardy looked for ultimate authority to Scripture rather than to church tradition, and the individual Lollard sought spiritual guidance not from the parish priest but from carefully preserved copies of parts of the Bible and of various Lollard writings. Over 235 manuscripts of the Wycliffe Bible have survived, though not all of them were originally in Lollard hands.[1] The church hierarchy, in turn, had made the suppression of Lollard Bibles and other books a major objective. As one historian has put it in reviewing the trials of Lollards at Coventry in 1511-12, 'The court displayed more interest in the heretics' books than in their doctrines'.[2]

The threat of the Lollard Bible later came to seem relatively minor to the authorities, since the Lollards had never had access to a printing press, while William Tyndale, translating his New Testament in Germany and in Antwerp from 1524 on, had ready access to print. For several years in the early Reformation, a large part of the English church's anti-Protestant activity consisted of efforts to suppress the vernacular Bible. According to one chronicler, the Bishop of London even resorted to preclusive buying of Tyndale New Testaments in Antwerp in his attempts to stop the influx.[3] In the years 1538-41 Henry VIII legalized another English translation of the Bible, and decreed that it was to be placed in all parish churches, but conservative fear of the vernacular Bible persisted. An attempt was made in a 1543 statue to define which classes of people might read it and under what circumstances, excluding the lower

---

[1] Anne Hudson, *Lollards and Their Books* (London 1985), pp. 182-83

[2] John Fines, 'Heresy Trials in the Diocese of Coventry and Lichfield, 1511-12', *J.E.H.*, XIV (1963), p. 165.

[3] Edward Hall, *Henry VIII* (1548), Charles Whibley, ed., 2 vols. (London, 1904), II, pp. 160-62.

parts of the social scale altogether. It was in the nature of Tudor society, however, that neither the decreed provision of Bibles in 1541 nor the restriction of 1543 was effectively implemented. A rough tabulation of the inventories made in Edward VI's reign of religious articles in London churches shows that only 55 out of 96 churches possessed a Bible of any description,[4] while Henry VIII himself complained to Parliament in December 1545 that 'the Word of God is disputed, rhymed, sung and jangled in every alehouse and tavern.'[5]

I am concerned here with the impact of the English Bible on some of those who, by the statue of 1543, were not permitted to read it. Predictably, their responses were varied. In some, contact with the Bible apparently stimulated the kind of alehouse disputativeness which Henry VIII denounced in his speech. Bishop Bonner's register for 1544, for example, contains the long recantation in which one Robert Ward, a shoemaker of St. Andrew's in Holborn, confesses among other things to the possession of 'unlawful bokes' on the basis of which he had

> dyverse tymes in alehouses and uncomelie and unmete places taken upon me to bable talke and rangle of the Scripture whiche I understode not, yea, and to expounde it after my folyshe fantasie . . .[6]

In a similar complaint a decade or so later, the Roman Catholic propagandist, Miles Hogarde, charged that rowdy London apprentices carried New Testaments about with them on holidays, using these to parade their own knowledge and to make fun of priests.[7] It is certainly true that in a city where anti-clericalism never lay far beneath the surface, the Bibles placed in churches for public reading lent themselves to the twitting of priests on points of doctrine by disrespectful parishioners.

In other recorded instances, however, the public reading of the Bible in the 'lower ende of the church' lent itself to more serious purposes. William Maldon, a Protestant from Chelmsford in Essex, has left a sizable account of how his first encounter with the Bible came in that manner as a lad of twenty in Henry VIII's reign, and how he returned 'everie sundaye' to hear more of the Bible read till his father prevented him. He then found himself so attached to the Gospel that he determined to learn to read it for himself, and some months later he and his father's apprentice combined their funds to buy a New Testament which he kept

---

[4] Compilation from H.B. Walters, *London Churches at the Reformation* (London 1939).

[5] Quoted in A.G. Dickens, *The English Reformation* (London: Batsford 1965), p. 190.

[6] Printed by John Foxe, *A. & M.*, V, p. 447 and Appendix XI. Evidently Ward's recantation was insufficient to win his release, for he died in prison.

[7] Miles Hogarde, *The displaying of the Protestantes*, 1556, (STC 13558) fol. 95. A conservative parish priest in Kent complained that even boys and girls fancied themselves as trained readers of Scripture, John Proctor, *The fal of the late Arrian*, 1549, (STC 20406) sig. A 8ᵛ.

hidden. Maldon felt compelled, however, 'to speke of the Scriptures' to his mother, insisting that the commandment against graven images made some of the current church processions 'plain idolatry' – which aroused his father's anger once more and this time so violently that it threatened Maldon's life. The narrative breaks off at this point, but it seems clear that Maldon considered that it was contact with the English Bible, practically unassisted, which made a Protestant of him.[8]

The Bible is described by John Foxe as having had a similar effect on the Wiltshire farmer, William Maundrel, who, after encountering Tyndale's translation, 'became a diligent hearer, and a fervent embracer of God's true religion.' Maundrel never learned to read himself, but carried a New Testament with him constantly, for use 'when he came into any company that could read'; having a good memory, moreover, 'he could recite most places of the New Testament.' For Maundrel, who was burned at the stake in Mary's reign, it seems to have been his memorized passages of the vernacular Bible which provided the core of his religion.[9]

A better known admirer of the vernacular Bible was the London bricklayer, John Harrydaunce, whose meetings in London in 1537-39 were described earlier in discussing the rise of the conventicle. Like Maundrel, he was unable to read the Bible himself but had a lifelong obsession with it. As one of the two Lord Mayors who interrogated him remarked, 'He hath the New Testament ever about him.' From the few bits of his discourses which have survived, it would seem that he simply recited passages of Scripture strung together in his own order, occasionally adding comments of his own. The popularity of his recitations makes it seem the less surprising that groups should gather in the 'lower ende of the church' to hear the Bible read aloud there when this could be done legally a year or two later.[10]

The cases of Maundrel and Harrydaunce testify to the strength of the vernacular Bible's appeal to those on the lower edge of literacy and suggest something about its extent but are too brief to say much about its nature, merely indicating the sense of assurance that direct access to the text gave them. A more detailed picture of this sense of assurance is to be found in a pamphlet called *The harvest is at hand*, published in 1548 by the radical Protestant, John Champneys. One persistent theme, appearing several times and stated in different ways in this not very coherent work, is that the English Bible now meets all a Christian's religious needs, because 'the Apostles lefte nothynge unwritten which was profitable to our fayth but have declared the whole counsell of God beyng nedeful for

---

[8] *Narratives of the Days of the Reformation*, J.G. Nichols ed. (London 1859), pp. 348-51.
[9] *A. & M.*, VIII, pp. 102-03.
[10] *L. & P.*, XII, ii, No. 594, No. 624; XIV, ii, No. 42.

us to know'.[11] Allied to this contention is his argument that the traditional clergy are now irrelevant because they tend to set up 'man's imaginings' against the clear text of God's Word. It is not reason and learning which will bring man to religious truth but reading the Scriptures in a reverent spirit. He then challenges the clergy to a contest like Elijah's with the priests of Baal, in which he, an unlearned layman, will show the Scripture's true meaning 'only by the Spirite of Christ'.[12]

While Champney's tract is instructive enough on one aspect of the vernacular Bible's appeal to the slenderly educated layman, a much more comprehensive picture of the subject is to be found in two other tracts written at about the same time by a man of similar background, namely Henry Hart. Though formally addressed to Hart's fellow Englishmen as a kind of homily on what true religion requires from them and offers to them, the two tracts can also be read as an account (in well over 100 pages) of how Hart himself discovered the Bible and what it has meant to him.

2

Hart is a figure of some importance in several contexts. He has been discussed earlier in this volume mainly as senior leader of the Freewillers and their spokesman in the debate on predestination with the orthodox Protestant cleric, John Bradford, in the King's Bench prison during the autumn of 1554. As noted in the Biographical Register of Freewillers,[13] the two tracts antedate this activity and indeed belong to almost the earliest known part of his career. The earliest surviving edition of the first (though the title suggests that it may not be Hart's first publication) is signed at the end 'Henry Harte' over the date of October 23, 1548, and was issued by the London printer, Robert Staughton, under the title:

> A godly newe short treatyse instructyng every parson how they shulde trade [lead] their lyves in ye imytacyon of vertu and ye shewyng [eschewing] of vyce, & declaryng also what benefyte man hath receaved by Christ through the effusion of hys most precyous bloude.

It is referred to below simply as 'the Treatyse'. The second edition, issued by John Day under a title-page date of January 1, 1549, calls itself:

> A godlie exhortation to all such as professe the Gospell, wherein they are by the swete promises therof provoked and styrred up to folowe the same in living, and by the terrible threates feared from the contrary.

---

[11] *Harvest at Hand* (STC 4956), E 6ᵛ; see also D 4ᵛ, E 2, E 4. For a similar case see I.B. Horst, *The Radical Brethren* (Nieuwkoop 1972), Appendix A, which prints a government report of a 1532 'Anabaptist' meeting in London where two of the eight men arrested are quoted as refusing to believe any interpretation of the Bible but only the text itself.

[12] *Harvest at hand*, sig. B4ᵛ, D 8.

[13] See chapter 3, appendix, above.

This edition, referred to below as 'the Exhortation', is sometimes mentioned as a new and different work,[14] but differences in the text go no further than minor changes of wording or punctuation and a somewhat greater accuracy in the marginal citation of biblical texts.

The second extant tract is somewhat longer, published in Worcester by John Oswen and dated January 30, 1549, on the title-page. It announces itself as:

> A consultorie for all Christians, most godly and ernestly warnying al people to beware lest they beare the name of Christians in vayne.

This work, referred to subsequently as 'the Consultorie' bears pronounced similarities to Hart's earlier one in both style and content; it precedes the 'H.H.' signature at the end with the rather curious formula, 'Yours as charitie bindeth me', employed in both editions of the other and also in the manuscript copies of Hart's letter to the orthodox Protestant prisoners in the King's Bench, and indeed no author other than Hart has been suggested. Further internal evidence suggests that his signature may simply have been reduced to initials by the printer, who had been granted a valuable royal monopoly for publishing on religious subjects in Wales and may not have wanted to flaunt the full name of a well known religious radical.[15]

The two tracts contain nothing like the explicit spiritual autobiography found later in John Bunyan or George Fox, but there is enough to suggest that Hart was one of those who went through the experience of discovering the Bible for himself and finding that, in George Fox's phrase, it spoke to his condition. In the opening statement of his first tract, the *Treatyse*, he asks his readers to 'Consyder . . . the greate goodness of God i[n] that he hath called you by his grace to the knowledg of himself through the worde.'[16] In his second tract, the *Consultorie*, he says in effect that it was Bible-reading which changed his life:

> For as muche as it hathe pleased the eternall God which seperated me from my mothers womb to lighten the inward eyes of my mynde withe hys grace, and thorowe the knowledge of his word and working of his holy spirite, to worke a perfect repentaunce in me and amendmente of my formour lyfe, love

[14] *E.g.*, George H. Williams, *The Radical Reformation* (London 1962), p. 780; W.K. Jordan, *Edward VI: the Young King* (Cambridge, Mass. 1968), pp. 228-29.

[15] The book reprints the royal licence in full, along with two Biblical quotations (Ephesians 4, 1-7 and 1 Peter 2, 13-14) which are strongly conservative in their political implications. These were apparently added by the printer, not the author, since they deviate considerably from the translations of Tyndale and the Great Bible of 1539, the versions which the author usually follows closely both here and in the *Treatyse*. E. Gordon Duff, *The English Provincial Printers, Stationers and Bookbinders to 1557* (Cambridge 1912), p. 113, assigns the tract without qualification to Hart.

[16] *Treatyse*, sig. Aii[r].

constraynethe me too wyl you (good brethren) to be partakers of this greate benefite.[17]

To Hart, as to others, the Bible brought assurance of salvation – but, it would seem, in a different way from its effect on those in the older church tradition. For him, its great appeal evidently lay in conveying sudden religious insights, not in providing detailed textual support for specific doctrines to be logically integrated into a theological system. Bradford was sharp but not unfair in saying of him during the controversy over predestination that 'he hath not learned his ABC concerning the Scriptures',[18] referring to Hart's lack of the formal training in theology and biblical exegesis needed for examining the contexts of statements, reconciling apparently contradictory texts, and drawing fine logical distinctions. Accordingly, his chief aim in both tracts seems that of conveying these insights as directly as possible to his readers by paraphrase or direct quotation of what he considers to be the relevant biblical passages. The great texts from Paul on faith and grace roll out, sometimes identified in the margin, sometimes not (and sometimes incorrectly identified), seldom presented in the kind of context a trained preacher would supply, and often joined to other biblical quotations in new combinations of Hart's. No other literary sources than the Bible are cited or readily identifiable.

The Bible in itself contains all man needs for salvation:

> Go not from the worde of God, declyne neyther to ye ryght hand neyther to ye left, lest ye perysshe from the ryghte way, for as the braunche can beare no fruyte of hym selfe excepte he abyde in ye vyne (sayth Chryste) no more can ye excepte ye abyd in me. Se that your faythe be lyvely, cleaving sure to the holy Word of God which is already grafted in you. Trewlye (except you have beleved in vayne) it is of power to save your soules, for it is quyck and myghty in operation, and sharper than any two edged sword . . .[19]

The Bible's recent release from its long imprisonment under the clerics of the medieval church is seen as the opening of a new era in history:

> God in tymes past . . . spake to the fathers by prophetes, but in these last daies he hath spoke to us, as S. Paule sayeth, by his Sonne . . . whose most excellent clear brightness hath long time been darkened, and as S. John saieth, hid as with a sackeclothe made with heyre, yt is to say with a fayned ryghtuousenes grounded upon naturall wysdome and carnal reason, invented and set fourth by man, so that the bright shynyng beames of Goddes truth contayned in the holy Scriptures might in no wise appere (by reason of that dark vaile or cloud) to the eyes or mynd of men, whiche is not yet wyth all men taken awaye.[20]

17 *Consultorie*, sig. Avi^v.
18 Bradford, I, p. 319.
19 *Treatyse*, Avii^v.
20 *Consultorie*, Aiiii^r.

The passage also suggests that part of the Bible's attraction for Hart is in its stimulation of his imagination, for in the text he attributes to St. John (Revelation 6:12) 'a sackeclothe made with heyre' provides a simple simile for the temporary darkness of the sun and not the complicated image Hart makes of it here.

Another persistent note in Hart – seen in the passage above, elsewhere in both tracts, and in the court depositions about his beliefs – is a distrust of human learning as a guide in spiritual matters. It is often not clear whether he is thinking historically of medieval clerics who kept the Bible from the people or of contemporary churchmen who would deny his own right as an unlearned layman to work out his own salvation from the Scriptures. Either way, he seems to see the Bible as the great equalizer: the man having a true understanding of it is better off than the worldly scholar. Those who 'thynk them selves wyse', Hart says, and with a 'blynded' understanding 'thynk they know God', really serve 'an ydoll and a false god'. Elsewhere he says:

> Truly knowledge is daungerous where love and obedyence is lackynge; for it tyckelyth the mynde of foles and lefteth them up in vanyty. But such as seke to encrease in vertu walk surely. Therefore searche not unreverently the sacred Worde of God, least ye stumbel in your way and take a sodeyn fal. Knowledge is a gyfte of the Spryte and in the hand of God, and he measureth hys gyfts to hys creatures at hys owne pleasure and wyll.

Nor do material worth and status weigh in the balance against a true knowledge of God; those with a false knowledge of Him 'deceyve them selves utterlye, thynkynge them ryche when the world favoreth them when in dede they are blynde and poore.'[21]

Despite some overtones in passages like this, Hart is much more the moralist than the social critic – more inclined simply to proclaim a course of action wrong and destructive of man's spiritual life than to look carefully at England's social structure and point to inequities in it. He does occasionally use ancient Israel as a frame of reference for looking at modern England, quoting, for instance, Isaiah's exhortation to 'deliver the oppressed, help the fatherles to hys right' and Jeremiah's denunciation of the powerful who 'judge not the poor according to equitie'.[22] But, on the whole, one can discover sharper social criticism in Hugh Latimer's sermons than in Hart's tracts – perhaps because Hart's horizon is narrower.

Ancient Israel seems to interest Hart most as an example of a people originally chosen by God and later rescued by him after a long intervening captivity, and with Israel thus conceived Hart finds identification on several levels. At one point he applies to all Christian

---

21 *Treatyse*, Bi.ᵛ, Aviiiʳ, Aiiiiᵛ.
22 *Consultorie*, Dvᵛ, Hiʳ; see also Eviiʳ-Fiᵛ.

nations the analogy between their pre-Reformation past and 'the
captyvitie of the Hebreues'.[23] At another point Israel, the elect nation,
has a more immediate parallel in England. Thus, a page or two after
quoting exhortations by Jeremiah and Isaiah that Israel should turn again
to God and there find deliverance, Hart says:

> Refuse not thou thy helth, O thou Englysshe nation, seeing God hath loved
> the[e] above many other and hath sent his worde . . . unto the[e] too call
> the[e] from thyne owne waies that thou mightest be made hys owne people
> . . .[24]

Elsewhere and less explicitly, the image of Israel as God's chosen is
applied to a smaller group. Hart does not specifically identify the modern
parallel he has in mind in his paraphrase from Exodus. 'Therefore the
Lord commandeth you to let his people go, ye heathen nations and
enemies of righteousness, that we may sacrifice unto the Lord our God
. . .', but much of the preceding page describes 'the humble and despised
nation of Israel' as a small 'remnant' of God's people, beleaguered by
larger heathen neighbours, and the page before that has a very
contemporary denuciation of

> . . . those bishops, pastours and lawiers, of what place and name so ever they
> be, whiche boast of power and auctoritie to rule and governe other and yet
> have no respecte to their owne soules . . . which seke holynes onely by
> outward sacramentes and signes, not regardyng what the hert & inward
> conscience bee . . .[25]

It would not be surprising if these pages are indeed a reference to
persecution of a separatist congregation by the ecclesiastical authorities,
for other references in the tracts indicate that Hart already had a
following of his own. One such reference occurs toward the end of his
first extant tract when he concedes that 'ye know the truth already, my
brethren . . . yet I think it not vayne by these letters to styre upp your
remembraunce.'[26] The second tract issues, in effect, an invitation to
outsiders to join his group, saying that the Gospel message 'declare we
unto you that ye may have felowship with us & oure felowship may be
with the Father and his sonne Jesus Christe . . .'[27] But as he had implied
above, the faithful and their religion of 'the hert & inward conscience' can
have little in common with the traditionalists who see religion in terms of
outward forms and imposed ecclesiastical authority. A whole middle
section of this tract is a kind of litany of denunciation under twelve
different heads (the previously quoted blast at bishops is part of the

---

[23] *Consultorie*, Bviii–Ci.
[24] *Consultorie*, Diii[r].
[25] *Consultorie*, Cviii[v], Cviii[r], Cvii[v].
[26] *Treatyse*, Bv[v].
[27] *Consultorie*, Cv[v] ff.

twelfth), calling down woe on the clergy in such terms as 'blynde guides' and 'deceytefull messengers of Sathan'. They are (under no. 1) 'Proude boastyng spyrites which, living wickedlye, teache their flockes by poure [power] and penaltie, and not rather by ensamples of vertue & godly lyving', or (under no. 6) 'paynted tombes and stinking sepulchres . . . which oftentimes spake of faythe, penance and love, and yet consume the tyme of their lyves in vanitie and idleness.'[28]

For his own followers' way of life Hart urges a sharply contrasting austerity. The initial statement on the title-page of the *Treatyse* promises to teach all how to pattern their lives on virtue and avoid vice; the title-page of its second edition – the *Exhortation* in 1549 – urges 'such as professe the Gospel . . . to followe the same in living'; and the title-page of the *Consultorie* 'ernestly' warns 'al people to beware lest they beare the name of Christians in vayne.' The texts of both tracts pursue this theme, citing various biblical admonitions on resisting the lusts of the flesh. 'Remember Esau,' Hart says in one passage, 'sell not your enheretaunce', and shortly thereafter he warns that through man's carnal appetites the Enemy leads 'the synner from one vanytye to another tyll he have so broughte hym in wooful bondage.'[29]

In contrast to his insistence on sincerity in religion and on virtuous personal conduct, Hart shows little concern in the two tracts over specific doctrines, even those provoking hot controversy at the time. Transubstantiation is never mentioned, nor is the heresy of the completely celestial flesh of Christ for which Joan Bocher was condemned to death in 1549. The issue of infant baptism arises only tangentially, when the rite of baptism is compared to circumcision and seen as a symbol meaningless in itself:

> What avayleth then a Christian name or baptisyng and receivyng of sacramentes, although it be never so many, yf there folowe not amendement of life . . . Have ye not then made your baptism, which signifieth repentaunce, the new regeneration and amendment of lyfe . . . of no value?[30]

Predestination, the issue responsible for his followers' popular nickname, is implicitly rejected and does not attract much of Hart's attention in the tracts. He sees Christians as having been given by God the promise of their salvation, but only a contingent promise; the important matter here as in other contexts is man's responsibility for virtuous conduct. 'Dearly beloved,' he says,

---

[28] *Ibid.*

[29] *Treatyse*, Bii[v] Biii[v]. See also Biiii[r], for the parable of the beggar Lazarus and the rich man; Bvii[r], for an exhortation of St. Paul's; *Consultorie*, Bv[v], quoting Jude's adjuration to 'hate the filthy vesture of the fleshe'; Bvi[v], a similar one from James; Giii[r], a denuncation from Isaiah of drunkenness.

[30] *Consultorie*, Eiii[v], Eiiii[r].

ye are called and chosen . . . ye are sanctyfyed by the bloude of Jesu through
the eternelle spyryte whyche dwelleth in you . . . Therfore worke owt your
salvacion and as the Apostle Peter sayeth, make your callynge and electyon
sure through good workes . . . And walke not from hencefourth as other
hethen people walke in vanytye of theyre myndes, blynded in theyr
understandyng, being straungers from the life that is in God.[31]

In his second tract Hart refers to the elect rather as the 'chyldren of
promyse'; for insufficient love of the truth, he says, 'weare ye geven
over, ye named [nominal] Christians, into the hands and power of your
enemies.'[32] Later on he insists again on the need for responsible
behaviour. It is folly, he maintains, for people to say:

We be safe, for we bee all Christians: we have Gods word and his holy
sacraments among us, and therefore ye great plagues and threatenynges of
God (declared by his prophetes and apostles) againste sinners shall not touch us
. . . Thinkest thou that they shal be preserved and defended of God that
continue and delite in sinne and wickedness?[33]

The marginalia of the two tracts can also be instructive. All of the
citations are to the Bible – Hart was evidently a one-book man – but in
the *Treatyse* the majority of these are to the New Testament while in the
Consultorie most are to the Old, suggesting that its influence came to Hart
more slowly than the New Testament's. The margins are also used on
occasion just to make an added point in the manner of the provocative
statements attributed to Hart in the Kentish depositions of 1551 – as, for
example, 'his faithe was not growndid upon Lernyd men, for all errors
were brought in by Lernyd men.' The pithiest of these marginal remarks
is: 'An idole is that whiche hath the love of the harte and is placed in the
roume of God.'[34]

3

It should not be assumed that English Roman Catholics in the mid-
Tudor years were insensitive to the religious utility of Scripture in the
vernacular. Take, for example, the 1533 tract, *A werke for housholders or
for them that have the gydynge of governaunce of any company*, by Richard
Whitforde a friend of Erasmus and Sir Thomas More, whose attachment
to the traditional church continued unshaken on to his death in Queen
Mary's reign. Ostensibly focusing on the education of young children, it
consists in effect of detailed prescriptions for household worship which,
though not involving the Bible as a whole, do centre very largely on

[31] *Treatyse*, Bvi^v.
[32] *Consultorie*, Bviii^v, Ci^r.
[33] *Consultorie*, Eii.
[34] Burrage, II, pp. 1-4; *Treatyse*, B 1^v.

detailed expositions of the Lord's Prayer and the Ten Commandments in English. It is emphasized that these readings will be beneficial to everyone in the household (the neighbours, it is suggested, might be invited in also on holy days) and there follows later the rather Protestant-sounding admonition about busy parishioners and holy day church services: 'let them ever kepe the prechynges rather than the masse yf by case [by chance] they may not heare bothe.'[35]

The church of Henry's later years and of Mary's, however, seems never to have understood how strong the desire was in many Englishmen to read the Bible for themselves, and it was only in the changed conditions of Elizabeth's second decade that the Catholic Douai-Rheims translation of the Bible emerged. The Marian church had indeed given formal approval to the preparation of an English New Testament, but the project apparently never got beyond the discussion stage.[36] In practice, the church's position remained essentially that set forth by its theologian, John Standish, in a 1554 tract. Though titled as a question, *A discourse wherein is debated whether it is expedient that the scripture should be in English for al men to read that wyll* – its text presents 50 reasons why it should not, and nearly half of these suggest in some way or other that lay Bible-reading is unsettling to the church or other institutions of society. It is not merely that the church's position is undermined as judge of the meaning of Scripture, but also that these 'teachers in corners and conventicles' tend to encourage disputes over the Bible 'betwene man and man, man and wife, maister and servant'.[37]

Standish, of course, was factually correct about Bible-reading stimulating disputes. In nearly all the cases this essay has examined, the laymen's excitement at discovering the Bible for himself led directly to a desire to expound it to others; the experience he had undergone was too powerful to be kept to himself. Much of the history of English Protestantism over the next century and more consists of efforts to cope with this situation. Henry Hart offers an unusually full picture of the English Bible's impact on one who stands near the beginning of the process.

[35] *Werke for housholders*, (STC 25424) sigs. B 2^r; D 4^v.
[36] Jennifer Loach, 'The Marian Establishment and the Printing Press', *English Historical Review*, Vol. 101, No. 398 (Jan. 1986), pp. 138-39.
[37] *Discourse wherin is debated*, (STC 22207) K 2^v-3^r.

Beinge in studie of the worldes estate
weyinge the workes of every wyghte
Alas my corage it did clene abate
Frome all joyfulnes, to joy in of righte
Penury his Pavilion had pighte
Heare forto remayne, wherbie I did see
Pore and riche punyshed, in theire degree.

All menne whiche are of noble progeny
Theire estate this day right well may bewayle,
Considerynge as thaie maye, if they vew thorowly,
Howe farre frome theire fathers theyre fame doth fayle,
Touchinge howse kepynge, for pore folkes availe
A Plage it may be, as trewly it is,
to the hartes of suche, as dothe thinke of this.

Pen-and-ink drawing in Miles Hogarde's long poem, *A mirroure of myserie*, in which Sodom and Gomorrah provide the distant mirror for England's sins. (Huntington MS. HM121, fol.6.)

Chapter 5

Miles Hogarde: Artisan and Aspiring Author in Sixteenth-Century England

1

Miles Hogarde[1] has been recognized, both by his Protestant antagonists in Queen Mary's reign and by modern historians, as the best of Roman Catholic propagandists in the bitter pamphlet war of 1553-58.[2] But there is more to Hogarde than the polemic brilliance of *The displaying of the Protestantes*, and little attention has been given to these other aspects – particularly that implicit in his characterization by Anthony Wood, the seventeenth-century Oxford antiquarian, as 'the first trader or mechanic that appeared in print for the catholic cause, I mean one that had not received any monastical or academic breeding.'[3] Whether or not Hogarde was statistically the first, he was certainly regarded (both by his opponents and himself) as unusual in his role, though Protestant lay preachers had been unobtrusively present in England for years past. He is unusual in various ways: for one thing, instances of sixteenth-century London artisans expressing themselves in print are certainly not numerous. At the same time, however, Hogarde exemplifies for the modern historian such trends as the gradual spread of literacy and printing, and the rising importance of the laity in religious affairs, not to mention the enlarging circle of aspiring authors. His situation and his outlook on the world seem worth a historian's attention.

---

[1] The name is variously spelled, *The Dictionary of National Biography* preferring 'Miles Huggarde' and the *Short-Title Catalogue of Books Printed in England, 1475-1640*, rev. ed. (London 1986) adopting 'Miles Hogarde'. Except within quotations, I have followed the latter spelling.

[2] *The lamentacion of England*, [1558] (STC 10015), refers three times to Hogarde's attacks on Protestants and to no other Roman Catholic pamphleteer more than once; the Protestant exile writer, William Plough, wrote *An apology for Protestants* in direct response to Hogarde's main polemic tract. (This is now lost, but see Edward J. Baskerville, *A Chronological Bibliography of Propaganda and Polemic Published in English between 1553 and 1558* [Philadelphia 1979], p. 82.) For modern judgments see D.M. Loades, *The Reign of Mary Tudor* (London 1979), *passim*; 'The Press under the Early Tudors', *Transactions of the Cambridge Bibilographical Society*, 4 (1964), pp. 29-50; Jennifer Loach, 'Pamphlets and Politics', *B.I.H.R.*, XXXXVIII (1975), pp. 31-45.

[3] The remark is made incidentally in Wood's article on John Plough, *Athenae Oxonienses*, Philip Blair, ed., 3rd ed. (facsimile, N.Y. 1967), p. 301.

Of Hogarde's biography we know very little. Hostile references to him are made by Protestants writing as early as 1540 and as late as 1558,[4] and there is a retrospective accusation in 1548 of his having been partly responsible for the burning of John Frith in 1533.[5] He published seven tracts in verse and one (in two somewhat differing editions) in prose, and two additional poems (one long and one short) survive in manuscript alone.[6] That he was a hosier is well established and also that he lived near the northern end of London Bridge in Pudding Lane.[7] In November 1553 he was made hosier to Queen Mary and allocated a shilling a quarter in addition to an unspecified daily wage,[8] and he was prosperous enough to present the Queen with manuscript copies of two of his long poems done in fine professional hands.[9] But he was apparently not prosperous enough to become a member of the Haberdashers Company, or a freeman of the City of London, or to leave a recorded will,[10] and his Protestant antagonist, Robert Crowley, taunts him on his lack of standing with the London aldermen.[11] No record of his birth, death or marriage has yet come to light.

Hogarde's own works and the hostile references to him, however, indicate clearly enough two dominant strains in his life. One is a strong attachment to the traditional church, along with a marked animus against Protestant preachers; the other is his passion for writing – writing on religious subjects. The tension in his life comes from the conflict between the two, for, as an artisan, he was generally considered not

---

[4] For 1540: Robert Wisdom (archdeacon of Ely under Elizabeth), when imprisoned in 1540, mentions Hogarde three times as one of his persecutors in a justificatory document printed in John Strype, *Ecclesiastical Memorials* (London 1816), VI, pp.223-239. For 1558: see n.2 above. In the late 1540s Hogard is attacked at more length in anti-Catholic satirical verses aimed chiefly at Bishop Gardiner, printed in Strype, *Eccl. Mem.*, VI, pp. 314-18, Stanza 10. I owe this reference to Dr. Baskerville.

[5] Robert Crowley, *The confutation of the misshapen aunswer to the misnamed wicked ballade called the abuse of the blessed sacramente of the altare, wherein thou haste, gentle reader, the ryghte understandynge of al the places of the scripture that Myles Hoggarde, with his learned counsell, hath wrested to make for the transubstantiacion of the bread and wyne,* 1548 (STC 6082), sig. A5.

[6] The full titles of Hogarde's surviving works (together with short referral titles) are listed in approximate chronological order in Appendix I.

[7] Hogarde affirms both facts in a first-hand account printed by John Foxe, *A & M* VII, p. 111.

[8] *Calendar of Patent Rolls*, 1553-54, p. 386. I am grateful to Dr. C.J. Kitching, then of the Public Record Office, for this reference.

[9] Harley MS. 3444 (British Library) and Huntington MS. 121. As Dr. Baskerville has noted (*op. cit.*, p. 45), the text of the former appears identical with STC 13560.5.

[10] His name does not appear in the index of members of the Company of Haberdashers, 1526-1607, Guildhall Library MS. 15857; or in the *Register of Freeman of the City of London in the reigns of Henry VIII and Edward VI*, C. Welch ed. (London 1908); or in *Index of Wills Proved in the Prerogative Court of Canterbury, 1558-83*, L.L. Duncan ed. (London, 1898).

[11] *Confutation*, sig. A6.

learned enough for writing on religion and, as a Roman Catholic, he was certainly expected to leave such matters to the clerics. In 1555 he defended himself stoutly, if somewhat speciously, against those saying that

> My calling is not bokes to write,
> Nor no faultes to reprove,
> But to folow my busynesse,
> As wisedome would me move.
> Before (say they) when men dyd preache
> Whiche artificers were,
> They were not calde thereto, say you,
> Gods word wyl them not beare.
> But now can ye suffer a man,
> Which no learning hath,
> Against his calling as it were
> To write upon our faith?
> To them I do answere againe.
> My selfe for to defende,
> If Gods precept dyd me forbyd,
> No bookes I would have pende.
> But God forbyds al men to preache
> The which he hath not sent:
> So hath he not all men to write;
> This is most evident.[12]

Not surprisingly, in view of the general clumsiness of his verse and his tendency to be a one-topic author, Hogarde has been passed over by historians of English literature, and I am not now concerned with challenging this judgement. Though I consider that Hogarde was by no means devoid of literary skill, my primary interest lies not in the quality of the product but in the person producing it and what his mental world was like. The contemporary references afford no ground for questioning Anthony Wood's statement that Hogarde lacked 'academic breeding'; he defends himself against various hostile charges, such as being a mere mouthpiece for clerics, but the jabs about his lack of learning bring only indirect replies and no assertions about his formal schooling. It is a fair inference to see him as one of the new phenomena of print culture, for without Caxton as a predecessor it is hard to imagine a London hosier, no matter how talented and energetic, having Hogarde's literary background and ambitions. Partly because of this circumstance, Hogarde's view of the changing society of sixteenth-century England comes from a somewhat new direction.

I will first look at the nature of Hogarde's works, then at some of his particular attitudes – his loyalties and his aversions – and finally at what light he may shed on his era.

---

[12] *Mirrour of love*, Preface.

2

For literary models, Hogarde turned first to the poetry of the late Middle Ages, much of which was by the mid-sixteenth century readily available in print. Most of his verse is written in rhyme royal or in an eight-line stanza, following the relaxed standards of late medieval verse. He has evidently read many romances and allegories and is familiar with such conventions as presenting the poem in the framework of a dream, with a mentor expatiating to the poet on its significant points. Hogarde's apparent feeling that a bird makes an especially appropriate mentor may reflect a fondness for Chaucer's *Parliament of Fowls*, as his writing a poem about a spiritual pilgrimage may mean that he has read Lydgate's translation of Deguileville's *Pèlerinage de la Vie Humaine*, but he makes no specific acknowledgement of sources. Hogarde was, of course, not alone in thus looking back to the Middle Ages for light on the current scene, or in using verse for purposes for which it would now be considered unsuitable; one may note the successive editions of *A Mirror for Magistrates*, popular chronicles partly in verse, and the activities of some of Hogarde's antagonists.[13] Protestant propagandists, alert to elements in medieval poetry which satirize clerical greed and hypocrisy or corruption in the church, had turned imitations of Chaucer to their purpose, converted William Langland into a kind of fourteenth-century Protestant, and made Piers Plowman into a contemporary one.[14]

Hogarde's imagination, in contrast, was caught by the possibilities of medieval knights and siege-warfare for polemic against Protestants on the doctrine of transubstantiation. Thus, in *The assault of the sacrament of the altar*, a work originally written in 1549 and dedicated to the then Princess Mary, Hogarde in his dream is conducted by 'Morpheus' into 'an hall long and wide' hung with tapestries portraying 'noble storyes' from the Old Testament, while his guide explains the New Testament

---

[13] *A mirror for magistrates*, 1559 (STC 1247), other editions following; see also *The chronicle of John Hardyn in metre*, 1543 (STC 12767), *The chronicle beginnynge at the vii ages of the worlde*, 1535 (STC 9984). C.S. Lewis notes that verse writing in the late medieval tradition continued through the reign of Edward VI, *English Literature in the Sixteenth Century excluding the Drama* (Oxford 1954), p. 64.

[14] E.g., *The plowman's tale*, 1540 (STC 5100), which attempts a Chaucerian flavour in its prologue and epilogue; *Jack up lande*, 1545 (STC 5098), which bears Chaucer's name in its title page and his portrait as frontispiece but consists entirely of satirical prose aimed at friars. On Langland's *Vision*, see John N. King, 'Robert Crowley's Editions of *Piers Plowman*: A Tudor Apocalypse,' *Modern Philology*, Vol. 73, No. 4, Part I (May 1976), pp. 34-52. On Piers rebuking the Roman hierarchy, see *I playne Piers which cannot flatter*, 1550 (STC 19903a); *A godly dialogue & disputacion betwene Pyers plowman and a popysh preest*, [c. 1550] (STC 19903); *Pierce the ploughmans crede*, 1553 (STC 19904); *Pyers plowmans exhortation unto the lordes, knightes and burgoysses of the parlaymenthouse*, [1550] (STC 19905).

analogues for these and how they support Roman Catholic dogma. Transubstantiation, the dogma of special concern, is externalized into a castle and six different assaults on it are described, commencing with that of Berengar of Tours in the eleventh century and proceeding through Wycliffe and Luther to Hogarde's own English contemporaries. These, led by Cranmer and some ten other bishops, and including as many more named Protestant clerics, are described as clad in 'armour blacke as any ynke' and each wearing on his helm 'a woman's foresleve', referring to their advocating a married clergy.[15] Hogarde's fondness for presenting doctrinal points visually was illustrated earlier, in his account of the Berengarians making their assault with arrows having 'heades very sharp, named error,/Feathered with scripture falsely understood.'[16]

This use of visual imagery is also prominent in *A treatise entitled the path waye to the towre of perfection*. In this allegory of the spiritual pilgrimage Hogarde makes much of the obstacles along the way; these include both the beautiful woman with braided hair 'shininge lyke gold', who reminds him of the pleasures he is leaving behind, and such physical hazards as a wood full of thorns and wild beasts or a lake called 'the pyt . . . of disperacion'.[17] Finally, after the narrator has called despairingly on God and looked in at a gate where

> Me thought I saw Christ with his woundes bleding
> Which said, come to me, thi lacke I wil supply,
>
> Come forward, quod Christ, & now folowe me,
> For I am the light, the lyfe, the truth & the way.
> Then perfitly the towre before me I did se,
> The glory whereof expresse I ne may.[18]

His descriptions of other people seen in groups along the way to the Tower sound as if Hogarde may also have encountered Langland's Field Full of Folk in his reading, and the narrator's mentor – a bird – is nearly always present to instruct and encourage him.

Hogarde relies on a bird as his mentor in two other of his verse publications also, but in these he is much less concerned with images and much more with direct discussions of religious and moral questions. The bird's role is to prod the poet constantly with questions, and then to formulate answers for him. For one of these tracts (which must have been published before Mary's accession, since it concludes with 'God Save the King'), the long title is accurately descriptive: *A new treatyse in manner of a dialogue which sheweth the excellencie of mans nature, in that he is made to the image of God, and wherein it restyth and by howe many wayes a man*

---

15 *Assault of the sacrament*, sig. E1ᵛ–E2.
16 *Ibid.*, sig. C3ᵛ.
17 *Path waye to perfection*, sigs. B1, B2ᵛ, C3.
18 *Ibid.*, sig. D4.

dothe blotte and defyle the same image. Like greater poets after him, Hogarde explores rhetorically the mystery of man's double nature, and each of the 122 stanzas concludes with some variation of the line, 'I say remember, thou man, what thou arte.' There is much discussion of divine grace and man's free will. The idea that God, by withholding his grace, can be considered responsible for man's sinning, is ridiculed in various ways; for example:

> Do lewde preestes lacke grace which kepeth not theyr vowes?
> Do ryche men lacke grace which help not the pore?
> Do lawers lacke grace which from the right bowes [incline, deviate]?
> Doth that man lacke grace which doth kepe an hoore?[19]

There is some discussion of other properties of man ('Reason and Understandyng') and even some contemporary social criticism about the removal of land from tillage, when the bird remarks that on her flights over the fields she used to feed 'many dayes upon swete corne' but that 'now is there nothyng, because the plough stayes.' But it is the question of *free will* which keeps stirring Hogarde's imagination; as the bird tells him,

> The hyest gyft which god to the[e] hath lent
> Is thy fre[e] wyle, by which thou mayste consent
> To vertue or vyce, both early and late.
> For if thou couldst not, fre wyl were frustrate,
> And all gods preceptes, in evry parte,
> In vayne to the[e], they were all promulgate [merely formal].
> Remember I say, thou man, what thou arte.[20]

The second of Hogarde's tracts consisting mainly of discourse with his mentor, the nightingale, is his 1555 *A mirror of love, which such light doth give/ That all men may learne howe to love and live*. The title here scarcely suggests the range of the dialogue which follows. Various kinds of love are covered by the nightingale's probing remarks, though there is some tendency to bring many of them around to the love owed by good Christians and good subjects to their church and queen. On the way, there is glancing attention to sexual love, some to love 'which from God doth procede . . . called charitie,' to love of country, with its exemplars in ancient Greece and Rome,[21] and then a long section devoted 'to the love that man ought to have to him selfe.' After much discussion the nightingale pronounces this basically good because man is made in God's image and Christ died for him.[22] Near the end is a section on 'the love that a pastor ought to extende toward his flocke.' This contains several

---

[19] *Excellencie of mans nature*, sig. D1.
[20] *Ibid.*, sig. C2, C3.
[21] *Mirrour of love*, sigs. B2, B3, B4.
[22] *Ibid.*, sigs. C4ᵛ-E1.

passages questioning the diligence of the clergy on Hogarde's side, noting also 'how diligent were they which did preach and teach eroniously' – and how confident of ultimate victory.[23]

One of the tracts which Hogarde presented in manuscript to Queen Mary was *A treatise declaring howe Christ by perverse preachyng was banished out of this realme, and howe it hath pleased God to bryng Christ home agayne by Mary our most gracious Quene.* The gift was presumably due more to Hogarde's pride in its form than in its content, since the latter consists mainly of conventional attacks on Protestants for rejecting the Real Presence, permitting the marriage of clerics, and exalting faith above works. The embracing image of the poem, however, is an implicit comparison of Edward VI's reign with that of Herod, when Joseph and Mary fled to Egypt with the infant Jesus, and the reference to the Queen's accession is periodically repeated in some variation of the line, 'Then Mary brought home Christ again.'[24]

Most successful poetically of Hogarde's works is probably a nine-stanza devotional lyric which survived only in one of the mid-century manuscript miscellanies and was printed with most of the other items in 1848.[25] Hogarde is in the company here of John Heywood, the writer of interludes and compiler of epigrams, along with John Redford and John Thorne, musicians and poets, and some anonymous writers. The selections vary in style and tone; Hogarde strikes about the most sombre note of any with his lyric commencing 'O Lord whych are in hevyn on hye', and concluding each of the five-line stanzas with 'O heare me, Lord, and graunt mercye'. But, at least in stanzas like the following, Hogarde's poem does not suffer from comparison with the others:

> No ryghtwysenes in mee doth rayne,
> But synne I knowe and wyckednes;
> Unles thy crace I doo obtayne,
> Dew unto mee is deth endles.
> O here me, Lord, and graunt mercye.

Two other poems of Hogarde's in print are, respectively, the latest and the earliest of his dateable printed works, and neither is of much interest artistically. His 1557 work, *A newe ABC paraphrasticallye applied*, is much in the manner of *An honest godlye instruction . . . for children* (STC 3281), which Bishop Bonner caused to be published the year before to provide children with a guide (in English) to the main parts of the liturgy and important Catholic doctrines. The task Hogarde has set himself is to produce, for each letter of the alphabet, four lines of religiously or

---

[23] *Ibid.*, sigs. F4ᵛ-G2ᵛ.

[24] Hogarde presented the Queen with a manuscript copy (Harley 3444), one evidently made from the printed text, since it includes the preface to the reader. Baskerville (p. 45) dates this prior to July 1554, since the Queen's titles are pre-marriage.

[25] See Appendix.

politically improving verse beginning with that letter. Those for the letter D are typical:

> Drede of Gode and eke his judgment
> Dryven have we from our heartes.
> Dearth without cause some doth invent;
> Divels can play no worse partes.[26]

Hogarde's earliest known work – a defence of transubstantiation against a Protestant 'ballad' attacking it – survives only in the extensive quotations which Robert Crowley's *Confutation* gives in refuting them. As found there, Hogarde's tract is a curious mixture. The preface tells the reader he will only end in error regarding the Eucharist 'If thou by reason seke to se/ How God can work this misterie,' but the argument is heavily sprinkled with marginal citations from the Bible in the manner of the Protestant preachers. At the end, perhaps so as not to try the forbearance of a Protestant regime too far, he prays for King Edward 'to defend the catholike fayth . . . and al heresy and popishnes to subdue.'[27]

Hogarde's only known work in prose, *The displaying of the Protestantes*, seems in various ways to belong to a different world from his tracts in verse. Where his verse style is clumsy and uncertain, his prose is assured, somewhat in the vein of Sir Thomas More's popular English prose. He can be racy at times and fond of contemporary colloquialisms – as when, assailing Protestant preachers for interpreting Scripture to suit their own purposes, he remarks, 'Thus of the Lordes Woorde in all their doynges, they make a Shypmans hoose [a seaman's broad britches] to use it as they like to do good or ill.'[28] And while in *Mirrour of love or Excellencie of man's nature* he discusses ideas about which much could be said on several sides, in *Displaying of Protestantes* he is simply attacking antagonists at whatever points they are vulnerable. Thus he insists, without admitting qualifications, that Protestants sent to the stake are not persecuted martyrs but common criminals to whom the magistrates have simply applied the penalties provided by law, just as they would to thieves or murderers.

There is perhaps another ground also for Hogarde's new air of assurance. In the verse tracts he apologizes repeatedly for his lack of learning, in statements which may be partly explicable as a convention he has picked up from medieval poetry, but which do find corroboration in the limited range of his marginal citations. With a very few exceptions, such as the references to the Book of Common Prayer and to some of Tyndale's writings in *Christ banished*, the only books specifically mentioned in the margins are scriptural. In *Displaying of Protestantes*, on

---

[26] *Newe ABC*, sig. A3.
[27] *Confutation*, sigs. A2^v, F3^v.
[28] *Displaying of Protestantes*, fol. 121.

the other hand, there are scores of nonbiblical marginalia: from Cicero, Seneca, Livy, Virgil, Plutarch and Xenophon, as well as from early Christian writers like Augustine, Jerome, Tertullian, and Eusebius. The Venerable Bede, Polydore Vergil, Martin Luther, and John Ponet are also cited. Some of the classical quotations, indeed, sound a little as if brought in mainly to parade Hogarde's present learning. The citations are nearly all in Latin and at one point in the text, when responding to a barbed query about his familiarity with Bishop Gardiner's antipapal classic, *De Vera Obedientia* (which the Protestants had first translated from the original Latin into English), Hogarde remarks that he has read the work in both languages, but does not undertake to dispute the the accuracy of the translation himself.[29]

His sense of being part of an established polemic tradition may also have lent him support. Hogarde had behind him a body of popular religious propaganda going back at least to the medieval friars, expanded in its audience by the spread of printing, and including such distinguished sixteenth-century practitioners as Thomas More and John Fisher. Among writers of the century's middle decades, however, it was his Protestant antagonists rather than his fellow Catholics who possessed the popular touch.[30] Those supporting Mary's regime, clerics themselves, for the most part wrote as if their audience were clerical also, concentrating on the doctrinal points then at issue with Protestants or on matters of church history, and making little effort to bring their arguments within the experience of their lay countrymen.[31] Bishop Bonner did indeed publish revised homilies and other works expounding the fundamentals of the faith, but the tone here is one of instruction, not of persuasion. The works of John Christopherson, Bishop of Chichester, and Thomas Watson, Bishop of Lincoln, commanded the respect of their Protestant opponents and still read impressively, but they tend to be official discourses, scorning the use of humour and other devices of popular controversy.[32] There is a marked contrast between such works and John Fisher's emotional sermon against Luther's heresies, preached from the open-air pulpit of Paul's Cross in 1521 and general enough in its

---

[29] *Ibid.*, fol. 108ᵛ.

[30] For more comprehensive treatment of the propaganda writers of Mary's reign, see the Introduction in Baskerville, pp. 1–30.

[31] *E.g.* John Angel, *The agreement of the holye fathers and doctours of the churche upon the chiefest articles of the Christian religion*, [1555?] (STC 634); John Churchson, *A briefe treatyse declaryng what and where the churche is*, 1556 (STC 5219); John Gwynneth, *A declaration of the state wherein all heretikes dooe leade their lives*, 1554 (STC 12558).

[32] Christopherson, *An exhortation to all menne to take hede and beware of rebellion*, 1554 (STC 5207); Watson, *Holsom and catholyke doctryne concerning the seven sacramentes of Chrystes church*, 1558 (STC 25112), *Two notable sermons made . . . before the Quenes highnes concerninge the reall presence*, 1554 (STC 25115). The last was still considered important enough in Elizabeth's reign for Robert Crowley to publish a reply in 1569.

appeal to be reprinted twice in Mary's reign.[33]

Deciding just where Hogarde learned the tricks of the propagandist's trade remains conjectural, but it is clearly the Protestant writers of his era who were the more enterpising and imaginative, not only in turning medieval literary works to their purpose but also in relating their religious message to men's everyday lives. Hugh Latimer, with his famous sermon declaring the preacher to be one of God's plowmen and his talent for the telling anecdote, was the best known, but there were younger men also who were eager to apply Gospel teachings to the responsibilities of lawyers and landowners. These included such figures as John Bradford, Thomas Lever, and Robert Crowley, who was a printer as well as a cleric.[34] Hogarde is reported to have been an attender (for whatever reasons) of Latimer's sermons,[35] and Crowley, author of a detailed reply to Hogarde's earliest publication, was certainly known to him. The greater liveliness of the Protestant propagandists in pushing their cause is, indeed, well illustrated in a number of the tracts Crowley published in Edward VI's reign. These, sometimes in verse as rough as Hogarde's, argue in effect that England's traditional society is to be preserved by each of the main components (the gentleman, the merchant, the lawyer, the yeoman, etc.) staying within his own 'calling' and strictly observing his obligations to his fellow men, under the immediate threat of God's punishment. Crowley is skilled at introducing bits of individualizing detail, not only in describing his various social types but also in throwing in a few specific numbers that illustrate the rise in rents and prices that has been driving the poor into vagabondage. The grasping landowner is his villain; the Gospel preacher, threatening damnation for the covetous, is his evident hero. Hogarde, as will be seen, apparently shared Crowley's admiration of the traditional social order but disagreed totally about the figure Crowley selected to help maintain

---

[33] *A sermon very notable, fruicteful and godlie . . . concerning the heresies of Martyne Luther*, 1554 (STC 10896) and 1556 (STC 10897). Hugh Glasier's Paul's Cross sermon of August 25, 1555 (STC 11916.5) was one of the few by Marian churchmen that reads with something of Fisher's broad appeal.

[34] Bradford, who was burnt at the stake in 1555, had little published in his lifetime but was widely known for having given up (under Latimer's influence) what he saw as the corruptions of a successful legal career and becoming a cleric. For Lever, see particularly, *A sermon preached the thyrd Sonday in Lent before the Kynges majestie*, [1550] (STC 15547), *A sermon preached at Pauls Crosse the xiiii day of December*, 1550 (STC 15546), *A meditacion upon the Lordes praier*, 1551 (STC 15544). For Crowley, see particularly *An informacion and peticion agaynst the oppressours of the pore commons*, [1548] (STC 6086), *The voyce of the laste trumpet . . . wherein are contened the xii letters to the twelve estats of men*, 1549 (STC 6094), *The waye to wealth, wherein is plainly taught a most present remedy for sedicion*, 1550 (STC 6096), *One and thyrtye epigrammes wherein are bryefly touched so many abuses that maye and oughte to be put away*, 1550 (STC 6088), *Pleasure and payne, heaven and helle, remember these foure and all shall be well*, 1551 (STC 6090).

[35] Crowley, *Confutation*, sig. A3ᵛ.

it. For Hogarde the Gospel preacher is an outstanding villain, along with the iconoclast, the Bible-quoting apprentice, and others whom John Foxe was to enshrine in his Protestant martyrology. But Hogarde seemingly did not disdain to learn from his opponents as a writer.

As the title of *Displaying of Protestantes* promises, Hogarde goes on the attack immediately. He is careful also to focus on Protestant religious practices and events with which a layman is likely to have some familiarity, giving little attention to points of theology. He plays rhetorically with the still new name, 'Protestants', defining them as 'disswaders of holsome lawes which touched the reparation of man's nature' (i.e. as encouragers of licence) and follows this shortly with a nostalgic reference to 'the happy tyme past' before the Reformation came to England.[36] He then describes various religious extremists who have been loosed upon Europe by Protestantism's destruction of the unity of the medieval church. There is little mention of Cranmer and other establishment figures except as those responsible for the relaxation of clerical celibacy and of fasting, or for the confusion caused in parish churches by changes in the communion service. Much of the middle of the book is directed at counteracting the effects which the burnings of Protestants have evidently been having on public opinion. He rejects any parallel with the martyrs of the early Christian church, insists that it is the rightness of the cause and not the courage of the sufferer which makes the martyr, and describes – satirically and quite without compassion – a number of particular burnings.

Later he returns to the nexus he has previously posited between religious freedom and social disorder ('O develysh libertie,' he exlaims, 'I wold to God Germany might have kept the[e] styll'),[37] recounting several instances of Protestants physically attacking priests and defacing statues of saints. He also sneers briefly at the exiled Protestant propagandists, citing a number of authors and works by name. Then, toward the end of the augmented second edition, there follows the vivid account of an illicit religious meeting in a stable in Islington, an occasion marked by much quoting of Scripture and presided over by a self-seeking charlatan named 'Father Browne'.

A mere summary of the book fails to do justice to Hogarde's skill. He has the true propagandist's feel for what a given audience will be interested in, where his opponent's weak points are, how far a line of argument can be pressed without losing credibility, and how to use the telling factual detail. His 'Father Browne' is a figure much like the character 'Zeal-of-the-Land Busy' in Ben Johnson's *Bartholomew Fair* over half a century later: fond of his food, given to unctuous language, fawned over by housewives of several different social levels. Hogarde's

---

[36] *Displaying of Protestantes*, fol. 8ᵛ.
[37] *Ibid.*, fol. 116.

effect is achieved mainly by shrewdly observed details presented in an even tone of voice, as when he describes the ending of Browne's conversation about 'persecutions' with his 'mother' (the most prosperous of the housewives) and the beginning of the formal service:

> Browne wente into the Stable where, tarrying a while belyke in doing his busynes, anone he called in the congregacion, & amonges them thrust we. Where Browne, leanynge upon hys horsebacke, which was a jade scarse worth sixe pence, sitting upon the maunger, he beganne to alledge certen places of *Ecclesiastes* without booke, one upon another in heapes. Then beganne he to talke of thre Religiones. The one he termed my lorde Chauncelors [Bishop Gardiner's] religion; the other Cranmers, Latymers and Ridleys religion; and the thirde he called goddes Religion. My lorde Chauncelors, he sayde, was nought; Cranmers & the others religion not good; but Goddes religion was best.[38]

Though faithfully reporting this separatist denunciation of the Edwardian church, Hogarde has previously spent some time describing the separatists' frequent use of biblical quotations, epithets like 'shavelyng priestes' and other turns of speech typical of the orthodox Protestants. Hence the reader is well prepared to accept his judgment now that 'with many such similitudes of Godlines many of the Protestants in our tyme be inspired',[39] and to be at least half inclined to blame Browne on Cranmer's reforms.

There is a certain parallel between this conventicle of Browne's and that described by Sir Thomas More as conducted by the Protestant Robert Barnes during his brief return to England from Germany in 1531. One of the women asking Barnes embarrassing questions in this meeting is the illiterate wife of the innkeeper 'at the signe of the botell at Botolfes wharfe' where Barnes is staying, and More evidently knows both place and person first-hand. But the questions themselves are hypothetical, as is the literate 'merchaunters wyfe' also asking such questions, and More's interest is not in the conventicle itself but in intellectually demolishing Barnes's concept of the church.[40] Hogarde's interest, a quarter of a century later, is in giving the reader a first-hand picture of a disorderly separatist meeting. If he was not present himself, as he asserts, he has certainly mastered the technique Defoe uses in *Robinson Crusoe* of choosing the individualizing details which carry this conviction to the reader.

This portrayal of Father Browne was added during the month or two between the first and second editions of *The Displaying of the Protestants*, and one wonders whether it reflects any considered view of Hogarde's

---

[38] *Ibid.*, fol. 124.
[39] *Ibid.*, fol. 125[v].
[40] *The confutation of Tyndale's answer*, Book VIII, in Yale ed. of More (New Haven 1973), Vol. 8, pp. 883–905. I owe this interesting parallel to Dr John Fines.

about contemporary religious separatists. He was probably aware that some of these groups, such as the Arians, were farther from orthodox Protestants in their theology than the latter were from the Roman Catholics, but there is no hint in him of anything like present-day scholarship's concept of a largely autonomous 'Radical Reformation' having its own roots in the medieval past.[41] Among Hogarde's Protestant contemporaries there was ambivalence about separatists. John Bradford and other orthodox prisoners in the King's Bench saw the Freewillers as a serious religious danger but also tried to maintain a united front with them against the Roman Catholic authorities.[42] Later on, John Foxe included men with separatist pasts in his account of the Marian martyrs, but he was very careful to conceal their separatist pasts in doing so.[43] Though differing from each other on how religious separatists should be treated, orthodox Protestants certainly agreed in seeing separatists as a Protestant propaganda vulnerability, and on this technical basis it is hard not to admire Hogarde's skill. He has been able at the same time to describe Father Browne denouncing orthodox Protestants and to imply that they are responsible for Father Browne's existence.

In other parts of the tract also, Hogarde achieves some of his effects simply by reporting checkable facts which tell against his opponents, as John Foxe was to do a few years later on the other side. Hogarde's instances of iconoclasm and of violence against priests are confirmed by various sources, and Foxe's own account of a particular burning gives factual support to one of Hogarde's sharpest barbs. The same Protestants, he says, who denounce as superstition the preserving of saints' bones as relics, themselves scramble in the ashes for the remains of comrades burnt at the stake, and treat these remains as sacred relics.[44] Elsewhere, directing his ridicule at the troubles of the Protestant bishops in finding an appropriate new location for the communion table, Hogarde reconstructs the scene in his imagination:

> Fyrst they placed it a lofte, where the hygh altare stode. Then downe it must come . . . In some places benethe the stepes, in the quier, covering it about with curtens for fears of bugges. Within a whyle after, it skipped out of the quier into the body of the churche. And in some places neyther in the quier, nor yet in the body of the churche, but betwene bothe. And some, because they would hitte it ryght, pulled downe the Rodelofte [choir screen], making such a confusion that neyther was there a quyer nor bodye of the churche, but making it lyke Westminster Hall.[45]

[41] E.g. George H. Williams, *The Radical Reformation* (London 1962); R. I. Moore, *The Origins of European Dissent* (New York 1977); Claus-Peter Clasen, *Anabaptism: a Social History, 1525-1618* (Ithaca and London 1972).
[42] See chapter 3, section 4 above.
[43] See chapter 9, section 3 below.
[44] A. & M., VIII, pp. 279-80; *Displaying of Protestantes*, fols. 62ᵛ, 64.
[45] Ibid., fols. 80ᵛ-81.

3

Some of Hogarde's persistent attitudes should now be evident. His loyalty to Queen Mary, which antedated her accession and was specifically mentioned in all but one of his books published after it, stands out as strong and uncomplicated.

His devotion to the beliefs and ceremonies of the traditional church was certainly as strong as Mary's and was something like hers, in that the church was evidently linked in his mind with the life of an earlier and more orderly England. What attracts him religiously is the solidity of a church 'of one faith, one spirite & one judgement, not lacerated, divided or tornc, but wholc and intier.'[46] Except for transubstantiation, clerical celibacy, and one or two other points, he ignores the specific issues then debated between Protestants and Roman Catholics.[47] His reference to 'the happy tyme' before the Reformation has already been mentioned – a time when England, as he says later, lived in 'mervylous love and amitie, in true dealing and honest simplicitie' because men held to the old religious ceremonies and observed the ancient boundaries of degree. Children were taught 'to use prayer mornyng and evening, to be reverent in the church, at their first enteraunce into the same to make the sygne of the crosse in their foreheades, to make beysaunce to the magistrates, to discover their heades when they mete with men of ancient yeres . . .'[48] But now, he goes on, 'apprentices and other servauntes' are no longer kept under proper discipline and 'no good man or priest passing by them in the streets can escape their mockes.' Their having Bibles to quote from in baiting the priests has apparently played a part in the situation, for, as Hogarde puts it, on holy days when they should be in church, the apprentices mill about the streets and markets, 'either skorning the passers by, or with their testamentes utter some wise thrust of their owne device.'[49]

Hogarde's verse tracts, besides looking back to the Middle Ages in their literary conventions, also praise certain aspects of that earlier society where, as remarked in *Excellencie of mans nature*, the farmer plowed his land instead of grazing it. One of the things Hogarde looks for from Mary's reign is restoration of the traditional social order, when once more he hopes, men

> gods law embrace,
> Such a common wealth god in his realme will place,

[46] *Ibid.*, fol. 20ᵛ.
[47] For example, purgatory, auricular confession, adoration of the saints, services in Latin, monasteries, and the papal obedience are scarcely mentioned.
[48] *Displaying of Protestantes*, fols. 92, 93.
[49] *Ibid.*, fol. 95.

> That king & quene in studie [desire] will not cease
> Tholde yeomanry of England againe to encrease.[50]

Mirrour of love closes with the nightingale expounding an organic theory of society. 'Christ, being head, ought to rule the bodie al,' and the various groups – nobles, merchants, yeomen – should stay within their respective callings (the merchant should not 'take fermes into his handes'), bound to one another by love. 'Because,' the nightingale concludes in a sixteenth-century version of William Langland's *Vision concerning Piers Plowman*, 'where love is, common wealth doth rayne.'[51]

Hogarde's aversion to the Protestant preachers (of all stripes, but primarily those of the Edwardian establishment) is as obvious as his warm loyalty to Mary, but by no means as uncomplicated. He dislikes them on several grounds, one of course being their part in destroying the pre-Reformation England which he idealizes. He sees them as pretentious in their knowledge and personally arrogant:

> Perching up in pulpittes, as thou dost see,
> Seeming to thignoraunt gods word to preache,
> Pretending to know that which they could never reache.[52]

Worse still, those who had originally been ordained in the traditional church are guilty of breaking their vow of celibacy. This was a matter of far-reaching importance, in that the celebrant who handled the body of Christ in the mass needed to be visibly set apart from ordinary men, and the Marian church made a great point of ousting from their posts clerics who had married.[53] Hogarde is even more severe on clerics with wives. He jabs at them in two of the verse tracts,[54] and turns to the subject in several parts of *Displaying of Protestantes*. In one passage he undertakes to refute John Ponet's defence of clerical marriage,[55] and in another he puts his finger on what was to be proved by experience in Elizabeth's reign to be a genuine practical difficulty posed by a married clergy: the strain on church finances caused by their having legitimate children to provide for.[56] But for a dozen or so pages elsewhere Hogarde writes about

---

[50] *Mirrour of love*, sig. F1.

[51] *Ibid.*, sig. G4.

[52] *Ibid.*, sig. D4ᵛ; see also *Displaying of Protestantes*, verse preface, and title page of *Christ banished*. On the 'foolishe arrogance' of Protestant mechanic preachers see *Displaying of Protestantes*, fol. 87.

[53] While those putting away their wives could be given different parishes, the rigor of the rule is seen in the case of Paul Bushe, whose *A brief exhortation . . . to Margaret Burgess,* 1556 (STC 4184), is one of the most effective defences of the Roman Catholic doctrine of the Eucharist for a lay public. Bushe, nevertheless, had had to resign as Bishop of Bristol because of his wife.

[54] *Assault of the sacrament*, sig. E2; *Mirrour of love*, sig. G1ᵛ-2.

[55] *Displaying of Protestantes*, fol. 23ᵛ; the Ponet tract is *A defence of marriage for priests*, 1549 (STC 20176).

[56] *Ibid.*, 84ᵛ-85.

married clergy almost as one himself obsessed by sex. He assumes no other basis for clerical marriage than the gratification of physical appetite, tries to establish a nexus between heresy and the influence of women in the ancient church, repeats some of the stock medieval attitudes toward women, and ends with jibes at Bible-reading wives in his own day who are 'ready to assure their husbands to dye in the lordes veritie because they would fayne have newe.'[57]

Furthermore, it was apparently the preachers and other Protestant controversialists who had most sharply questioned Hogarde's right, as a mere artisan, to discuss religious questions. Crowley's attitude in his *Confutation*, the detailed answer to Hogarde's now lost tract defending transubstantiation, is instructive on this point. In addition to the tracts of social criticism mentioned earlier, Crowley wrote works of theological controversy roughly parallel to the *Confutation* – one, for example, in 1569 against 'the subtyule sophistries' of two sermons which Thomas Watson had preached before Queen Mary, and another replying to a recantation sermon preached by the former Protestant bishop, Nicholas Shaxton, in 1546.[58] But the tone taken toward Hogarde is harsher than that taken even against the apostate Protestant; he is repeatedly reminded of his menial occupation (being told on one occasion that he writes 'lyke an Hosyar') and of his lack of the formal qualifications to discuss transubstantiation.[59] When Crowley says, 'You are to[o] yonge, maister Hoggarde, to defend thys matter,' he refers to Hogarde's educational shortcomings, since there was no notable difference in the two men's chronological ages.[60] Over a disputed point of logic Crowley tells him that 'a man had nede to have you to the universitie to teach you to understand your errour in this argument,' and elsewhere Crowley ostentatiously translates a critical bit of Latin so that Hogarde can be sure of understanding the point. Crowley's punning on his name to address him as 'maister Hogherd' was of course common practice in sixteenth-century controversy.[61] What Hogarde seems to have really resented are the insinuations that he is no more than a mouthpiece for Bishop Gardiner or some other cleric.[62] He ends another of his early tracts with

---

[57] *Ibid.*, 72–78.

[58] *A setting open of the subtyle sophistrie of Thomas Watson . . . in hys two sermons, Anno 1553*, 1569 (STC 6093); *The confutation of xiii articles whereunto N. Shaxton, late by shop of Salisburye, subscribed,* [1548] (STC 6083).

[59] *Confutation*, sig. C7ᵛ.

[60] *Ibid.*, sig. A3ᵛ. Crowley may even have been chronologically younger than Hogarde, if one accepts 1518 as his year of birth and assumes that there was some substance to his charge (sig. A5) that Hogarde had had 'a parte' in the execution of Protestants from the time of John Frith in 1533.

[61] *Ibid.*, sigs. F1ᵛ, B7, regarding Hogarde's learning; sigs. D1, E4ᵛ, F1, for punning on Hogarde's name.

[62] *Ibid.*, sigs. A5ᵛ, A8ᵛ, B1ᵛ, D2ᵛ.

an explicit challenge to anyone to prove that 'Myles Hogarde . . . settes his name/ To that which other man myght clame.'[63] In his preface to another verse tract he argues somewhat defensively that he does not aspire to eloquence and learning because he writes for 'the simple folke,' and reiterates that 'in matter of faith I have assurance.'[64]

In an incident which understandably rankled Hogarde even more, a Protestant broke off an oral discussion with him on the ground that his occupation made him incompetent to debate religious questions. In a first-hand account printed by Foxe, the Essex country gentlemen, Thomas Haukes, who was subsequently burnt for heresy, describes his questioning in July 1555 in Bishop Bonner's residence by Bonner and other clerics, with Hogarde joining in also. After the first exchange with Hogarde over the biblical basis for the baptism of children, Haukes cuts him off with a query about his name and whether he is not a hosier living in Pudding Lane. To Hogarde's affirmative answer Haukes replies with what sounds like a much-used jingle: 'It would seem so, for ye can better skill to eat a pudding or make a hose than use Scripture either to answer or oppose.' Hauke's account then adds with a certain air of surprise, 'With that he was in great rage, and did chafe up and down.'[65]

Another indication that Hogarde was well recognized as a foe by Protestants, even before *Displaying of Protestantes* appeared in mid-1556, is seen in a flagrantly seditious Protestant pamphlet attributed to the year 1555. In this the anonymous questioner repeatedly asks, in ostensible innocence, whether various alleged betrayals of the country's interests by Mary's marriage to Philip of Spain have not released the Queen's subjects from their allegiance, and the title page, perhaps mimicking Hogarde's fondness for describing himself as the Queen's servant, announces that it is 'Imprinted at the earnest requeste and sute of youre graces trewe and faythfull servaunt Myles Hogherde.'[66]

Of the clerics on his own side Hogarde has nothing directly to say. There is neither praise of their actions (the credit for the church's revival all goes to the Queen) nor defence against Protestant attacks, and it is not easy to define the relationship. They presumably recognized his usefulness in a propaganda war where pro-regime pamphleteers were not plentiful, and gave him support, whether or not in the direct form that Hogarde's opponents insinuated. His special patron seems to have been Bonner. The story told by Haukes indicates that Hogarde had ready access to Bonner's episcopal residence in London and, as noted earlier, Hogarde's 1557 tract, *Newe ABC*, fits in well with Bonner's other

---

[63] *Excellencie of mans nature*, sig. D4ᵛ.
[64] *Path waye to perfection*, sig. A2.
[65] *A. & M.*, VII, p. 111.
[66] *Certayne questions demaunded and asked by the noble realme of Englande of her true naturall chyldren and subjects of the same*, [1555] (STC 9981).

projects for expounding Roman Catholic beliefs to children and the slenderly educated. The statement on the title page of the first edition of *Displaying of Protestantes*, 'Perused and set furth with thassent of authoritie, according to the ordre in that behalfe appoynted,' points to the Bishop of London as the responsible official, and could imply his active encouragement. (The irony of the situation is that after the success of that tract, no better use for Hogarde's propagandist talents could apparently be found than the journeyman task of *Newe ABC*.) Gardiner, despite Protestant insinuations of Hogarde's dependence on him, is a less likely patron because of Gardiner's limited interest in propagandizing or even in formally instructing the ordinary laity. In any event, no direct references to Hogarde have come to light in ecclesiastical records.

It is rather in his attitude toward the Protestant preachers that the key to Hogarde's outlook is to be found. As has been seen, he denounces them harshly, yet he also admires the 'diligence' with which they spread their views, and he seems secretly impressed by their confidence that they will win in the end.[67] Also, as has been noted, he was a repeated attender of Latimer's sermons, and the vein of social criticism in his works is not unlike that of various radical Protestants, despite the doctrinal gap between them. For despite the disclaimer in the preface to *Mirrour of love*, Hogarde was himself essentially a lay preacher, fond of words and feeling a deep need to discuss religious questions. The years of religious controversy and the availability of printing presses provided both stimulus and opportunity for giving his views expression, and he evidently felt he had things to express that were both important and his own.

Two parallel cases to Hogarde's may be cited, both almost exact contemporaries, one of them a Protestant separatist and the other an orthodox Protestant. The separatist, Henry Hart, resembles Hogarde in showing special interest, in part of his writing, in the question of free will. His contemporary reputation, indeed, is as leader of the sect of Free-willers in the controversy with orthodox Protestants imprisoned with them in the King's Bench prison in 1554-56, though his two known printed tracts pay relatively little attention to the question of free will.[68] The orthodox Protestant is a bitter opponent of Hart's in the prison controversy, one John Careless, a weaver from Coventry, where he performed in the traditional Coventry plays and had even been temporarily released from prison for this purpose before being sent to London for trial as a heretic. He was a voluble writer of letters and, to judge from the 18 which Foxe prints, felt a compulsion to describe what his religion meant to him, and to encourage others (both those in prison

---

[67] *Mirrour of love*, sig. G2.
[68] *A godly short treatyse*, 1548 (STC 12887), *A consultorie for all Christians*, 1549 (STC 12564).

with him and those outside it) to stand firm in a time of trial. Though the letters have little of the interest of Hogarde's writings, Careless evidently had an engaging personality, which tempted one of the presiding Roman Catholic clerics to a long effort to convert him, and influenced John Bradford and another important Protestant cleric to exchange letters with him.[69] Nor do these three provide the only such cases.[70]

The point here is the compulsion felt by each of these three men of the artisan class to set down his religious feelings in writing for others to read. Theologically, they were divided from each other by what each considered an unbridgeable gap, but each had the same conviction that it was important and even necessary to express his own religious views.

4

Does Hogarde's story represent no more than a footnote to ecclesiastical history with a few human sidelights on in-group snobbery? This examination suggests that it does mean more. Though it is only one piece of evidence, it is a striking one in that this kind of lay participation in sixteenth-century religious life is normally seen as a Protestant rather than a Roman Catholic phenomenon. It is noteworthy also that this sixteenth-century layman, insistent on airing his religious views to a wider public, should be drawn not to the new learning from Italy but attracted rather by the medieval order in church and society.

The origin of individualism, or the sense of the self, is a complicated phenomenon, placed by Burckhardt in the fifteenth century and by others more recently in the twelfth.[71] In sixteenth-century England it is traceable in such varied manifestations of a slowly changing upper class sensibility as the rising interest in portrait painting, in mirrors, in

[69] *A. & M.*, VII, pp. 691-93, VIII, pp. 163-200, includes Careless' long dialogue with the Roman Catholic, Dr Martin, and his correspondence with John Bradford and John Philpot, as well as his letters to lesser figures; two additional Careless letters are printed in Bradford, II, pp. 354-58, 406.

[70] Foxe prints various letters of religious exhortation by Ralph Allerton, Richard Woodman and other Protestant laymen awaiting execution in Mary's prisons. Among the anti-Protestant tracts of her reign, George Marshall's *A compendious treatise in metre declaring the firste originale of sacrifice and of the buylding of aultares*, 1554 (STC 17469), reads more like the work of a layman deeply devoted to church tradition in the Hogarde manner than like the writings of the regime's clerical propagandists, though (as the *DNB* article on Marshall notes) we know nothing about the author beyond what he says in the work itself.

[71] *E.g.* Jacob Burckhardt, *The Civilization of the Renaissance in Italy*, Book II; R.W. Southern, *The Making of the Middle Ages* (London 1973), pp. 217 ff; Walter Ullman, *The Individual and Society in the Middle Ages* (Baltimore 1965); C.W. Bynum 'Did the Twelfth Century Discover the Individual?' *J.E.H.*, xxxi, No. 1 (January 1980), pp. 1-17; Colin Morris, 'Individualism in Twelfth Century Religion: Some Further Reflections', *ibid.*, No. 2 (April 1980), pp. 195-206.

sequences of love sonnets, in a greater provision for privacy in country house architecture. The subject is too large for discussion here beyond the reminder that there may be plebeian parallels also. It may be little more than coincidence that this insistence on airing their personal religious views, differing as these views were, should appear at almost the same time in three Englishmen of the artisan class. But the coincidence still suggests that the century's growing interest in individual identity may be found on levels lower than where we have been accustomed to look. The spectacular version of this desire to discuss religion is all too familiar in the contentious sects committed to new or revived heretical doctrines. Miles Hogarde, quite the reverse, clings to traditional doctrines and institutions, but the growing individualistic germ is detectable in him also.

Appendix I

Miles Hogarde's Surviving Works

Hogarde's earliest known printed work was titled, at least in part, *The abuse of the lessed sacramente of the altare*, but it survives only in the very extensive quotations given by Robert Crowley in the tract (STC 6082, dated 1548; full title given in n. 5 above) which he devoted to refuting it.

The assault of the sacrament of the altar containyng as well sixe severall assaultes made from tyme to tyme against the sayd blessed sacrament, as also the names and opinions of all the heretical captaines of the same assaultes: written in the yere of oure Lord 1549 by Myles Huggarde and dedicated to the Quenes most excellent majestie, then being ladie Marie, in which tyme (heresie then raigning) it could take no place. Now newly imprynted this present yere. London, Robert Caly, 1554 (STC 13556). Referred to here as *Assault of the sacrament.*

A new treatyse in manner of a dialoge which sheweth the excellencie of mans nature in that he is made in the image of God, and wherein it resteth and by howe many wayes a man dothe blotte and defyle the same image. London, Robert Wyer, [1550] (STC 13560). Referred to as *Excellencie of mans nature.*

A treatise declaring howe Christ by perverse preachyng was banished out of this realme. And howe it hath pleased God to bryng Christ home againe by Mary our moost gracious Quene. London, Robert Caly, 1554 (STC 13560.5). Referred to as *Christ banished.*

A treatise entitled the path waye to the towre of perfection. Compiled by Myles Huggarde, servant to the Quenes most excellent majestie. London, Robert Caly, 1554 (STC 13561). Referred to as *Path waye to perfection*.

The displaying of the Protestantes and sondry their practises, with a description of divers their abuses of late frequented within their malignaunte churche. Perused and set furth with thassent of authoritie, accordyng too the ordre in that behalfe appoynted. London, Robert Caly, 1556 (STC 13557). Citations here are to the augmented second edition.

The displaying of the Protestantes and sondry their practises, with a description of divers of their abuses of late frequented. Newly imprinted agayne and augmented with a table at the ende of all matter as is specially contained within this volume. Made by Myles Huggarde servant to the Quenes majestie. London, Robert Caly, 1556 (STC 13558). Referred to as *Displaying of Protestantes*.

A newe ABC paraphrasticallye applied, as the state of the worlde doeth at this day require. London, Robert Caly, 1557 (STC 13559.5). Referred to as *Newe* ABC.

A mirroure of myserie, newly compiled and sett forthe by Myles Huggarde, servaunte to the quenes moste excellente majestie, A° Domini M.D.lvii. Huntington Library MS. HM 121.

'O Lord whych art in hevyn on hye', nine-stanza poem bearing Hogarde's name, in MS. miscellany, *Songs and religious poems*, British Library Add. MS. 15233; printed in J. O. Halliwell, ed., *The moral play of wit and science . . . and early poetical miscellanies* (London 1848), pp. 107–109.

Appendix II

A Note on A Mirroure of Myserie

Little is known about Hogarde's last substantial work, *A mirroure of myserie*, which survives only in a single manuscript (now in the Huntington Library) bearing the date 1557 and containing an elaborate eight-stanza dedication to Queen Mary. It could be argued that only some kind of official assistance would have enabled Hogarde to put a poem of nearly 900 lines into such a handsomely transcribed and illustrated manuscript, including the royal arms on its title page and a

pen-and-ink drawing to introduce the text proper. Some points which
the poem emphasizes, moreover, accord very well with the regime's
efforts to recatholicize England – as, for example, the passages attacking
persons (i.e. Protestants) who take 'a lewd libertie / Not to come to the
church materiall / With others to praie' and also those who flout the
church's traditional rules on fasting.[72]

The main thrust of the poem, however, would hardly please official
readers, for it holds up Sodom and Gomorrah as a distant mirror of
England's present condition, denouncing in particular the way material
abundance is worshipped for its own sake and none of it devoted to the
needy poor. In one of his frequent comparisons of his own country with
these Old Testament cities Hogarde declares:

> Lesse mercie, I thynke, there was never seene
> In all thies contries, whyche so wicked were,
> Then is nowe in Englande & late hath bene.
> Pore folk hath sterved,[73]

A whole society is under attack, and in a tone reminiscent of that found in
the 'Commonwealth men' of Edward VI's reign. One thinks of Robert
Crowley's pamphlets in prose and verse attacking greedy landowners
who exploit the poor, or Thomas Lever's sermon before the King and
Council, denouncing the neglect of the poor and calling England to
remember Sodom and Gomorrah.[74]

In form, the work follows the pattern of some of Hogarde's earlier
poems in which he falls into a dream and is conducted by 'Morpheus' to a
distant scene whose varied features, explained by a mentor there, convey
the message of the poem. In this case Morpheus places him on a hill from
which he can observe both the fruitful land of Canaan and the devastation
which had once been the flourishing cities of Sodom and Gomorrah. A
mentor stands by him to answer his questions, which mainly concern the
four basic sins causing God to destroy these cities. These are identified as
pride, gluttony, preoccupation with worldly wealth, and idleness in the
sense of improperly using one's time. In the detailed description of each
sin Hogarde's fondness for discussion of religious questions is again
evident. Despite his earlier controversy with Crowley and his strictures
on Protestant preachers generally, he follows their practice of making
frequent marginal references to the Bible (and to no other works besides
the Bible) and agrees with Crowley to a considerable extent on social
policy. Like Crowley, he hits specifically at the oppression of the poor by
raising their rents, and calls for a price-freeze by way of remedy.[75] For

[72] *Mirroure of myserie*, fols. 22[r] and 15.
[73] *Ibid.*, fol. 23[r]; see also 11.
[74] *A sermon preached the thyrd Sonday in Lent*, [1550] (STC 15547), sigs. B5[v], B8[v].
[75] *Mirroure of myserie*, fols. 23[v], 24[r]; for Crowley see chapter 8, section 2 below.

him, as for Crowley, it is the greed of the few which misuses the wealth God has given: 'wicked possessoures,' as he puts it, 'maie cause Englandes fall.' Society is in danger of disruption from those seeking to rise above their appointed stations in life: 'Pride theire wicked hertes doth so elevate / That prowdlie they wolde clyme above theire estate.'[76] The poem closes on a note of deep pessimism, concluding that only God's action can remedy England's social condition and that God will not act till men turn to him in contrition.[77]

[76] *Mirroure of myserie*, fols. 18ᵛ, 11ᵛ.
[77] *Ibid.*, fol. 24ʳ.

Chapter 6

The Marian Regime's Failure to Understand the Importance of Printing

1

Recent research has shown that, contrary to earlier historical judgements, Mary Tudor's reign was a period of substantial achievement in a number of matters, including finance and local administration. It has, however, left unchallenged earlier verdicts on the two policies closest to the Queen's heart: the Spanish alliance and the restoration of Roman Catholicism in England.[1] I am concerned here with one factor that seems to have gone into the latter policy's failure, namely, the regime's incomplete awareness of the difference printing had made in matters where public opinion was substantially involved. I will suggest first that the regime did not sufficiently understand how the new technology could be used for influencing public attitudes and, second, that it did not appreciate how the gradual spread of literacy and printing had helped increase the importance of the laity in religious affairs.

One may note initially a *prima facie* difference or two in the role of the printing press in Mary's reign from its role in previous and succeeding reigns. No member of Mary's Privy Council took the positive interest in printed propaganda shown, on occasion, by Thomas Cromwell in her father's reign or by William Cecil in her sister Elizabeth's.[2] And, unless there is a serious distortion for the mid-century years in the *Short-Title Catalogue of Books Printed in England, 1475-1640,* there were markedly fewer books published in England during Mary's five years than in the five full years of her Protestant brother, Edward VI, who immediately preceded her. This was despite the general upward trend in publication for the century as a whole. Counts of STC-recorded items have been

---

[1] See, for example, D.M. Loades, *The Reign of Mary Tudor* (London 1979), and Jennifer Loach and Robert Tittler, eds., *The Mid-Tudor Polity, c. 1540-1560* (London 1980).

[2] See G.R. Elton, *Policy and Police: the Enforcement of the Reformation in the Age of Thomas Cromwell* (Cambridge 1972), Chap. 4, and Robert L. Kingdon, ed., *William Cecil's The execution of Justice in England* (Ithaca, N.Y. 1965), Introduction. For Edward VI's reign, see John N. King, 'Freedom of the Press, Protestant Propaganda and Protector Somerset', *Huntington Library Quarterly*, XL (1976-77), pp. 1-9.

made independently by me as well as by several other investigators – Patricia Took, John N. King and Philip R. Rider.[3] The frames of reference differed somewhat, as did the resulting annual averages of books published, but all investigations agreed in finding a decline in Mary's reign as compared to Edward's. My figures give an average of 125 items per year for 1548-52 inclusive, as against only 90 annually for Mary's years of 1554-58. The contrast becomes sharper when one remembers that in Mary's reign the pro-Protestant tracts comprise a considerable part of the STC total while very few pro-Catholic tracts appear on the record for Edward's reign. The disparity is further underlined by Dr. Took's finding that only 41 printers were active in Mary's reign and over 80 were in Edward's.

In justice to Mary's regime, however, one should recall something of the state of England on her accession and also note that appreciation of the new technology's potential came rather more slowly in England than is sometimes thought. A story by a contemporary chronicler about one of her elder statesmen, Cuthbert Tunstall, is instructive in this respect. It relates to an early part of Tunstall's career, when he was Bishop of London, and shows that in 1529, at least, he had no clear idea of the capabilities of the printing press. Tunstall was always anxious to prevent copies of the heretical New Testament of William Tyndale, which was printed in the Low Countries, from filtering into London. Consequently, when in Antwerp on diplomatic business in 1529, he arranged with an English merchant to buy up all existing copies for destruction. The transaction, which would have made good sense if the New Testaments had come from a scriptorium or a commercial workshop for hand-copying manuscripts, had its predictable result. Afterward, when the influx of Tyndale Bibles had resumed in London, the merchant explained to Tunstall that he should have bought up the type.[4]

[3] Patricia Took's research, recorded in her unpublished London University Ph.D. dissertation, 1977, *Government and the Printing Trade,1540-1560*, is the most comprehensive and thorough; see particularly p. 245 and Appendix III. I am grateful to her for permission to quote and for helpful comment. See also King, *op. cit.*, pp. 1, 2, and Philip R. Rider, *A Chronological Index to the Revised Edition, Vol. II, of the Pollard and Redgrave Short-Title Catalogue, 1475-1640* (1978). My own estimate is based on an informal count of the 452 cards in the Northwestern University Library's chronological catalogue of the STC for the years 1554-58 inclusive, checked against a similar count of 447 cards for those years in the British Library''s chronological catalogue of the STC, plus a count of the latter's 625 cards for 1548-52 inclusive. With varying bases of calculation (*e.g.*, the King figures include the year 1547, the Rider count includes only about half of the STC), none of the annual averages agree in absolute numbers, but in percentages of decrease from Edward's reign to Mary's they are reasonably close together. It must be remembered, of course, that all such twentieth-century figures depend on the accidents of book survival in the sixteenth century.
[4] Edward Hall, *Henry VIII* (1548), Charles Whibley, ed., 2 vols. (London 1904), II, pp. 160-62.

As to the situation facing Mary when she came to the throne in July 1553, perhaps the most important thing to remember is that for two previous decades England had experienced various kinds of instability – religious and social, economic and political. Under her father, Henry VIII, England had swung toward Protestantism in the 1530s and then in a more conservative direction in the years before his death in 1547, but it had held quite consistently to the replacement of the pope by the monarch as head of the English church. Under Edward VI the trend to Protestantism was consistent and strong. The changes related not just to doctrine, but to how parish churches looked and worship sounded. Images and stone altars were removed as idolatrous and services were no longer held in Latin but in English. Parish priests could now become legally married and many former monks and nuns became part of the general population. Religious and social changes were paralleled by steadily rising prices and a physically deteriorating coinage. Armed rebellions had broken out against Henry in 1536 and against Protector Somerset's government in 1549. In mid-July 1553, Mary had to rally armed supporters to gain the throne from the Duke of Northumberland's nominee, the Protestant Lady Jane Grey.

The policy of Mary's government was, roughly speaking, to return order and stability to English affairs. In ecclesiastical matters it was to restore the English church of Mary's girlhood in the 1520s. This seemed relatively simple to Mary, who had the courage of her father and her half-sister Elizabeth, but none of their political astuteness. It also seemed simpler than in fact it was to her principal ecclesiastical adviser, Reginald Pole, who had been out of England almost continuously from the late 1520s to the closing months of 1554. Others of Mary's senior churchmen, such as Stephen Gardiner, Edmund Bonner, and Cuthbert Tunstall suffered from the opposite handicap of having been Henry VIII's trusted servants in England during his conflict with the papacy two decades before. Cardinal Pole was a man known throughout much of Europe and, as Archbishop of Canterbury he had aims more extensive than just the restoration of Roman Catholic doctrine and the papal allegiance. He sought particularly to provide a better educated, better distributed, and better financed parish clergy.[5] This last, however, was not a policy which explained itself and during the first quarter of Mary's reign the church's constitutional position remained essentially the same as under Henry and Edward. Government priority during this time went not to ecclesiastical matters but to Mary's marriage to her cousin, Philip II of Spain, a marriage most of her countrymen strongly disliked.

---

[5] See Wilhelm Schenk, *Reginald Pole, Cardinal of England* (London 1950) and Dermot Fenlon, *Heresy and Obedience in Tridentine Italy: Cardinal Pole and the Counter-Reformation* (Cambridge 1972); also Rex H. Pogson, 'Reginald Pole and the Priorities of Government in Mary Tudor's Church', *The Historical Journal*, XVIII (1975), pp. 5-20.

2

Some of the regime's public actions, propaganda in the larger sense of the term, were well conceived and effective. Despite the attacks by militant Protestants on what they called revived 'idolatry' and 'superstition', Mary's church apparently found much favourable response to its reinstatement of the old ceremony in worship – not merely the altars and masses within the churches, but the elaborate full-dress processions outside. Many Englishmen evidently welcomed these occasions for a certain colour and drama which had been largely lacking in the Edwardian Church of England. Elizabeth's succeeding regime, if we may go by the periodic references in diaries, took some care to provide substitutes for these public ecclesiastical ceremonies with occasional military displays and, of course, Elizabeth's royal progresses. The Marian church also had its effective preachers, among them John Feckenham, who was to be the last Abbot of Westminster. In 1554 more use seems to have been made of Paul's Cross, the famous outdoor pulpit in the Cathedral grounds, than in any year preceding the reign of Queen Elizabeth.[6]

On one occasion of great meaning to the regime, the first Sunday after England's formal return to the papal obedience, both sermon and ceremonial combined to produce a moment of high emotion. On that day, December 2, 1554, Pole as Papal Legate came to St. Paul's Cathedral with his ecclesiastical retinue by boat from Lambeth Palace, while Queen Mary and King Philip came in an equivalent procession by land from Westminster. After mass and Te Deums within the Cathedral, Stephen Gardiner, Bishop of Winchester and Lord Chancellor of England, preached from the Paul's Cross pulpit on the theme of restoration – of the final awakening of England from the bad dream which had plagued it ever since Henry VIII had broken the tie with Rome. At the conclusion his 15,000 hearers, many of these described as in tears, knelt down to receive absolution.

Thus one cannot say that the regime's efforts to influence public opinion were ineffective, but one must say that they were incomplete. Little attempt was made to enlarge the effect by the printed page. Though texts of other sermons by Marian clerics were disseminated in England in print, this one never was. Our knowledge of it comes partly from a Latin version published the next year in Rome, partly from the hostile John Foxe in his *Actes and Monuments* in 1563, and partly from the summary account printed in January 1555 in John Elder's *A copie of a letter*

---

[6] In the chronological table contained in Millar Maclure, *The Paul's Cross Sermons, 1534-1642* (Toronto 1958) 14 sermons are noted for 1554, as compared with 12 in the critical year of 1536 and 13 in 1559.

sent unto Scotland (STC 75552), a work mostly devoted to the pageantry surrounding the marriage of Mary and Philip the previous summer and to extolling Philip's virtues.[7]

The regime, of course, was by no means blind to the threat posed by hostile printing. As English governments had done for decades before Mary, it routinely banned any publications it saw as endangering sound belief and practice and, as Dr. Took has shown, it managed to make this ban generally effective as regards the Protestant printers at home, though it failed notably to stop the influx of exile publications.[8]

On the positive side, the reign did see publication of the handsome comprehensive edition of the English works of Sir Thomas More, who in various ways symbolized the church that Mary tried to restore. Similarly, a number of the important sermons preached during these years were later issued in print as was customary. One of these was a sermon preached by James Brooks, Bishop of Gloucester, at Paul's Cross on November 12, 1553, which likened Mary's restoration of the traditional church to Christ's raising of Jairus's daughter from the dead. Another was *Two notable sermons made . . . before the quenes highnes . . . concernynge the reall presence*, by Thomas Watson, Bishop of Lincoln, a publication considered still important enough in Elizabeth's reign to warrant a point-by-point reply by a Protestant cleric.[9] Other substantial set-pieces included John Harpsfield's sermon in St. Paul's Cathedral on the first anniversary of England's return to the papal obedience, also *A bouclier of the catholike fayth of Christes church, conteyning divers matters now of late called into controversy by the newe gospellers* by Richard Smith, the Oxford theologian, and several sermons by John Feckenham.[10] On a different level, Edmund Bonner, as Bishop of London, carried on in a Roman Catholic direction the publication of printed homilies which Archbishop Cranmer had inaugurated in 1547 in order to supply inadequate preachers with discourse of what was then considered sound doctrine.[11]

In the early months of Mary's regime, moreover, there appeared a number of pro-regime publications which reflect mainly gratification at

[7] A.J. Muller, *Stephen Gardiner* (New York 1926), pp. 264–66, 384–86.

[8] Took, p. 295.

[9] Brooks, *A sermon very notable, fructfull and godlie made at Paules Crosse the xiii of Novembre,* 1554 (STC 3838); Watson, 1554 (STC 25115). For the reply to Watson see Robert Crowley, *A setting open of the subtyl sophistrie of Thomas Watson . . . in his two sermons . . . anno 1553,* 1569 (STC 6093).

[10] Harpsfield, *A notable sermon . . . made upon Saint Andrews day last past,* (STC 12795); Smith, 1554 (STC 22816); Feckenham, *A notable sermon made within S. Paules church . . . at the celebration of the exequies of the . . . Quene of Spain,* 1555 (STC 10744), *Two homilies upon the first, second and third articles of the crede,* 1555 (STC 10745).

[11] Bonner, *A profitable and necessarye doctryne with certayne homelies adjoyned therunto,* 1555 (STC 3281.5), other eds., STC 3282–3285.10.

failure of Northumberland's attempt to change the succession, or even just a printer's desire to exploit dramatic events for an honest penny. 'Poore Pratte' writes as a Protestant loyalist in his *Copie of a pistel . . . sent . . in the tyme when he was in prison for speaking on our most true quenes part, the Lady Mary*, as does Thomas Watertoune, whose *An invective agaynst treason* virtually ignores religion except to say of Edward VI that he 'sought and mynded goddes glory.'[12] Similarly with *The saying of John, late of Duke Nortumberlande uppon the scaffolde*; the tract could hardly have been more useful propaganda for Mary's ministers had they written it themselves. Yet its whole account agrees closely with the independent narrative of Antonio de Guaras, a Spanish merchant long resident in London, who summarizes Northumberland's speech, 'which I heard from being very near him.'[13]

Whether these early months persuaded them that the output of the press needed no more than a censor's attention or for some other reason, Mary's supporters were markedly less energetic at publishing than her Protestant opponents, despite the latters' handicap of having to publish in foreign cities and disseminate their works surreptitiously in England. Even in these controversial years, of course, a large proportion of the recorded publications were religiously and politically neutral: translations from the classics and other works of literature, scientific works, and the like. By my rough figures, nearly half those in Mary's reign are in this neutral category and this count gives the government the benefit of the doubt. I rate as pro-regime such things as royal proclamations on various subjects, liturgies, and visitation articles. Even so, the pro-regime items outnumber the illegal anti-regime publications by not much more than two to one.[14] Edward J. Baskerville, who confines himself to explicitly controversial works in his *Chronological Bibliography of Propaganda and Polemic* for Mary's reign, gives a total of 114 Protestant items and only 93 Roman Catholic for the reign as a whole.[15] Insofar as simple numbers indicate, disputatious Catholics were less likely to appear in print than were Protestants.

One possible reason for the disparity, as Dr. Took's research has established, is that the more enterprising mid-century printers were mostly Protestant in inclination. After Mary's accession, government pressures forced out of business those printers who were most zealously Protestant but there were few Roman Catholics of equivalent zeal to

[12] STC 20188 and STC 25105.

[13] 1553 (STC 7283); Antonio de Guaras, *The Accession of Queen Mary*, Richard Garnett, ed. and trans. (London 1892), pp. 105–09.

[14] Estimate based on an informal scanning of the 452 cards in the Northwestern University Library's chronological catalogue for 1554–58 inclusive. Of these I assigned 169 to a pro-government category as liberally defined, 69 to anti and 214 to neutral.

[15] *A Chronological Bibliography of Propaganda and Polemic Published in English between 1553 and 1558* (Philadelphia 1979), p. 6.

replace them. Robert Caly, who transferred his activities abroad during Edward's reign, was, in her view, the only Roman Catholic printer who used his trade to propagate his faith with the ardour shown by Protestants.[16] This might have made a significant difference, since most sixteenth-century publications depended on the initiative of the printer and on his belief that a particular item would bring him a satisfactory return. Outsiders could, of course, influence the process by subsidy or other means but about this our knowledge for Mary's reign is no better than inferential.

Such evidence as we have shows Mary's regime as markedly less imaginative than its opponents were in using the press and in identifying propaganda opportunities which printing could exploit. Protestants early seized such an opportunity to embarrass Gardiner, whose classic attack on papal authority, written for international consumption in 1535, had hitherto remained in Latin only. Within the first four months of Mary's reign an English version of *De Vera Obedientia* appeared as from the press of Michael Wood of Rouen. It also included a preface which Edmund Bonner had contributed to a subsequent Latin edition, further denouncing the Bishop of Rome.[17] Sometime after February 1555 there appeared an anonymous volume (twice reprinted) which was derisively attributed to the Marian government's official printer and which reprinted a few selected quotations from *De Vera Obedientia* along with Bonner's preface and two or three pages from a sermon preached before Henry VIII on Palm Sunday, 1539, by Cuthbert Tunstall (now Bishop of Durham), violently attacking both the pope and Reginald Pole.[18] On the government side, a similar effort was made in late 1553 against the lesser Protestant figure, William Barlow, Edwardian Bishop of Bath, by reprinting intact a rather less damaging anti-Lutheran tract he had published in 1531.[19]

Normally, the government side was not adroit at using the press in this way. A more characteristic performance on their part occurred in

---

[16] Took, pp. 215, 224 ff., 313, 333.

[17] *De Vera Obediencia . . . nowe translated into English*, 1553 (STC 11585, also 11586, 11587).

[18] *A supplicacyon to the quenes majestie* (STC 17562, also 17562a, 17563).

[19] *A dialogue describing the original ground of these Lutheran facions and many of their abuses*, 1553 (STC 1462). This publication may be connected with the recantation through which Barlow was released from the Tower and was able to escape abroad. It reprints the whole text of the 1531 tract (STC 1461) with a new preface broadening the attack to Protestants generally. As Baskerville points out (*op. cit.*, p. 13), the pro-government printer, in reproducing the original text entire, overlooked the fact that it attacked not merely Lutheran factions but also the papacy and some of the regular clergy. The addition of a new preface, however, was done skillfully enough, referring to the author this time in the third person and employing at one point a favourite Protestant phrase, 'synful synagogue of Sathan'. I am grateful to John Fines for bringing this phrase and its significance to my attention.

1556 when government agents succeeded in kidnapping a leading Protestant exile, Sir John Cheke, who had been Edward VI's tutor and who was thought, correctly or incorrectly, to be one of those chiefly responsible for the exiles' propaganda. Cheke lacked the martyr temperament of Latimer or Ridley and the regime obtained his written recantation without too much difficulty. But, in an omission hard to credit, it then neglected to print and disseminate the document.[20]

3

One underlying reason for this relative ineffectiveness with the printing press is probably to be found in the regime's estimate of the public it had to influence in order to recatholicize England: that is, the laity. In most respects the regime was evidently unable or unwilling to recognize that laymen by mid-century had gained an importance in religious affairs which they had not had when the century began. Part of this new importance consisted of greater economic power seen in the possession of former monastic lands. This was a change the government was forced to acknowledge before it could get its needed religious legislation through Parliament. But the lay role in the world was enhanced in other ways also. Luther had spoken of the priesthood of all believers, and the Holy Scriptures had been made available to a large sector of the community to read for themselves. In these psychological changes the gradual spread of literacy and printing had played a part. Once a book was committed to print it became much harder to restrict access to it, as Henry VIII had found when, after first authorizing the English Bible for placing in churches, he then tried to determine what groups might actually read it. If enough copies were in existence, the determined person, even if illiterate, could usually find someone to read some of it aloud.

Where the new Protestant church, with its emphasis on the preaching function and the text of the Bible, had tended to decrease the distance between clergy and laity, the restored traditional church tended to increase that distance again. Religious services went back into Latin and stressed not Bible-reading but the mass, which only the clergy could perform. It was important, moreover, that the priest who administered the sacrament be set apart from ordinary men by celibacy; priests who had married under the Protestant regime were therefore compelled to put away their wives and, even so, move to a different parish. The role of

---

[20] John Strype subsequently printed the Latin statement on transubstantiation obtained from Cheke, *Eccl. Mem.*, 1816 ed., VII, pp. 264-66. In a parallel omission pointed out by Loades, *op. cit.*, p. 165, the government made no attempt to publish its version of the staged debate between Ridley and Cranmer and the Roman Catholic theologians at Oxford in April 1554.

the laity was simply to follow clerical instruction and conform.

The Marian church seems never to have understood the strength and extent of the laity's desire to read the Bible. Instead of an authorized Roman Catholic translation of the New Testament, such as was to be provided in the Douai/Rheims Bible some two decades later, the reading public was offered a book by John Standish whose title asked the question whether 'the scripture should be in English for al men to reade that wyll' and whose text expounded 50 reasons why it should not.[21] Standish, who had the well-trained mind of a disputant on theology and church history, as seen in his 1540 tract against the Protestant Robert Barnes and his 1556 work justifying the papal supremacy,[22] has in this tract produced a curious mixture of reasons. They range from such simplistic assertions as that Jesus had used the spoken and not the written word, to sophisticated points about the inherent difficulties of the translation process. Nearly half of them argue in one way or another that making the Bible accessible to laymen tends to disrupt the established order in church or society. The main purpose of those translating the Bible into English, Standish asserts, is to displace the church as judge of the meaning of Scripture and that as a result 'these wretched yeres' recently have seen an epidemic of 'teachers in corners & conventicles,' with disputes over the Bible having arisen 'betwene man & man, man & wife, maister & servant.'[23] Further, 'women heretykes have taken upon them the office of teaching' and servants have become 'stubborne, frowarde and disobedient to theyr masters & mistresses.'[24]

Keeping the Bible away from the multitude was, of course, a position favoured by others beside Standish. Stephen Gardiner, until his death in November 1555 the strongest figure in Mary's government, wrote nothing in these years except short notes on immediate questions but various references in his copious writings of the preceding decade leave no doubt as to his attitude. He was generally cautious about putting the Bible into English, saw 'the discussion of the Scriptures' as requiring 'further giftes of erudicion,' and on one occasion questioned whether the English language, which had not lasted for 200 years 'in one forme of understanding,' was a fit vehicle for the Christian religion.[25] He tended to see himself as writing, whether in Latin or English, for a small group

---

[21] *A discourse wherin is debated whether it be expedient that the scripture should be in English for al men to read that wyll*, 1554 (STC 23207).

[22] *A little treatise*, 1540 (STC 23210); *The triall of the supremacy*, 1556 (STC 23211).

[23] *A discourse wherin is debated*, sigs. F2^v-3^r, K3^r, K2^v.

[24] *Ibid.*, H7^r.

[25] Gardiner, *Letters*, J.A. Muller, ed. (Westport, Conn. 1970), p. 164 (from the preface of STC 11588, part of his controversy with George Joye) and p. 289 (from a letter to Protector Somerset).

divided by its literacy from the public as a whole, a group which constituted, as he wrote on another occasion, 'not the hundredth part of the realme'. The 'letters' of the great majority were 'images' such as crucifixes and statues of saints in churches, nobles' coats-of-arms, and the King's seal. To his military correspondent on this occasion, he put the case against iconoclasm not on grounds of sacrilege but on the need to keep open the lines of communication with the mass of the people.[26]

In a similar vein, James Brooks, in the Paul's Cross sermon previously mentioned, spoke of not everyone being capable of understanding the Scriptures,[27] and John Christopherson, Bishop of Chichester, in his learned work, *An exhortation to all men to take hede and beware of rebellion*, portrayed the translating of the Bible into English as Protestantism's opening move to disrupt the church, and the general reading and discussion of the Scriptures as something setting children against parents.[28] In the heat of controversy, at least, the regime's writers never seem to have asked themselves if there might be more positive reasons for the English Bible's popular appeal.

The government's unawareness of changed attitudes in the laity is seen most dramatically in the burnings which became fixed as a permanent stigma on Mary's reign. Of the 282 persons burnt alive in somewhat under four years, scarcely more than a score were clerics; the great majority were working class men and women.[29] The burnings had apparently been undertaken simply as the way the late medieval church had dealt with the Lollards, and the differing response with Marian Protestants had not been foreseen. Most Lollards, faced with the psychological pressures of trial and execution, had recanted; but out of 22 persons arrested in June 1558 at an unauthorized religious meeting at Islington, 13 chose the stake instead of recantation.[30] There were, of course, various differences between the Lollards and the 'Gospellers' of Mary's reign. The former evidently felt themselves to be a small persecuted sect, while the latter often saw themselves as members of a true national church temporarily ousted from power. But another difference was that Lollards had never controlled a printing press and had comparatively few and incomplete copies of the Bible, while Marian Protestants had had relatively free access to the Bible for over a dozen years prior to Mary's reign and then possessed organized networks

---

[26] *Ibid.*, pp. 273-74 (letter to Capt. Edward Vaughan).
[27] Brooks, sig. C1^r.
[28] 1554 (STC 5207), R7, T2^r.
[29] A.G. Dickens, *The English Reformation* (London 1966), p. 266.
[30] *A. & M.*, VIII, pp. 468-86.

bringing in books from abroad.[31] Not all those defying Catholic judges could themselves read, but they still spoke confidently of what the Bible contained.

The regime's unawareness of how the attitude of many laymen had changed is seen less dramatically in contemporary controversial tracts, but one cannot read extensively in these without encountering it. Pro-regime writers were effective enough when treating matters where a change in lay attitudes did not enter in: for example, when writing for those laymen who simply sought instruction in Catholic doctrine and practice. Bonner's book of homilies was aimed in this direction, as was another work he sponsored, *An honest godly instruction . . . for the . . . bringing up of children.*[32] Though the tract was ostensibly directed to schoolmasters for teaching children their ABCs, only a page or two was actually on this elementary level; most of the conveniently small volume consisted of expositions of Roman Catholic doctrine and English translations of the main parts of the liturgy.

Pro-regime writers on political matters also seem to have been in touch with their audience, stressing the importance of obedience to authority in evident confidence that their readers shared the same desire for external order and stability as they did. John Christopherson is eloquent in his massive *Exhortation . . . to beware of rebellion*, which continually links political and religious dissidence but seems to find its main inspiration in the need for order in society generally. In his catalogue of wicked uprisings against constituted authority he even includes two revolts – the Pilgrimage of Grace in 1536 and the Cornish rising of 1549 – which were raised against the Crown in ostensible support of the traditional church.[33] John Proctor's *The historie of wyates rebellion* (which had been directed against the Spanish marriage) makes the same association of political and religious dissidence in terms of a particular instance.[34] So successful is this tract in giving an organized factual account of the 1554 Kentish revolt from the regime's point of view that direct government inspiration has been suspected, and there is indeed a good circumstantial case to be made for this. Proctor was

---

[31] See particularly the report by an agent of Mary's government, printed in *A. & M.*, VIII, p. 384, identifying specific persons who spread heretical tracts and doctrines in London. The many accounts of heresy trials, prison discourses and letters of mutual encouragement which Foxe prints are testimony to the extensive traffic of written materials (in both directions, handwritten as well as printed) between imprisoned Protestants and exiles. The government's repeated proclamations and warnings against heretical books are another such testimony.

[32] Nov. 28, 1555 (STC 3281).

[33] Christopherson, *Exhortation*, 1554 (STC 5207), sigs. CC6ʳ ff.

[34] *The historie of wyates rebellion . . . whereunto . . . is added an earnest conference with the degenerate and sedicious rebelles for the serche of the cause of their daily disorder*, 1554 (STC 20407).

known as a strong Roman Catholic cleric and was established as schoolmaster in Tunbridge throughout Mary's reign; many people at Sir Thomas Wyatt's execution on April 11 tended to treat him as a martyr, dipping handkerchiefs in his blood, and someone a few days later stole his head from the pike where it had been impaled.[35] On April 21 a 'John Proctour' is recorded as appearing before the Privy Council on summons,[36] and the book when it was published in December had obviously profited from access to various official documents. The relevant point here is Proctor's evident confidence that his readers, whatever their religious views, share his disapproval of rebellion.

But writing to persuade laymen on religious questions, not merely to instruct them on doctrine, was something which Roman Catholics of Mary's day did not do well. Where Protestant clerics address their readers more as fellow Christians (as in Thomas Becon's *A comfortable epistle to Goddes faythfull people in England*),[37] Mary's churchmen tend to talk down to them, as in *A plaine and godlye treatise concernynge the masse . . . for the instruction of the symple and unlerned people*,[38] or, at least, to insist very strongly on the gap between the cleric in the pulpit and the layman in the pew. The treatise proceeds to discuss specific Protestant arguments against transubstantiation but with repeated reminders that this is 'for the instrucyon of the unlearned and ruder sort.' John Standish had cited church fathers against 'the common ignorant people' who presume 'to meddle with the mysterie of Scripture.'[39] Even the generally humane Roger Edgeworth, in the book of sermons covering 'the space of fortie years and more' which he published in 1557, repeatedly attacks laymen who, from a knowledge of the Scriptures in English, dare to question the cleric's superior knowledge. He is also somewhat apologetic in his preface for publishing 'in such language as might

---

[35] D.M. Loades, *Two Tudor Conspiracies* (Cambridge 1965), pp. 115–16, quoting contemporary accounts by the French ambassador and *The Chronicle of Queen Jane*.

[36] *A.P.C.*, V, pp. 12, 13.

[37] 1554 (STC 1716). See also *A letter sent from a banished minister of Jesus Christ unto the faithfull Christian flocke in England*, 1554 (STC 10016), and Thomas Sampson, *A letter to the trew professors of Christes gospell in the parishe off Alhallows . . . London*, 1554 (STC 21683). There were, of course, insensitive Protestant clerics also, like the Edwardian Bishop of Chichester, John Scory, who had escaped abroad by means of a temporary recantation and then wrote *An epistle . . . unto all the faythfull that be in prison in England*, 1555 (STC 21854), exhorting them to face martyrdom bravely.

[38] Anonymous, 1555 (STC 17629). 'Simple' was a word of varied connotations; that Marian clerics used it rather disdainfully is suggested also by Richard Smith's offering his *Bouclier of the catholic fayth*, 1554, for 'the edifying of the simple and rude people' (preface). A tone of condescension is evident also in the text of Cardinal Pole's 'Speech to the citizens of London on behalf of religious houses', as printed by Strype, *Eccl. Mem.*, III, ii, pp. 482–510.

[39] Standish, *A discourse wherin is debated*, A7ᵛ.

presentlie best edifie the multitude.'[40]

Such theological writers as Richard Smith and John Gwynneth make few concessions to the new Protestant ways of Biblical quotation, preferring still to cite early church fathers[41] and to argue fine points of doctrine.[42] A number of the works sound like clerics writing for other clerics. Thus John Angel, one of Queen Mary's chaplains, in *The agreement of the holye fathers and doctours of the churche upon the chiefest articles of the Christian religion*, provides a kind of handbook for parish priests on the main points of doctrinal controversy with Protestant theologians.[43] Dr Thomas Martin devotes a substantial book to arguing that marriage for clergy is 'altogether unlawful, and in all ages and all countries of Christendome bothe forbidden and also punyshed.'[44] John Churchson, another of the Queen's chaplains, shows a tendency (of which he is not the only exemplar) to write against sixteenth-century Protestants by equating them with the Donatists and other heretics of the early church. He apparently never asked himself how many English laymen either knew or cared about the ancient Donatists.[45]

Not all Marian publications, of course, were similarly preoccupied with churchmen's technicalities. One or two of the reprintings of older works were well chosen – as, for example, John Fisher's eloquent Paul's Cross sermon of 1521, which was sufficiently general in its attack on the heresies of Luther to seem still current in 1554.[46] There was both eloquence and fire in the Paul's Cross sermon, printed in October 1555, of another of Mary's chaplains, Hugh Glasier, which (somewhat in Latimer's evangelical manner) inveighed against men's obsession with material luxuries and against the plundering of the church.[47] There was Paul Bushe's *A brief exhortation . . . to one Margaret Burges*, which presented the Roman Catholic doctrine of the Real Presence forcefully and without concession but without talking down to his reader.[48] This

---

[40] Edgeworth, *Sermons very fructfull, godly and learned* (STC 7482), fols. 31^v, 32^r, 34^r, 36^v, 280^r, 304^r.

[41] Smith, *A bouclier of the catholike fayth*. See also Leonard Pollard, *Fyve homilies*, 1556 (STC 20091), sigs. C2 ff.

[42] Gwynneth, *A declaration of the state wherin all heretikes dooe leade their lives*, 1554 (STC 12558). This, along with two other Marian publications of his (STC 12559, 12560), is actually a continuation of Gwynneth's old polemic against John Frith, burnt at the stake in 1533.

[43] Angel, [1555?], (STC 634).

[44] Martin, *A traictise . . . plainly proving that the pretensed marriage of priestes and professed persons is no marriage*, 1554 (STC 17517).

[45] Churchson, *A brefe treatyse declaryng what and where the churche is*, 1556 (STC 5219), sig. H7. See also James Cancellar, *The pathe of obedience*, 1556 (STC 4564), E1^v.

[46] Fisher, *A sermon very notable, fructeful and godlie*, 1554 (STC 10896).

[47] Glasier, *A notable . . . sermon made at Paules crosse the xxv day of August*, 1555 (STC 11916.5).

[48] Bushe, 1556 (STC 4184).

may be attributed partly to Bushe's feeling that he was on the same social level as Margaret Burges but partly also to his having been out of clerical life for some two years after having to resign as Bishop of Bristol because he had married. And there were also one or two Catholic laymen writing: George Marshall, of whom nothing is known but a single tract which reads as if of lay origin,[49] and Miles Hogarde, recognized both by his Protestant antagonists at the time and by modern historians as the most effective of the regime's propagandists.

4

Hogarde, who is discussed more fully in the immediately preceding chapter of this volume, is indeed the exceptional case which highlights the shortcomings of the regime in communicating with the public at large. His talents as a propagandist and his personal outlook on life, that of a mere artisan intent on having his say in print, are both relevant to the Marian regime's unacknowledged problem. From his published works and the little that is known about his life, it seems clear that he was himself one of the articulate laymen whom the regime tended to ignore and a product of the new print culture which it only partly understood.

All that we know of Hogarde's biography is that he was a hosier in the City of London, was referred to as a strong anti-Protestant at various times between 1540 and 1558, and was the author of seven printed tracts, all but one in a rough verse. He evidently learned the style and artistic conventions of his verse tracts from the late medieval romances and allegories which Caxton and others had made available in print, but his propagandist's feel for a situation was probably not to be learned from anyone. This is strikingly evident in his one tract in prose, *The displaying of the Protestants*,[50] where he shows appreciation of his audience's own concerns, a sharp nose for his opponent's weak points, and an ability to relate each of these to the other. His underlying assumption is that his readers are as irritated as he is by the aggressiveness of the Protestant preachers who claim superior knowledge of the truth with incessant quotations from the Bible, that people are tired of the ecclesiastical and social disorders of the past two decades, and that they are ready to be convinced that the orthodox Protestants are responsible for the disorder.

Further, he is careful to keep his main emphasis on things within his readers' own experience. Hogarde has much to say about the radical

---

[49] *A compendious treatise in metre declaring the firste originall of sacrifice and of the first receavinge of the Christian fayth here in England*, 1554 (STC 17469).

[50] *The displaying of the Protestantes and sondry their practices*, 1556 (STC 13558). The appearance of this augmented second edition in July, so soon after the June first edition (STC 13557), suggests the success of the work.

sectaries, who were perceived by most people as elements making for disorder. Some of them – the Arians – were as severely dealt with by orthodox Protestants as by the Roman Catholics. Hogarde, however, blames all the sectaries on the Henrician and Edwardian hierarchy, implicitly or explicitly, for disrupting the unity of the medieval church. He keeps the focus on contemporary heretics rather than ancient Donatists while saying enough about the latter to make his point that heretics are no new thing in church history. He devotes several pages to figures like Joan Bocher, whose eventual burning by Edward's government had made her widely known, and toward the end of the expanded second edition of the tract he gives a first-hand account of a separatist meeting presided over by one 'Father Browne'.[51] From time to time, moreover, he draws a nostalgic contrast between these present disorders and the era when 'so long as this Realme was in unitie [with Rome] it continued in unspeakable welth and prosperitie, in merveylous love and amitie, in true dealing and honest simplicitie, and in al godlines and pietie.'[52] But he was careful not to make this contrast too specific or press it too hard.

In his more direct attcks on orthodox Protestantism Hogarde is similarly mindful of the interests and capabilities of laymen readers. He does not avoid doctrinal points, particularly the key issue of transubstantiation, but he tends to be brief and relatively simple, though citing scriptural texts rather liberally in the margin. His emphasis is less on theology than on religious practice, a subject also offering scope for his satiric talents. Knowing that most of his readers would have directly observed the confusion in their parish churches as the Protestant bishops, a few years before, had sought to revise the celebration of the communion service, he pokes fun at the use of two different prayer books within a short space of time, at changes in the bread, and particularly at how the communion table 'skipped out of the quier into the body of the churche' and how in some instances it was displayed as in 'a Cockpytte, where all the people might see them and their communion.'[53]

Hogarde's verse tracts, three of which preceded Mary's accession, all support the traditional church and its beliefs. The two earliest are devoted to the doctrine of transubstantiation. The second of these (*The assault of the sacrament of the altar*) is an allegory in the medieval manner which externalizes the doctrine as a castle attacked by successive waves of armoured heretics, ending with the Protestant bishops of Edward's

---

[51] *Ibid.*, fols. 121 ff.
[52] *Ibid.*, fol. 89ᵛ.
[53] *Ibid.*, 80ᵛ–82ᵛ.

reign.[54] Another is an allegory of spiritual pilgrimage; two others, also using some of the conventions of medieval poetry, discuss a variety of religious and ethical questions.[55]

Hogarde, though he was accused indirectly by his Protestant opponents of being a mere mouthpiece for Gardiner and other clerics, did not at all fit into the view of England, expressed by Gardiner, as a country divided between a small literate group of leaders and a mass of obedient subjects content with a religion which consisted largely of a liturgy in a foreign language and beautiful stone images before which to pray.[56] Hogarde, though lacking the status and formal education of the clergy, was a widely read man (as the marginal references in *The Displaying of the Protestants* bear witness). Though wholly committed to the traditional church and its ceremonies, he still had a strong desire to discuss his religious beliefs and opinions on morals, and to air them in print. Mary's church really did not know how to use this lay talent which came to it apparently as an unsolicited bonus.

Hogarde seems to have been kindly treated up to a point. He was given a small stipend as hosier to the Queen, and allowed free entry to Bishop Bonner's London residence.[57] But, after the propaganda success of *The Displaying of the Protestantes*, no more appropriate use for his talents could apparently be found than the journeyman work seen in his last printed tract, *A newe ABC*.[58] It is a kind of parallel to the elementary work of Bonner's previously mentioned, designed for children and the slenderly educated. That Hogarde himself was not satisfied with the treatment he received is suggested by a rather bitterly defensive preface he wrote in 1555 for *The mirrour of love* in which he recognized the charge that, as an artisan, 'my calling is not books to write', but insisted that God had forbidden only unauthorized preaching, not writing, 'upon our faith'.

[54] The first survives only as extensively quoted in the point-by-point refutation of Hogarde's published tract in Robert Crowley, *The confutation of the mishapen answer to the misnamed ballade called the abuse of the sacraments of the altare*, 1548 (STC 6082). *The assault of the sacrament of the altar*, 1554 (STC 13556), says later on its title-page that it was 'written in the yere of oure Lord 1549 . . . in whiche tyme (heresie then raigning) it could take no place.'

[55] *A treatise entitled the path way to the towre of perfection*, 1554 (STC 13561); *A new treatyse in maner of a dialog which sheweth the excellency of mannes nature*, 1550 (STC 13560); *A mirrour of love which such light doth give / That all men may learn how to love and live*, 1555 (STC 13559).

[56] See also Gardiner's letter, cited in n. 26 above, where he refers approvingly to images as a language 'suche as all men can reade'.

[57] *Calendar of the Patent Rolls, 1553-54*, p. 386, notes Hogarde's allocation of a shilling a quarter in addition to an unspecified daily wage; Foxe records (*A. & M.*, VII, p. 111) an encounter between Hogarde and a Protestant prisoner in Bonner's London residence.

[58] *A new ABC paraphrastically applied as the state of the world doeth at this daye require*, 1557 (STC 13559).

5

On the larger question of the role of the press in Mary's reign, what may be said in conclusion? On the level of simple coincidence, one could say that a regime which paid surprisingly little attention to printing was markedly unsuccessful in achieving one of its major aims. This is, of course, too simple. But one may suggest that this neglect and the regime's failure to understand some of the changes printing had helped make in England did aid its opponents to fix an unfavourable public image on Mary's reign and make the task of the evangelizing Protestants in Elizabeth's reign a little easier. The investigator of printing's impact on society might further see in the attitude held on printing a kind of mental barometer. For a regime which in various respects looked backward and not forward, the imperfect understanding of one of the dynamic elements in its world neatly symbolizes a state of mind.

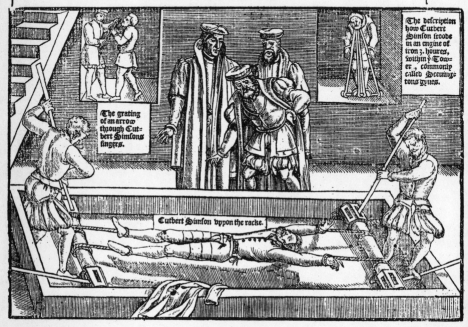

Woodcut of the attempt to make the deacon of the main London underground congregation of Mary's reign surrender his roll-book of members. (*A. & M.*, 1570 ed., p.2229.)

Chapter 7

The Protestant Underground Congregations
of Mary's Reign

1

In contrast to the extensive research devoted to the Marian exiles, little detailed attention has been paid by modern historians to the Englishmen who simply tried to continue Protestant worship during 1553-58 within the country. Yet developments in these years provide unusual insights into mid-Tudor Protestantism at its grass roots, particulary into what remained after the Edwardian Church of England had suddenly had the power of the state not merely removed from its support but actively turned against it. Not surprisingly, the change from Edward to Mary is referred to in contemporary Protestant tracts in something of the tone used toward an inexplicable natural disaster like an outbreak of the plague, for Mary's measures to return England to Roman Catholicism were indeed radical in their impact. Among other things, most of the Protestant hierarchy was soon in prison or in exile, and men and women intent on continuing the communal worship of the Edwardian church were in effect cast into the same boat with religious groups like the Freewillers which that church had previously repressed. Legally, all of them were now religious separatists – that is persons who persistently conducted worship apart from the established church. Any gatherings for Protestant worship were mere conventicles – that is, periodic meetings of self-selected persons worshipping without the participation of an authorised cleric. The conventicle, of course, had been an unobtrusive part of the English religious landscape during generations of activity by the Lollards – who did not, however, regard holding their own meetings as necessarily precluding all participation in the rites of the established church.[1] It was apparently thought familiar enough as an institution to be mentioned in a royal proclamation of 1529 which

---

[1] See J.A.F. Thomson, *The Latter Lollards, 1414-1520* (Oxford 1965), especially the three sketch maps of varied Lollard activity; also Gordon Rupp, *Studies in the Making of the English Protestant Tradition* (Cambridge 1949), p. 4. In the 1570s the radical sect of Familists professed conformity to the Church of England while at the same time clinging to its own meetings and ceremonies. See chapter 10 below.

denounced heretical activity of various kinds.[2]

The need for some such gatherings to sustain the faith of Protestants was early recognised by at least some of the leaders of the Edwardian church. John Hooper, writing from prison in the early months of Mary's reign to 'certain . . . lovers of the truth, instructing them how to behave themselves in that woeful alteration and change of religion', said:

> There is no better way to be used in this troublesome time for your consolation than many times to have assemblies together of such men and women as be of your religion in Christ; and there to talk and renew amongst yourselves the truth of your religion, to see what ye be by the word of God, and to remember what ye were before ye came to the knowledge thereof . . .
> It is much requisite that the members of Christ comfort one another, make prayers together, confer with on another: so shall ye be the stronger . . .[3]

A sustained effort was made (we do not know by exactly whom) to have one such congregation maintained continuously in London under orthodox clerical leadership. The success of this effort has monopolised most of the attention given to the underground congregations, not only in John Foxe's *Actes and Monuments* but in other sources in the sixteenth century and later. Even so, the implications of evidence about this group can be a bit puzzling. Near the end of his massive work, Foxe describes 'the congregation in London' as meeting throughout Mary's reign in numbers ranging from 40 to 200, always presided over by an ordained cleric (those he names include two future bishops) and assembling in a variety of places ingeniously chosen to avoid apprehension by the authorities. Two or three of these gatherings, he says, were on a ship in the Thames, where the service nevertheless included 'after their accustomed manner, both sermon, prayer and communion'. He also prints a report submitted to Bishop Bonner by an agent who had attended two of the congregation's meetings, stating that 'commonly the usage is to have all the English service without any diminishing, wholly as it was in the time of King Edward the Sixth'.[4]

After Foxe's description one reads with some surprise the account of the London congregation's situation in the early months of Elizabeth's reign, as given by Thomas Lever, who was master of St. John's College, Cambridge, in Edward's reign and archdeacon of Coventry under Elizabeth. Writing on 6 August 1559 to Henry Bullinger, his friend and former host in Switzerland, Lever says that the congregation which met in London secretly throughout Mary's reign, where 'the gospel was always preached with the pure administration of the sacraments', has, under Elizabeth, been no more than tolerated, permitted to meet 'in open

---

[2] *Tudor Procl.*, I, p. 183.
[3] *A. & M.*, VI, pp. 602-04; see also VII, p. 688, for a somewhat similar recommendation by John Philpot, Edwardian Archdeacon of Winchester.
[4] *A. & M.*, VIII, pp. 558-59, 458.

private houses but in no public churches'. He reports the official explanation that all public 'preaching and exposition of holy scripture', with a few exceptions, is to be prohibited till parliament has 'come to a decision respecting religion', but his surprise and indignation are unmistakable. He recalls in particular that celebration of the mass was allowed to continue in parish churches during this period, and he elaborates on the contrasting nature of the communion service he has frequently attended in the congregation that was excluded from the parish churches.[5]

As regards this principal London congregation, Elizabeth's government evidently took a different view from that held by two of her respected ecclesiastics, and the present discussion will try to shed some light on that difference. Primarily, however, it seeks to examine, as precisely as the data permit, the different kinds of underground congregations, using this term generically to include all groups of persons assembled for illicit religious worship ('conventicles', of course, in the government's terminology). It will examine how such groups arose, the nature of their activities, and their relationship to other aspects of the Protestant resistance to Mary. It will look also at how they were regarded by Mary's government and what residues they may have left for her successors. The intent is simply to describe the behaviour of these groups of committed Protestants in Marian England, not to assign them places in any of the theoretical frameworks for separatism and conventicles which were constructed by others later on in the rather different conditions of late Elizabethan and Stuart England.

It should be noted that, though conventicles proliferated during Mary's reign, specific contemporary information on them is nevertheless scarce, the groups themselves having naturally sought obscurity and largely avoided written records. Most data come from Foxe and must be read remembering not only his personal biases as a loyal but radically inclined member of the Elizabethan Church of England but also the attitudes he shares with his century. The sixteenth century, of course, saw religion as much more of a public and civic matter than the twentieth century does, and tended to regard certain acts of public behaviour as the critical test of a man's religious state. Since the Marian church's main effort was directed toward getting all Englishmen to attend and participate in its rites (as indeed was that of the Elizabethan church in the following decades), the main effort of committed Protestants was, necessarily, to refuse such participation. Many tracts were written on the theme of John Bradford's 'The Hurt of Hearing Mass', denying that separation between inner belief and outer behaviour was possible. The secret religious gathering could be a good way of sustaining one's faith, but was not to be equated with public testimony; it

[5] *Zurich Letters*, H. Robinson, ed. (Cambridge 1846), pp. 57-59.

was a means, not an end. Individual members of congregations are memorialised by Foxe not for their participation in such worship but for their sharp retorts to interrogating bishops or their bravery at the stake. All of the congregations combined get less space in *Actes and Monuments* than the story of one gifted lay evangelist, a prosperous Sussex iron maker named Richard Woodman, who organised no known congregation but who was examined 32 times by several different bishops before finally being burned in 1557.[6]

2

Hooper's prescription includes the basic features of all the underground groups: that is, periodic gatherings of the like-minded for fellowship, prayer, reading and expounding the Bible, and for reaffirming opposition to the revived Roman Catholic establishment. Strictly speaking, all were separatists, but some of the groups saw themselves as carrying on the tradition of the Edwardian church, while others were varying kinds of radicals who had parted from the national church well before Mary's accession. Three basic types may be distinguished.

First, there is the fully orthodox congregation presided over by an ordained minister and celebrating communion and other services as prescribed in the Edwardian Book of Common Prayer. The best known example is the London congregation which had John Rough and Thomas Bentham as pastors, but other instances may be cited also. Foxe tells how another London congregation, comprising about 30 people, met periodically under the leadership of the elderly minister, Thomas Rose, and was surprised by government officers at a service held in a house in Bow Churchyard on New Year's night 1555; he also prints the letter of encouragement which Hooper sent to its members in prison a few days later.[7] In the remote Lancashire village of Shakerly, one Jeffrey Hurst, the brother-in-law of an executed cleric and in hiding himself, made a practice of arranging night meetings of 20 or so people as he was able to find itinerant Protestant ministers (four are specifically named) to preach and sometimes to celebrate communion.[8] A somewhat similar practice obtained among a Protestant group in the small Devon market

[6] *A. & M.*, VIII, pp. 332-77. Foxe also tells (VIII, pp. 553-57) as worthy of celebration how a group of Protestants in the Suffolk parish of Stoke-by-Nayland managed to avoid attending mass throughout Mary's reign and how two individual gentlewomen, in Norfolk and Sussex respectively, did likewise. Foxe's fondness for extensively printing government documents and other primary material somewhat compensates for his own attitude toward conventicles. For example, the five reports by government agents about the principal London congregation during Rough's pastorate run to greater length than Foxe's own account of the congregation's entire history.

[7] *A. & M.*, VI, pp. 579, 584-87; see also *Original Letters*, p. 773.

[8] *A. & M.*, VIII, p. 562.

town of South Molton (and possibly among other groups nearby) watched over by the cleric William Ramsey.[9]

The second main type is the radical sectary congregation, providing its own lay leadership and following its own pattern of worship, usually with Bible-reading, prayer and discussion of religious questions. Such groups seemed insistent on maintaining an identity distinct from the orthodox Prayer Book Protestants. They tended to be restrictive in their membership and in most cases had probably had previous experience in underground religious activity. The best documented of these groups is the one known subsequently as the Freewillers. It had attracted the alarmed attention of Edward VI's Privy Council by a gathering in the Essex village of Bocking at Christmas time 1550, and later conducted both doctrinal controversies and negotiations (ultimately unsuccessful) for a joint communion service with orthodox Protestants who had been imprisoned with them in the King's Bench prison in 1554.[10] A second example is the Familist congregation whose two disgruntled ex-members made depositions before a Surrey magistrate at Guildford in May 1561. These described in detail the doctrinal views, secret night meetings and miscellaneous proceedings of their group of about 30 which, they noted, dated from 'the beginning of Queen Mary's reign.' They stated also that there were similar congregations in half a dozen additional counties.[11] Still another group is described by the Roman Catholic propagandist, Miles Hogarde, as holding a meeting which he attended in Islington in 1555. Its leader, one 'Father Brown', Hogarde says, quoted liberally from the Bible and spoke disrespectfully of both Roman Catholic and orthodox Protestant clerics.[12]

The third, and apparently most prevalent, category is the mixed type – a group that was orthodox Protestant in the backgrounds of its members and in their expressed belief that the religious practice of the Edwardian church was 'good and godly' but which lacked the cleric needed for the full Prayer Book rites. Necessarily, therefore, they followed something more like the sectaries' pattern of worship: Bible-reading, prayer and discourse on religious questions. The best-documented example is the 'company of godly and innocent persons to the number of 40, men and women', whom Foxe describes as engaged in prayer and 'the meditation of God's holy word' in a field near Islington in May 1558 when arrested by the constable. Foxe gives the names and sometimes the occupations of the 22 who were sent to prison, and also fairly detailed

---

[9] See Ramsey's letter of 1561 to the congregation, as quoted in Patrick Collinson, *The Elizabethan Puritan Movement* (London 1967), pp. 21-22.

[10] Detailed information on the Freewillers in chapter 3 above.

[11] Depositions printed in J.D. Moss, *'Godded with God': Hendrik Niclaes and his Family of Love* (Philadelphia 1981), Appendix I, pp. 70-74.

[12] *The Displaying of the Protestantes*, 1556 (STC 13558), fol. 124ff.

accounts of the interrogations of 16. The answers of one or two may indicate a separatist past. Thus, Robert Southam insisted that he had not taken communion from 'your curate or any other priest' for ten years past, i.e., since the beginning of Edward's reign. The rest, however, expressed complete satisfaction with the creed and worship of the Edwardian Church and one of them, a young merchant-tailor named Roger Holland, had had his first child baptised by Thomas Rose early in Mary's reign.[13]

A similar example is the group at Great Bentley in Essex, a few miles from Colchester. During the long examination of its leader, the layman Ralph Allerton, in April 1557, the local parish priest complained to Bonner that 'a great sort of the parish will be gathered one day to one place and another day to another place to hear him, so that very few will come to the parish church'. Yet Allerton affirmed in his interrogations that the Edwardian Prayer Book and the opinions of Cranmer and Ridley were entirely 'good and godly' and nothing said of him, or of the other six persons named in connection with the Great Bentley congregation, suggests that any had separatist views.[14] Another such instance is the meeting at Brighton held in October 1554 in the house of Dirick Carver, a beer-brewer described as quite illiterate at the time of his arrest. Here twelve persons, according to the confession of one of them, were seized as they were praying and 'saying the service in English set forth in the time of King Edward the Sixth'.[15]

Of mixed groups in the sense of a membership that was in substantial parts both orthodox and radical sectary, there is only one specific instance, and that probably due to exceptional circumstances. This is described by the orthodox Protestant, Henry Orinel of Willingham, Cambridgeshire, in a letter written in the late 1570s, telling how he had visited Colchester in late September 1555 in search of spiritual sustenance and had attended a conventicle at one of the inns there. Doctrinal disputation was evidently a main purpose of this gathering. Orinel remarks that the principal spokesman for the orthodox, one John Barry, had brought along 'two women gospellers' to hear him debate with an artisan named Christopher Vitel, who on this occasion was a proponent of Arian and other radical views and in the mid-1570s became the chief English leader of the Familists. (To Orinel's dismay, Barry was worsted in the argument.)[16]

The circumstances described suggest that meetings for such disputations may have occurred periodically in strongly Protestant

---

[13] *A. & M.*, VIII, 468–82.
[14] *Ibid.*, VIII, pp. 409–12.
[15] *Ibid.*, VII, pp. 321–27.
[16] William Wilkinson, A *confutation of certaine articles delivered unto the Familye of Love*, 1579 (STC 25665), prefatory historical material; see below chap. 11.

Colchester. There, as one of Bonner's subordinates wrote to him about a year later, 'priests are hemmed at in the street and called knave', and Protestants 'assemble together upon the Sabbath day at the time of divine service, sometimes in one house, sometimes in another, and there keep their privy conventicles'.[17] But it is doubtful whether the meeting Orinel describes can be equated with ordinary congregations meeting for worship. The normal situation was more likely that found in the King's Bench prison, where the Freewillers engaged often enough in theological debate with orthodox Protestants but still maintained their own group and regarded the holding of a joint communion service at Christmas as something requiring careful negotiation. It the event, most of the Freewillers decided that the area of their religious agreement with the orthodox was not great enough to justify taking the sacrament together.[18]

As to how many underground congregations existed in all, or how numerous their members, no firm figures are possible. That they were considered a familiar pheonomenon in Marian England is suggested by the way people refer to them. Hooper, in recommending that Protestants gather in their own religious assemblies, does not write as one proposing anything unusual, and Foxe, describing the arrest of Thomas Rose's congregation, refers to them and others like them as engaging in a practice frequently repeated 'to the comfort of their consciences'.[19] Orinel recounts his journey to find an underground religious meeting in Colchester as a normal way for him and 'dyvers of mine acquaintaunce' to seek inner support against defilement by 'the popish pitch'. The subsequent martyr, Robert Smith, tells Bonner at his trial in July 1555 that persecuted Christians in apostolic times held their religious meetings 'in houses and privy places as they now do',[20] and the diarist Henry Machyn notes the detection of underground congregations as casually as he does the placing of men and women in the pillory.[21]

The congregations mentioned as examples above can all be explicitly documented. Various others lie on the borderline with household worship, or their existence depends on merely circumstantial evidence.

---

[17] *A. & M.*, VIII, p. 383.

[18] John Trew, 'The cause of the contention in the King's Bench,' in *Authentic Documents*, Richard Laurence, ed. (Oxford 1819), pp. 57-63.

[19] *A. & M.*, VI, p. 775.

[20] *Ibid.*, VII, p. 348.

[21] *Diary*, J.G. Nichols, ed. (London 1858), pp. 59, 160. See also the reference of the Roman Catholic cleric John Standish to a recent epidemic of 'teachers in corners and conventicles,' *A discourse wherin is debated*, 1554 (STC 23207), sig. F. 2^v-3^r; also a magistrate's remark to a Protestant prisoner to the same effect, *A. & M.*, VII, p. 119. Parliament's 'Acte for the punishment of traterous woordes against the Quenes Majestie' (I Philip and Mary, 9) assumes the prayers offered in London conventicles to be a frequent occasion for such words.

For example, Foxe says that 22 persons, many of them subsequently executed as heretics, were 'apprehended at one clap' in Colchester in August 1556, and he prints the government document listing their names and places of origin. Since the latter distribute around Colchester at distances of four to fifteen miles, as well as in the town itself, it is hard to imagine how all could have been arrested at one time except at a religious meeting.[22] Another congregation of orthodox Protestants, probably restricted to Colchester itself, may be inferred (though somewhat less confidently) from various statements printed by Foxe about five residents burned together on 2 August 1557, plus another whose execution was delayed by a few days through a legal technicality.[23] Another congregation may be similarly inferred in the nearby town of Coggeshall, where six artisans were arrested on the same day in May 1555 and sent to Bonner for trial.[24]

Since the interest of the present study lies in the nature of the congregations' activity, it has considered only those two dozen or so where a few details, such as the surname of a presumed member, have survived. For one or two congregations enough data exist to permit a partial reconstruction of the membership, but actual names usually get into the record only when their possessors suffer at the hands of the law. Thus, in my file of 171 names of persons (often with accompanying occupations) whom there is some reason to connect with an underground congregation, the most fully described group is that surprised at Islington in May 1558, since of the 40 men and women meeting there, 22 were sent to Newgate and 13 eventually burned. For no other group has even a bare majority of names survived. For the principal London congregation identified members total only 19, including the five who were successively ministers, whereas Foxe says attendance sometimes reached 200 and describes specific meetings where 40 were present. Those arrested while worshipping under Thomas Rose in January 1555 are numbered as about 30, but we have names for only Rose himself and five others. Of the 12 arrested at the Brighton meeting in October 1554, only four are specifically identified. Among the radical sectaries, the Familist group near Guildford was numbered at 30 by two of its ex-members in 1561, but we have names for only those two, and their membership may not stretch back to Mary's reign.

Congregations of all sorts, were probably more numerous than Foxe's accounts record. For example, in the Protestant heartland of East Anglia no parallel Protestant record survives of the 'secret conventicles' in Harwich and neighbouring Dovercourt whose detection the Privy

[22] *A. & M.*, VIII, pp. 303-07.
[23] *Ibid.*, VIII, pp. 386-90, 411-14, 422-23.
[24] *Ibid.*, VII, pp. 139-42.

Council noted in August 1556,[25] nor of congregations in Ipswich, where a government document of 1556 lists by parishes the names of some 80 obdurate Protestants, over half of whom had gone into hiding.[26] For Colchester, despite its reputation as a Protestant stronghold, there is specific evidence of only two congregations for secret worship. The activity of radical sectary groups was likewise probably greater than the written record indicates. In my file of 171 probable congregation members only 18 come from sectary groups and all but two of those from that of the Freewillers in the King's Bench prison. Yet is seems likely that at least some of the 'Anabaptists' whom John Hooper decribed as disturbing his lectures in St. Paul's in 1549, and went to preach against in Essex and Kent in 1550, were still in existence in Mary's reign.[27] It is likely also that the 'horrid monsters of Arianism' that John Parkhurst went to Guildford to contend against in May 1559 had not all arisen in the previous six months.[28]

In their social composition the underground congregations, like the Marian martyrs generally, were predominantly working class men and women. Only 19 clerics' names occur in connection with the congregations, and most of these only for very brief periods, as England became an increasingly hazardous place for ordained Protestants. Of the 152 lay persons (109 men, 43 women) named in connection with all types of congregation, some 67 have indications of occupation. Among these, 18 are artisans in the textile trades, plus seven women for whom 'spinster' is evidently an occupational term; 13 are artisans in other trades, four are small merchants and eight of such varied designations as husbandman, herder and mariner. Gentry and wealthy merchants figure in a very minor way, mainly in two small separate groups that will be mentioned later.

3

Underground congregations came into existence in a variety of ways. One fairly frequent pattern was that of a committed Protestant trying to continue as much of the previous evangelising programme of his parish church as the new circumstances permitted. Thus, two ejected ministers in East Anglia, Robert Samuel and William Tyms, continued to teach Protestant doctrine secretly – Tyms even preaching on two occasions to a hundred people assembled in the woods – and after their arrest wrote

---

[25] *A.P.C.*, V, p. 334.
[26] *A. & M.*, VIII, pp. 598–600. One of these Protestants surfaced two years later as a member of the underground congregation at Islington.
[27] *Original Letters*, pp. 65–66, 86–87.
[28] *Zurich Letters*, p. 39.

letters of exhortation to their parishioners till they were executed.[29] In the Suffolk parish of Hadleigh, which Dr Rowland Taylor had made a model for the Edwardian church, Taylor himself was put under detention after his initial denunciation of the restored Roman Catholic rites. His seventy-year-old curate proved unable to replace him effectively, but a young artisan, John Alcocke, provided the needed leadership. With a successor not yet installed in the living and the parishioners continuing to come to the empty church, Alcocke, who was 'singularly learned in the holy scripture', read to them regularly from the Edwardian Prayer Book and 'gave them godly lessons and exhortations out of the chapters that he read unto them'. When arrested and sent to Newgate (where he died), Alcocke also wrote letters to his parishioners, but after the authorities installed a priest in the church this particular underground congregation came to an end.[30]

In the case of Great Bentley, mentioned earlier, an underground congregation grew up more gradually and entirely under lay leadership. Ralph Allerton had tried to keep Protestantism alive in his parish church by exhorting the people periodically 'to prayer and meditation of God's most holy word' and by reading them a chapter of the New Testament. When told 'that he might not do so by the law', he desisted, with one lapse into 'reading' in a nearby parish that occasioned his temporary arrest. From then till mid-1556 his pattern of life was to 'keep himself in woods, barns and other solitary places', apparently in some inner confusion ('yet not thoroughly staid upon the aid and help of God', Foxe says), but also doing some preaching in unspecified places which presumably included Great Bentley. He was once again arrested and this time sent up to London where Bonner succeeded in getting him to recant publicly at Paul's Cross on 10 January 1557.[31] Meanwhile, three other local Protestants, William Mount, his wife Alice and his step-daughter Rose Allin, had been released from temporary imprisonment and become so active in the Great Bentley underground congregation as to figure in a letter of complaint to the authorities by the curate of the parish, Thomas Tye, and others – a complaint repeated orally by Tye to Bonner in April after Allerton had again become active in the village.[32] We do not know what happened to the congregation after the spring of 1557, for the Mounts were arrested in March and burned in August, a few weeks before Allerton was, but at that time it had clearly become a rival parish church.[33]

Other cases described by Foxe may be categorised as 'incipient

[29] *A. & M.*, VII, pp. 371-80, VIII, pp. 107-21.
[30] *Ibid.*, VI, pp. 676-81, VIII, pp. 731-36.
[31] *Ibid.*, VIII, pp. 405-06, 411.
[32] *Ibid.*, VIII, pp. 382, 409.
[33] *Ibid.*, VIII, pp. 391-92, 405.

congregations', since they show the early stages of what could have become groups such as Great Bentley's, if more effective leadership had been available and the government's repression less prompt. The nineteen-year-old apprentice, William Hunter, undertook the public reading of the Bible at a chapel near his father's home at Brentwood outside London; the sixty-year-old fisherman in South Wales, Rawlins White, gathered the like-minded more privately for prayer and the reading of scriptural passages. Both men were among the earliest to be burned, going to the stake in March 1555.[34]

Incipient congregations can also be seen sometimes in expanded household worship. Looking back in old age to her youth in Marian London as the wife of the wealthy Protestant merchant, Anthony Hickman, the octogenarian Rose Throckmorton described how they had given shelter to various endangered Protestants and how all would assemble for meals and Bible-reading together, 'keeping the doores shut for feare of the promotours [informers]'.[35] Less cautiously, James Trevisam, an old man in one of the London parishes, had his servant read the Bible to him and admitted others from outside the household.[36] Both sets of meetings were cut off in 1555, the former by the merchant's being imprisoned and later escaping abroad, the latter by the old man's dying of natural causes after a professional informer had obtained an arrest order. Still another kind of religious gathering which was cut off in its early stages is to be noted in Mancetter in northern Warwickshire. There the gentlewoman, Joyce Lewes, who went to the stake for taking a public stand against Roman Catholic ceremonies, had apparently found support for her stand in meetings with a number of friends (men and women), eleven of whom were later summoned before the Bishop of Lichfield, 'for that they did pray and drink with the said mistress Lewes'.[37]

Among the orthodox congregations there was an evident effort to find clerics for expounding the Scriptures as well as for administering the sacraments. The layman Jeffrey Hurst, who ran the Shakerly congregation in Lancashire, held meetings only when he could secretly bring in one of the clerics still in England. Besides those going to Shakerly, there was also John Pullan, formerly rector of St. Peter's

[34] *Ibid.*, VI, 722–29; VII, pp. 28–33. See also VIII, pp. 102–03, for the case of William Maundrel, the Wiltshire husbandman who felt he must give testimony against the restored Roman Catholic ceremonies but could not read the Bible himself.

[35] Printed in 'Religion and Politics in Mid-Tudor England', M. Dowling and J. Shakespeare, eds., *B.I.H.R.*, LV (1982), pp. 97–102.

[36] *A. & M.*, VIII, pp. 286–87.

[37] *Ibid.*, VIII, pp. 401–05, 429. For another incipient congregation see the account sent to Foxe, *c.* 1575, by 'John Kempe, then of Godstone in Surrey, now minister in the Isle of Wight,' telling how he was almost apprehended by an informer on 'Sondaye as hee conferred in Scripture with three or four of his neighbours,' *A. & M.*, 1575 edn., p. 1975.

Cornhill, who celebrated communion on two successive Easters at his London house. He is also identified by a government agent as being one of three Edwardian pastors based at the King's Head in Colchester and travelling thence to London and elsewhere.[38] Another, Simon Harlestone, is described in the same report as based partly at a house in Dedham (possibly because he had a small congregation there),[39] and the activities of other clerics are seen incidentally from time to time.[40]

In most cases it is implied to be the lack of clergy which impelled laymen to take over as substitute preachers. But in at least one case the congregation's leader, a miller named Edmund Allin, had apparently been expounding the Bible for some time as a matter of right. Foxe describes Allin as having helped the poor in Frittenden not only by means of moderate grain prices in times of dearth but 'with the food of life, reading to them the scriptures and interpreting them'. Responding at his trial in 1557 to the magistrate's peremptory query, 'Who gave thee authority to preach and interpret? Art though a priest?', Allin insisted that God had done so, as He had 'to all other Christians'. This position and a vein of anti-clericalism later in the exchanges suggest that Allin may have had a past among the radical sectaries, but no such question is raised in the extensive account of the trial printed by Foxe.[41] In the Essex town of Billericay no suggestion arose of any but lay leadership in the undeground congregation when the magistrate denounced the linen draper, Thomas Wats, at his trial in April 1555: 'Ye will not come to the church, ye will not hear mass, but have your conventicles, a sort of you in corners.'[42] As may be noted from these varied instances, the lifetime of any individual congregation was likely to be short. A determined leader could apparently start one without formality or delay, but his arrest was likely to mean its end.

4

The activities of the underground congregations cannot be definitively set forth, but a rough mosaic can be constructed from the occasional glimpses provided of particular groups. As noted earlier, worship centred on prayer, reading and expounding the Bible. Concerning the lines preaching took there is no direct evidence, though it may be assumed, for example, that the sermons of Robert Samuel and William

[38] *A. & M.*, VII, p. 738; VIII, p. 384.

[39] Ralph Allerton had sent farewell messages to 'the congregation' in Dedham and two other places, and a Dedham weaver had been one of the group arrested together in Colchester in August 1556, *A. & M.*, VIII, pp. 411; 306.

[40] *E.g.*, Thomas Whittle, who was an itinerant minister between the time he was ousted from his Essex parish and his burning early in 1556, *ibid.*, VII, pp. 718 ff.

[41] *Ibid.*, VIII, pp. 321-25.

[42] *Ibid.*, VII, pp. 118-23.

Tyms to their illegal congregations were somewhat similar to the letters of exhortation written to parishioners from prison afterwards. These prison letters, as printed by Foxe, remind them of God's spiritual mercies to them, call on them to keep the faith against 'these idolatrous Egyptians here in England' and cite various biblical figures whom God preserved from their persecutors.[43]

For members of most underground congregations (i.e., those of the third type) the sacraments were apparently observances to be enjoyed when possible but were usually precluded by the emergency conditions under which underground congregations met. Jeffrey Hurst in Lancashire seems to have been exceptional in convening meetings only when he had obtained a cleric to officiate. Some scattered evidence suggests, however, that arrangements were sometimes made for the sacraments to be administered privately, as in the cases previously noted of communion by John Pullan and in the case of a baptism in 1557 by an otherwise unidentified cleric, Thomas Saunders.[44] Roger Holland, previously mentioned as one of the group arrested at Islington in May 1558, perhaps illustrates the attitude of many orthodox Protestants. His first choice was evidently the congregation of Thomas Rose, who baptised his first child, but, when this congregation was disbanded in January 1555, he went to a group whose worship was confined to Bible-reading, prayer and exhortation. No instance is recorded of laymen in orthodox Protestant congregations undertaking to administer the sacraments themselves, though there were apparently some hostile accusations to this effect.[45]

Members of the congregations looked to their leaders, lay or clerical, for pastoral counsel as well as preaching. In one celebrated case Thomas Bentham, who was to be Elizabeth's Bishop of Lichfield, wrote to his friend Thomas Lever in Switzerland for Henry Bullinger's advice on three problems of conscience raised by members of the principal London congregation.[46] But the layman Ralph Allerton of the Great Bentley congregation also had his advice sought, in this case on the admissibility of Roman Catholic baptism for a fellow villager's child.[47]

In matters of internal organisation, particularly financial and security arrangements, the orthodox congregations had to strive for a competence which some of the radical sectaries had already achieved. Guildford Familists held night meetings with passwords, and a government agent reported of the Freewillers that 'there come none into

---

[43] *Ibid.*, VII. pp. 374 ff. (Samuel); VIII, pp. 117-21 (Tyms); p. 414 (Ralph Allerton).

[44] *Ibid.*, VIII, p. 727.

[45] Richard Woodman, the intinerant lay preacher, strongly denied the charge 'that I baptized children and married folks,' *ibid.*, VIII, p. 334.

[46] Letter printed in *Eccl. Mem.*, III, ii, pp. 133-35; see also Rough's counselling a member of the congregation, *A. & M.*, VIII, p. 726.

[47] *Ibid.*, VII, p. 412.

their brotherhood except he be sworn'.[48]

In contrast, the government had five different informers reporting on meetings of the principal London congregation when John Rough was pastor in 1557 – probably because Rough had recently returned from an exile group overseas. In meeting financial needs, which were especially heavy because of the many Protestants needing support in London prisons, Rough's congregation was more successful. Its collectors of funds are named in several of the agents' reports and Foxe indicates that, besides the main roll-book of members, there was a shorter second list of those delinquent in their payments.[49] It is noteworthy that the person chiefly responsible for the London congregation's finances (and possessing also an executor's responsibility for the property of executed Protestants), a tailor named Cuthbert Symsom, is referred to as 'deacon of the Christian congregation in London'. The title 'deacon', which is used both in the agents' reports and by Foxe himself, suggests that the congregation may have been organised at least partly on Genevan lines and not those of the Edwardian church, where a deacon occupied the lowest order of ordained clergy.[50]

What the minister's powers were, and what the congregation's, we do not know. One instance is recorded in which John Rough as pastor excommunicated a member (Margaret Mearing) 'in the open face of the congregation . . . and cut her off from their fellowship' – not, however, on any doctrinal grounds but because he considered her too lax in admitting strangers and too incautious in her speech.[51] In what is perhaps a more significant case, Rough, in counselling another member of the congregation who was greatly troubled in spirit for having been persuaded to attend two Roman Catholic services, followed his citations of 'comfortable sentences of Scripture' with the advice that she 'confess her fault' to the whole congregation 'and so be received into their fellowship again'.[52] The bond of fellowship in the group seems very important here, though the incident says nothing about the congregation's formal powers.

The external relationships of the congregations are far from clear. The principal London body certainly had ties with the Protestant exiles, for two of its ministers – Rough and Bentham – returned to London from safety abroad, and Bentham, as already noted, remained in

[48] *Ibid.*, VIII, p. 384.

[49] *Ibid.*, VIII, pp. 454, 458-60.

[50] *Ibid.*, VIII, p. 454. I am grateful to John Fines for drawing my attention to the significance of Symson's title. That others bore the title also is indicated by a nearly contemporary reference to Symson as 'one of the fyrst deacons of the congregation' in Robert Crowley's 1559 edn. of *An epitome of cronicles* (STC 15217.5), fol. 308[v].

[51] *A. & M.*, VIII, pp. 450-51. In fact, one of the government's reports (p. 459) came from James Mearing, her husband.

[52] *Ibid.*, VIII, pp. 727-28.

correspondence with the exiles. But we do not know the precise relationship of the London group to those overseas. Mary's government evidently believed that dangerous links existed between the congregation and plotters abroad, for the arrest of Rough (along with other members) came within a few months of his arrival. There were, of course, contacts between the congregations and imprisoned leaders of the Edwardian church. Hooper had written his encouragement to the arrested members of the Thomas Rose's congregation, and Augustine Bernher, the Swiss who had been Latimer's disciple and served as liaison between various Protestant figures in England, filled in temporarily between the pastorates of Rough and Bentham.

For a variety of reasons, including the danger from professional informers, the congregations apparently attempted little or no proselytising of the general public, though both orthodox Protestants and radical sectaries were ready enough in special circumstances to seek converts among other religious dissidents. Various individual conversions were made as a result of such disputations as occurred in the King's Bench prison, but, with one possible exception, the congregations themselves seem to have held to their original allegiances.[53] A government agent's report indicates that the directing centres for Protestant activity within England were located at various named inns and similar locations in the City of London and in the Colchester area.[54] Those travelling back and forth from these bases evidently represented divergent tendencies among Protestants, and over a dozen persons are specifically named. The orthodox Protestants' centre is characterized as the most influential. This was presided over by an Essex gentleman named Laurence whose 'servant' John Barry, attended the 1555 session at a Colchester inn to dispute with radical sectaries. Two of the other London centres are described in the report as concerned with propagandising prisoners in the King's Bench and circulating religious tracts.

The congregations seem to have had no role in the distribution of exile tracts, though they would of course have provided some of the readers. Two persons arrested for the suspected smuggling of Protestant books into England gave no hint, in the extensive interrogations which Foxe prints, that their contacts within the country were in the underground congregations.[55] The impermanence of most of the groups would in any

[53] The Guildford congregation may have been 'captured' by the Familists from another group in the second year of Mary's reign. At about that time, according to the deposition of the two ex-members in 1561, the congregation relaxed its ban on participating in parish church services and decreed both attendance and complete outward conformity, 'although inwardly thay did professs the contrary.' (See n. 11 above.) Familists were virtually unique at that time in taking such a position.

[54] *A. & M.*, VIII, p. 384.

[55] *Ibid*, VIII, pp. 521-24, 536-48.

case have made them less preferable outlets than ordinary trade channels. Nor, despite the government's occasional suspicions, are there signs of their concerning themselves with any kind of political activity.

Similarly, they had little to do with the informal network for the sheltering of co-religionists on the run from the authorities, an internal migration which Foxe refers to as comparable in scope to the flight of Protestants overseas.[56] Such arrangements had been part of Lollard practice and were of course needed by someone like Jeffrey Hurst to bring itinerant ministers secretly to his small group at Shakerly. But it was apparently individual Protestants, and not the congregations as such, who provided this assistance.[57] From time to time, also, a member of the congregation might need to take temporary refuge in 'the woods' – that kind of rural Alsatia composed of varied sorts of outlaws, from occasional religious refugees, to the vagabonds created by Tudor England's economic stresses, to common criminals. 'The woods', however, seem to have been regarded as only a temporary expedient, suggesting that congregation members saw themselves as generally law-abiding solid citizens. Ralph Allerton readily admitted under interrogation that he had known 'Trudgeover', the itinerant preacher whom the government had executed as a traitor, but he denied that he had 'read unto the people abroad in the woods' except on one occasion which he took pains to describe.[58]

In short, the life of the congregations seems to have centred almost entirely on providing the inner support and consolation which Hooper had defined as its purpose. Each congregation apparently undertook such organisation as it felt necessary for itself and had the most informal of relations with other groups.

5

Mary's government in its upper levels, in contrast to the professional informers, paid only incidental attention to the underground congregations as such. In the 68 months of the Privy Council register for her reign, only one item specifically mentions 'secret conventicles', and this is a commendation of an official who had apparently stumbled across some in the Harwich area while prosecuting an urgent search requested

[56] *Ibid.*, VIII, Appendix Document VI, which prints a passage that appeared only in the 1563 ed. (at p. 1679).

[57] Foxe remarks of a carpenter in rural Suffolk that he was a 'harbourer of straungers that travailed for concience,' (*A. & M.*, VIII, p. 630) and makes similar statements about William Pikes, a tanner in Ipswich (VIII, p. 481) and William Wood, a barber in Stroud who became a rector in Suffolk in Elizabeth's reign (VIII, pp. 729-30.

[58] *Ibid.*, VIII, pp. 410-13. Similarly, the lay preacher Richard Woodman insisted to the Bishop of Winchester in 1557 that the sheriff's men did not capture him 'in the woods' but at his own house (VIII, p. 364).

by the Council for the itinerant preacher 'Trudgeover'. That figure, in contrast, appears seven times in the register, evidently because he was thought to be some kind of political agent for plotters abroad.[59] Nine other items in the register apparently refer to itinerant preachers of one sort or another whose activities were regarded as disturbing to good order generally,[60] but the preaching and other activities of the Edwardian clerics apparently concerned the Council more. Of 22 items about Protestant clerics below the level of bishop, four concern the arrest of Thomas Rose and one the case of John Rough, but in none of the items is there any reference to the numerous members of their congregations who were arrested with them.[61] Conventicles likewise received little attention in visitation articles and similar ecclesiastical documents in Mary's reign: only one out of approximately 50 items in the 1554 articles for London diocese and two in about the same number in another inquiry of April 1558, though both documents showed considerable interest in the varied means used to evade full participation in Roman Catholic worship.[62]

These Marian attitudes differ appreciably from those of the preceding and following Protestant governments. The Privy Council register for the 78 months of Edward's reign shows about the same number of items as in Mary's concerned with hostile activity by lower clerics and, if the Marian items regarding 'Trudgeover' are excluded, almost as many items about itinerant preachers.[63] But in the attitude toward secret religious meetings there is a contrast. The register for Edward's Privy Council has six detailed items reflecting the alarm aroused in early 1551

[59] The conventicle reference (*A.P.C.*, V, p. 334) occurs part way through a series explicitly mentioning 'Trudgeover': V, pp. 310, 312, 318; VI, pp. 18, 129-30, 142, 215. The furore over Trudgeover is also reflected in the Venetian ambassador's report of Aug. 25, 1556 (*Calendar of State Papers, Venetian*, R. Brown, ed. (London 1877), VI, i, pp. 578-79) and in the account of the fugitive Protestant, Thomas Mowtayne (*Narratives of the Reformation*, J.G. Nichols, ed. (London 1859), pp. 210-11). Though Foxe considers Trudgeover a religious martyr, the government executed him as a traitor, *A. & M.*, VIII, pp. 393-97.

[60] *A.P.C.*, IV, pp. 369, 375, 377, 383, 387, 403; V, p. 110.

[61] *Ibid.*, V, pp. 86, 123-24, 126 for Rose; VI, p. 216 for Rough; IV, pp. 321-22, 333, 340, 384-85, 389, 420-21, V, pp. 17, 30, 77 for other Protestant clerics below the rank of bishop. The government apparently saw a political aspect to Rose's meeting in January 1555 (*A. & M.*, VI, p. 584; VIII, pp. 584-85), possibly suspecting that his prayers violated a recent statute (I Philip and Mary, 9) against asking God to shorten Queen Mary's days.

[62] *Documentary Annals of the Reformed Church of England, 1546-1716*, Edward Cardwell, ed., 2 vols. (Oxford 1844), I, p. 139; *Interrogatories . . . for search . . . of all such things as now be . . . amysse*, 1558 (STC 10117). See also Archbishop Pole's 1557 visitation articles, Cardwell, I, pp. 203-08.

[63] For lower clerics, *A.P.C.*, II, pp. 401, 451-52, 465, 483; III, pp. 137, 237, 287, 295, 305, 316-17, 400, 404, 431, 476, 482; IV, pp. 129, 136, 197-98, 225, 257, 268. For itinerant preachers, III, pp. 19, 20, 32, 81, 217, 228, 413.

by the Freewillers' gathering in Bocking, and then three in late 1552 relating chiefly to an unidentified sect 'newly sprung in Kent' which Cranmer is asked to investigate.[64] Also, the 1550 visitation articles for London diocese have seven items directed at secret religious meetings and radical religious activity.[65] Elizabeth's Privy Council, at least in the first four or five months before sizeable gaps appear in the register, shows a marked inclination to police the activity of the lower clergy and itinerant preachers, and the holding of any unauthorised meetings.[66] The 1559 ecclesiastical visitation articles focus mainly on Roman Catholic activity but contain also an inquiry on 'unlawful conventicles'.[67] It looks, therefore, as if Mary's government may not have much cared about 'secret conventicles' except in special circumstances.

Later on, in Elizabeth's reign, the accusation was to be heard from Church of England Puritans that the sectaries had been less severely persecuted than orthodox Protestants had[68] – and indeed there seems to be some basis for the charge. It was a standard line of Marian propaganda to emphasise the excesses of the sectaries and to charge that Cranmer and Ridley, by breaking the tie with Rome, had loosed the sectaries on the country,[69] and the spectacle of a few eccentric lay preachers might conveniently support this argument. The lay preacher Richard Woodman, who was arrested early in Mary's reign for denouncing his parish priest as a turncoat and finally burned toward its end, was released from prison in December 1555 in circumstances which left him surprised and somewhat defensive about his own reputation for constancy.[70] Henry Hart, known to the authorities as the Freewillers' senior leader, was apparently able to move rather freely in and out of the King's Bench prison.[71] While there he debated with John Bradford, the leading Protestant cleric in the prison, on the doctrine of election. Later on, a

[64] *Ibid.*, III, pp. 196-99, 306-07; IV, pp. 131, 138.

[65] Cardwell, *Annals*, I, pp. 89-93; *Articles to be inquired of in . . . the byshopricke of Norwyche*, 1549 (STC 10285).

[66] See the royal proclamation of Dec. 27, 1558 against unauthorized preaching (*Tudor. Procl.*, II, pp. 202-03) and the immediate action ordered against a perceived violation (*A.P.C.*, VI, p. 32).

[67] *Articles to be enquyred*, 1559 (STC 10019), sig. B 2^v.

[68] In the course of arguing against English Jesuits in 1581 that it is Rome which is responsible for the proliferation of sects, Percival Wilburn asserts that 'in the late days of poperie here' England was overrun with 'Arians, Anabaptistes, Libertines & c., though none in effect were persecuted but the poore Protestantes as ye call them. These mens peculiar heresies in examinations were commonly never touched; peruse the records: of these there was little or no accompt made in those dayes of ignorance and darkness,' *A checke or reproofe of M. Howlets*, 1581 (STC 25286), fol. 15.

[69] *E.g.*, 'The declaration of the Bishop of London to the lay people,' 1554, in Cardwell, *Annals*, I, pp. 170-74; Hogarde, *Displaying of the Proestantes*, fol. 16-20, 116-25.

[70] *A. & M.*, VIII, pp. 333-34.

[71] *Ibid.*, VIII, p. 384.

Roman Catholic interrogator used another statement of Hart's views for seriously upsetting the orthodox layman, John Careless.[72]

6

Fragmentary though the evidence assembled on the underground congregations is, it does suggest a few tentative conclusions. The best known of the congregations, the principal London one, now looks like the exceptional case, exceptional both in its having outlasted Mary herself and in its degree of clerical planning and control.[73] Most of the congregations, compatible though they were with Hooper's guidelines for them, seem to have arisen quite spontaneously and on lay initiative. The latent ability for religious leadership which the emergency revealed was, moreover, surprising. Few could have expected to find a Ralph Allerton or a John Alcocke in a sixteenth-century English village.

All of the congregations were autonomous to a degree none of their members had experienced before; even the principal London congregation had an independence known to few Edwardian or Elizabethan religious bodies. It was an autonomy deriving partly from financial self-sufficiency and the remoteness of higher authority but also, it may be suggested, from a certain shift in religious focus. Larger civic matters and problems of social discipline which sometimes preoccupied parish churches gave way to more immediate and personal religious concerns. This evidently did not affect the willingness of members of orthodox groups to give public testimony to their faith. Foxe's roll of martyrs contains over a third of those probably connected with underground congregations of all types. But for some of the survivors the experience of autonomy could leave lasting effects.

It is noteworthy also that all the orthodox congregations were apparently able to maintain their positions against the radical sectaries by various kinds of argument rather than by the powers of the state wielded by the Edwardian church. The new relationship was by no means one of equality or avowed toleration. The orthodox tended to see themselves as a true national church still, and viewed many of the doctrines of the sectaries as abominable and dangerous in the extreme.[74] The Freewillers, indeed, reported of the disputation in the King's Bench prison that the orthodox not only termed their beliefs damnable heresy 'but also threatened us that we were like to die for it if the Gospel should reign

[72] Bradford, I, pp. 307-30; *A. & M.*, VIII, pp. 164-65.
[73] Though the Shakerly and South Molton congregations also survived, their sizes and levels of activity were much less.
[74] See John Philpot's prison tract, 'Apology for spitting on an Arian', in *Eccl. Mem.*, III, ii, pp. 363-80.

again'.[75] But orthodox leaders in the prison apparently continued to share with them the relief funds, which came mainly from orthodox sources, and to maintain a united front against the Roman Catholic authorities. There survives from this period an open letter by a Freewiller converted to orthodoxy but none with the positions reversed.[76]

Elizabeth's accession affected the underground congregations in differing ways. Some, such as the two in South Molton and Shakerly respectively, evidently became ordinary parish churches again without unusual incident.[77] The Familist congregation near Guildford merely continued as before. The Freewillers are not heard of as an active group after Mary's reign and their senior leader, Henry Hart, was reported dead in 1557.[78] The cold-shouldering of the principal London congregation which aroused Lever's indignation did not necessarily spring from prescience of the way its memory was to be invoked by separatists in later years. The cause could have been either dislike of a 'Genevan' influence detectable there, or simply rigour in enforcing the proclamation of 27 December 1558 against unauthorised preaching.[79]

From the government's point of view the first decade of the new reign was full of trouble from nonconformists within the Church of England and separatists outside it, a story it is not necessary to retell here. It is, however, pertinent to recall one particular episode which has been examined in detail by H. Gareth Owen. This concerns the independence asserted for some years in the 1560s by the London parish church of the Minories, and the way religious dissidents moved back and forth between it and private conventicles with apparent ease.[80] Various factors helped produce this situation, notably the constitutional one that the Minories was a 'peculiar' which was not brought fully under the control of the Bishop of London till 1578. However, it is hard to ignore the influence of the five Marian years when Protestants desiring communal worship within England had perforce to become separatists. One must remember also that the lines between separatist group and established church were not then so sharply drawn as they became for Henry Barrow and John Greenwood in the late 1580s.

The experience of the underground congregations had not been forgotten, especially by the separatists of the 1560s, and their most pointed appeal to it as a precedent is worth quoting again. A spokesman

[75] Trew, 'Cause of the contention', *Authentic Documents*, pp. 56–57.
[76] Bradford II, pp. 180–81; *Eccl. Mem.*, III, ii, pp. 325–34.
[77] Ramsey writes in 1561 as one satisfied with the transition in South Molton. Foxe describes how Jeffrey Hurst, until his untimely death, worked with the Queen's commissioners to establish Protestantism more firmly in the Shakerly parish church, *A. & M.*, VIII, p. 564.
[78] *Archdeacon Harpsfield's Visitation, 1557*, L.E. Whatmore, ed. (London 1950), p. 120.
[79] See n. 66 above.
[80] 'A Nursery of Elizabethan Nonconformity,' *J.E.H.*, XVIII (1966), pp. 65–76.

for the separatist congregation arrested at Plumbers Hall in 1567 justified
to Bishop Grindal their assembling there:

> But when it came to this point, that all our preachers were displaced by your
> law . . . and then were we troubled and commanded to your courts from day
> to day for not coming to our parish churches; then we bethought us what
> were best to do, and we remembered that there was a congregation of us in
> this city in Queen Mary's days . . .[81]

The 'us' was figurative. None of the 72 names of arrested members of the
Plumbers Hall congregation matches any of those in my file of probable
members of the Marian underground congregations.[82] It was the
prestige of the London congregation which was being invoked – and its
autonomous character.

The memory of that congregation, indeed, became part of the
separatist tradition and was enshrined nearly a century later in the
Dialogue written for the instruction of younger members of Plymouth
Colony by Governor William Bradford. 'In the days of Queen
Elizabeth', he wrote, 'there was a Separated Church whereof Mr. Fitz
was pastor, and another before that in the time of Queen Mary, of which
Mr. Rough was pastor or teacher and Cuthbert Symson a deacon . . .[83]
There is a certain irony in separatist tradition choosing as its chief Marian
ancestor the group which of all the underground congregations had been
the nearest to be being externally controlled, but at least Governor
Bradford avoided mentioning the two of its pastors, Scambler and
Dentham, who became Elizabethan bishops. It is easier to see how
Church of England Puritans could look to it as a model, since it had
always worshipped under ordained ministers and, at least in the office of
deacon, had apparently followed Genevan lines. Leaving the Church of
England for a separatist conventicle remained a step which no cleric took
lightly, but when one felt he could no longer tarry for reformation, the
memory of this and other Marian congregations perhaps strengthened
his confidence that there would be a separatist group to provide him with
an alternative.

The story of the underground congregations also contributes to the
understanding of sixteenth-century popular religion, a phenomenon
sometimes referred to as if it included only elements rooted deeply in
tradition, such as the use of pagan charms and the veneration of Christian
relics and saints' images. The veneration of images, as recent research has
emphasised, was indeed an element in the religious life of many Tudor
Englishmen, but so also, for others, was the persistent holding of

---

[81] Edmund Grindal, *Remains*, W. Nicholson, ed. (Cambridge 1843), p. 203.
[82] Burrage II, pp. 9-11.
[83] Quoted from *Plymouth Church Records, 1620-1659*, Pub. Colonial Society of
Massachusetts, XXII, pp. 115 ff. (Boston 1920) in B.R. White, *The English Separatist
Tradition* (Oxford 1971), p. 2.

conventicles for the discussion of religious concerns.[84] In both elements, of course, the influence of official religion is often evident and there seems to be no way of drawing a sharp line between this influence and what is fully indigenous.

The experience of the five Marian years further suggests something about the essential nature of the conventicle. As has been seen, it was likely to be short-lived in individual instances but possessing as an institution the resilience to spring up whenever felt need and a measure of natural leadership coincided. At various times in later decades and on through the following century English separatists were to elaborate the conventicle's organisation by such means as congregational compacts, attach it to controversial points of doctrine like believers' baptism, or even make it the vehicle of social and political radicalism. In Mary's reign, however, it appears predominantly as a simple gathering of those feeling close enough to each other in their religious concerns to worship together and find spiritual support in so doing.

---

[84] Robert Whiting, 'Abominable Idols: Images and Image-breaking under Henry VIII', *J.E.H.*, XXXIII (1982), pp. 30-47.

Chapter 8

Robert Crowley in Two Protestant Churches

1

Robert Crowley, a cleric whose active life stretched from the last years of Henry VIII to the year of the Spanish Armada, has been examined from various points of view: as one of the so called Commonwealth Men of Edward VI's reign, as a significant influence on Elizabethan and Stuart literature, and even as the first English university man to set up as a printer.[1] My concern here is primarily with the way Crowley illustrates the changes occurring in Tudor Protestantism, especially in the mid-century decades.

Elizabeth's Church of England was separated by the mere five years (1553-1558) of the Roman Catholic Mary from the national church of Edward VI, and it consciously sought continuity with that church, yet the two Protestant Churches of England differed in a variety of ways. Elizabeth's church was run by an almost entirely new set of leaders, since those burned by Mary included not merely Cranmer, Ridley and Latimer but such other influential figures as Hooper, Bradford and Philpot, while others such as Ponet and Bale died in exile or soon after, and Knox was not allowed back in England. Elizabeth's first bishops had nearly all of them been in rather junior positions in Edward's reign; those later on were necessarily clerics who had grown up as Protestants, tending to accept ecclesiastical affairs as they found them. Their Edwardian counterparts, in contrast, had many of them gone through a personal religious conversion and, having experienced great change within themselves, inclined to see great change in the external world as also possible. With an enthusiastically Protestant monarch on the throne,

---

[1] *E.g.*, J.W. Allen, *A History of Political Thought in the Sixteenth Century* (London 1941), Part II, Chap. III; Quentin Skinner, *The Foundations of Modern Political Thought* (Cambridge 1978), I, pp. 224-226; G.R. Elton, 'Reform and the "Commonwealth-Men" of Edward VI's Reign', *Studies in Tudor and Stuart Politics and Government* (Cambridge 1983), III, pp. 234-253; John N. King, *English Reformation Literature: Tudor Origins of the Protestant Tradition* (Princeton 1982), Chap. 7 and Appendix V, the latter a comprehensive bibliography of Crowley to which I am much indebted; J.W. Martin, 'The Publishing Career of Robert Crowley', *Publishing History*, XIV (1983), pp. 85-98.

they felt ready to undertake a transformation of the liturgy (twice, in fact) a revision of the canon law, the founding of Reformation-oriented grammar schools, a purging of church buildings of their 'idolatrous images' (furnishing them with vernacular Bibles instead), and even the provision of a 'godly preaching ministry' throughout the land. Two young clerics, Edmund Grindal and Richard Cox, who survived the Marian years to take on the burdens of Elizabethan bishoprics, still looked back on the Edwardian church with nostalgia; similarly, John Foxe in 1570 revised the introduction to Edward's reign carried in the 1563 edition of his *Actes and Monuments*, and inserted a glowing encomium of the boy monarch prefaced by an elaborate woodcut setting forth schematically the special virtues of the Edwardian church.[2]

Crowley was only a secondary figure in the sense that he never became a bishop or even a dean, but he was talented as a preacher and both talented and versatile as a writer. His 20 or so published works range from formal theological controversy to social satire in a popular doggerel verse. A convert to Protestantism in his student days, he stood out at two different periods in his life as an advocate of two particular religious causes. The first of these, which he urged in Edward's reign, was a Christian society's obligations to its poor; the second, early in Elizabeth's reign, was the right of Protestant clergy to refuse to wear the traditional vestments of the old church. Disparate as the two causes appear to the twentieth-century eye, Crowley seems to have been equally devoted to them both and the historian, curious to discover why, looks to the surviving data on him for help. What kind of man emerges from the publications and the miscellaneous details? How different, apart from his writings, was he from other Protestant clerics of his time? No personal letters have come to light, but there are biographical inferences to be drawn from his own works and from some of those he published or wrote prefaces for. There are also mentions of him in a variety of contemporary sources, most of them relating to London, where Crowley spent nearly all his working life.

2

The outline of his life presented in the *Dictionary of National Biography* is essentially accurate, though subsequent research has corrected or

[2] Patrick Collinson, *Archbishop Grindal* (Berkeley, California 1979), pp. 48, 49; Foxe, *Actes and Monuments*, 1570 (STC 11223), pp. 1483-85. The woodcut, reproduced as this volume's frontispiece, was carried along with the new text in the two subsequent editions in Foxe's lifetime but dropped by his nineteenth-century editors; for the 1570 text see *Actes and Monuments*, J. Pratt, ed., 8 vols. (London 1870-77), V, pp. 698-702.

amplified it in various details.[3] Miscellaneous documentary references to his age, for example, indicate that the year of his birth (in Gloucestershire) was 1517. He entered Magdalen College, Oxford, about 1534, became converted to the new faith in the later 1530s and was one of a somewhat persecuted Protestant minority there, along with his friend John Foxe, the future martyrologist. A remark he made in the last few years of his life suggests that he was one of those like John Bale whose conversion came suddenly after active devotion to the old church. Addressing a young man of about 20, who was a recent convert to Roman Catholicism, he says: 'I my selfe was at your age a more skilful Papist than you bee.'[4] After having proceeded B.A. in 1540, he gave up his college fellowship about 1544[5] and apparently spent some time as tutor to the children of Sir Nicholas Poyntz of Iron Acton, Gloucestershire. By the end of 1546, however, Crowley was in London and writing.

The earliest picture of his religious views comes from *The opening of the wordes of the prophet Joell*. This tract, which is in doggerel verse, was printed only in 1567, but announces on the title page that it was written in 1546, a dating reinforced by a reference or two later on to 'our King' and one to the contemporary existence of chantry priests.[6] It, along with several immediately succeeding works, reflects the impact both of Crowley's religious conversion and of the social dislocations of contemporary England. He is acutely conscious of the way enclosures and the trading in former church lands have driven many of the poor from their homes, and of how they have suffered from the persistent rise in prices. England, as he sees it here, suffers from both spiritual and material famine. London's lack of 'ghostly food' he attributes to a corrupt and indolent clergy, over-concerned with their financial perquisites and inattentive to their teaching duties, whom the royal measures have not yet sufficiently reformed.[7] No less persistent is his demand for social justice to cope with the material famine: 'This worlde call I / Gods familie / Wherein the riche men be / As stewardes stout / To

[3] I am indebted to Olga Elizabeth Illston, 'A Literary and Bibliographical Study of Robert Crowley' (London University M.A. thesis, 1953), regarding his relationship with the Poyntz family and his will. References to Crowley in various contemporary documents appear in Mark Eccles, 'Brief Lives: Tudor and Stuart Authors', *Studies in Philology*, Vol. 79, Texts and Studies Issue (1982), pp. 27, 28; more such data are found in Eccles, 'William Wager and his Plays', *English Language Notes*, Vol. 18 (1980–81), pp. 258–59; I am grateful to Kathy Pearl for bringing these to my attention. See also A.B. Emden, *A Biographical Register of the University of Oxford, 1501 to 1540* (Oxford 1974).

[4] *Fryar John Frauncis of Nigeon in France*, 1586 (STC 6091), fol. 5ᵛ.

[5] J.F. Mozley, *John Foxe and His Book* (London 1940), pp. 22-25, quoting contemporary letters by Foxe.

[6] Legislation abolishing chantries was passed in Edward's 1547 Parliament.

[7] *Opening of the wordes of Joell*, 1567 (STC 6089), sigs. A7ʳ, D6ʳ ff, F7ʳ.

rule the rout / And succour povertie.'[8] It is human greed which prevents
rich men from doing so; to persuade them that they must, Crowley
hopes partly that the King will set them a good example and partly that
they will remember that God's justice cannot be avoided.[9]

Crowley is writing here in a genre already established by Simon Fish's
1529 work, *The supplication of the beggars* (STC 10883), which
concentrates almost entirely on the financial extortions and other
misdeeds of the clergy. The tradition was carried on by *Supplication of the
poore commons* of 1546 (STC 10884), which urges that Henry VIII's
reform of the clergy has not gone far enough, and especially by two
works of Henry Brinkelow. The first of these, in 1542, is *The complaynt of
Roderyck Mors . . . unto parliament* (STC 3760). This writes more
extensively than Crowley attempts to do regarding the varied injustices
of civil life as well as those attributable to the clergy. The second, in 1545,
The lamentacyon of a Christian agaynst the cytye of London (STC 3164), is a
fairly conventional denunciation of Londoners for not having accepted
Protestantism more widely. None of these tracts, however, is quite in
Crowley's vein of coupling his new faith with the social conditions
which need changing and calling for their correction as a matter of
religious obligation. His message is roughly what would be known in
English-speaking countries around 1900 as 'the social gospel:' a call for
religious concern about the state of the poor and the way they are treated.
Who is to protect them? What should Christian teaching mean for the
remedying of social ills?

Crowley's earliest appearance in print, *An information and petition
agaynst the oppressours of the pore commons* (STC 6086) is a direct appeal (in
prose) to Parliament as the body responsible for remedying these
conditions – and, as he says in his opening statement, there is no more
important question for Parliament to consider. The tract was apparently
published sometime in 1547, for its Latin version, *Explicatio petitoria
adversus expilatores* (STC 6085), a somewhat longer work translated by
John Heron, dates its preface January 15, 1548. The provision of this
Latin version and its dedication to a well-connected member of the 1547
Parliament suggest that Crowley took his tract's appeal to Parliament
more seriously than Brinkelow had in 1542.[10] Though the tract opens on
the theme of the spiritual famine which the mercenary-minded clergy do
nothing to abate, the focus soon shifts to the material exploitation of the
poor. Crowley is quite specific on some things, such as the degree of

[8] *Ibid.*, B1ᵛ.
[9] *Ibid.*, G4, ʳ & ᵛ.
[10] Neither title page has a date or printer's name, but each tract bears Crowley's name
in the preface. The Latin version is dedicated to Kenelm Throckmorton, a member of
Parliament with ties to Queen Catherine Parr's household and a brother of Sir Nicolas,
who was later to be Elizabeth's first ambassador to France.

inflation which has occurred in lower class London rents, and excessive funeral fees charged the poor by the old clergy, and he argues at some length the responsibility of England's rich and powerful to relieve the hunger and homelessness of the dispossessed. 'If there were no God,' he asserts, 'then would I think it leaful [lawful] for men to use their possessions as they list. Or if God would not require an account of us for the bestowynge of them.'[11] Returning to this theme, he tells the landowners:

> By nature . . . you can claim no thynge but that whiche you shall gette with the swet of your faces. That you are Lordes and gouvernours, therefore, cometh not by nature but by the ordinaunce & appoyntment of God which gives responsibilities for the multitude . . . If the impotent creature perish for lacke of necessaries, you are the murderers, for you have their enheritaunce and do not minister unto them. The whole earth . . . (by byrth ryght) belongeth to the chyldren of men. They are all inheritours thereof indifferently by nature. But because the sturdy shoulde not oppresse the weak and impotent, God hath appoynted you stuards to give mete unto his household.[12]

They must never forget that they are both fellow members of one body (the realm) and also fellow Christians.[13]

Crowley, in his presentation of the social gospel to Parliament had apparently envisaged sanctions of two sorts for the needed changes: the legal sanction of royal edict or parliamentary statute; the religious sanction of the 'possessioners'' own fear of divine punishment. 'Be merciful to your selves,' he tells them, 'destroye not youre own selves to enriche your heires. Enlarge not your earthly possession wyth the losse of eternall enheritaunce.'[14] Neither sanction, of course, materialized to any effective degree and Crowley turned to other ways of trying to arouse the Christian conscience on which his call for social justice depended. During the years 1549–51 he tried two different approaches: the presentation of his message in several tracts written in Crowley's facile verse, and the establishment of a publishing business to exploit more fully the still relatively new medium of print.

He did not become his own printer in this enterprise, but some variant of the colophon, 'Imprinted at London by Robert Crowley dwelling in Elie rents in Holbourne,' appears on about 20 works, 8 of them by Crowley himself, the rest being things he apparently thought likely to advance Protestantism generally. Though his own imprint disappears after September 1551, when he was ordained by Bishop Ridley of London, his contacts with the printing trade continued in one way or

---

[11] *An informacion and peticion*, sig. A 4ᵛ.
[12] *Ibid.*, A 8ʳ.
[13] *Ibid.*, B 3ʳ.
[14] *Ibid.*, A 7ᵛ.

another throughout his life, and he formally became a freeman of the Stationers Company in 1578.

One of the earliest of the publications devoted to the Protestant cause was *The psalter of David newely translated into English metre in such sort that it may the more decently, and with more delyte of the mynde, be reade and song of al men*, 1549 (STC 2725). Crowley, who did the translating himself, evidently intended it as a Protestant service book, for its type is relatively large and well leaded, it contains some additional canticles and has a table of the moveable feasts projected well into the future. He likewise issued several books evidently intended to assist in the evangelization of Wales, reprinted William Tyndale's *The Supper of the Lord* (STC 24469), supplying a preface himself, and published what is now known as the General Prologue to the Wycliffite Bible, *The true copye of a Prolog written about two C yeres paste by J. Wyclife*, 1550 (STC 25588). Most important of all, he put into print the celebrated fourteenth-century poem by William Langland, *The Vision of Piers Plowman*.

In these last two publications Crowley was working in another established genre, different in kind from that he had written in with *An informacion and peticion*. Because *Piers Plowman* satirized clerical pretensions and strongly attacked corruption in the church, it was widely regarded as a proto-Protestant work, and the character of Piers had become a recognized mouthpiece for Protestant propaganda. In such tracts as *I playne piers which can not flatter* and *A godly dyaloge & disputacion betwene Pyers plowman and a popysh preest*, the simple peasant confounds the priest with questions which the priest cannot answer without absurd stumbling.[15] Other Protestant propagandists sheltered behind Chaucer's name, as in the strongly anti-clerical *Plowman's Tale* which they got inserted at the end of the *Canterbury Tales* in the 1542 printing of Chaucer's complete works.[16] Before Crowley, however, no one had dared to put Langland's long poem into print.

Crowley's three editions of *Piers Plowman* in 1550 are much more than an effort to use a respected name for Protestant propaganda.[17] The poem as a whole has clearly impressed him and he wants to make it more accessible to sixteenth-century readers. Accordingly, he sometimes modernizes the language and in the preface tells his readers something about the poem's authorship and assures them that, once the alliterative verse tradition is understood, 'the meter shall be very pleasant to read.' In this, as in his other printings of fourteenth-century works, Crowley's

---

[15] *C.* 1550, STC 19903a and 19903; see also *Pierce the ploughmans crede* (STC 19904) and *Pyers plowmans exhortation* (STC 19905).

[16] STC 5069; see also *Jack up Lande*, [1536?], (STC 5098). Additional anti-clerical material apparently circulated in manuscript, *e.g.*, *God spede the plough*, W.W. Skeat, ed. (London 1867).

[17] STC 19906, 19907, 19907a.

respect for his manuscript originals has been declared unusual for his time.[18] Nevertheless, his main interest in the poem is in the support it lends to Protestantism and in the lessons it contains. The preface recommends it to the reader for its moral teaching and to help 'amend thyne owne misse.' To this end, he adds a marginal comment now and then, and makes a few textual changes but, as a modern scholar has pointed out, it was important for his purpose that his edition remain as close to the original as possible. Accordingly, he limited himself to such emendations as seemed really essential – in some cases purely linguistic changes to avoid archaisms, and in others the omission of lines indicating a belief in purgatory or transubtantiation or praising the high ideals of monasticism.[19]

Looked at in a longer perspective, Crowley's effort here, as in printing the General Prologue to the Wycliffite Bible, seems to have been to provide Edwardian Protestants with an answer to the Roman Catholic taunts which in effect asked, 'Where was your church before Luther?' That mid-century Protestants felt a need of such reassurance is suggested not merely by Crowley's three editions in 1550 but by the appearance of still another edition in 1561, shortly after Elizabeth's accession returned the press to Protestant hands.[20]

The first of the Crowley verse tracts aimed at men's social consciences was *A new yeres gyfte, wherein is taught the knowledge of our selfe and the feare of God*, issued in 1549 over his own imprint. He promises the reader early in the text to show him all 'that Christ in his Gospel requireth of the[e],' and tries constantly to keep him aware of the Day of Judgment. Specific implications for the social scene are also pointed to – quite literally, indeed, with a printer's pointing finger placed opposite the following:

> In fine, all estates, what so ever they be,
> That do know them selfe, & thinke on their end,
> Wyll seke to walke ryght in their owne degre
> And all their enormities for to emende.[21]

It is his next verse tract, *The voyce of the laste trumpet blowen bi the seventh angel*, which gives the reader a comprehensive picture of what Crowley sees wrong with English society through a dozen selected cases – what he calls the 'several estates of men:' that is, groups with established ways of life, such as the yeoman, the lawyer, the merchant, and the gentleman.

Like Luther, Crowley is deeply conservative about social structure,

---

[18] Anne Hudson, ' "No Newe Thyng": the Printing of Medieval Texts in the Early Reformation Period' in *Lollards and Their Books* (London 1985), pp. 230, 233, 247.

[19] John N. King, 'Robert Crowley's Editions of Piers Plowman: a Tudor Apocalypse,' *Modern Philology*, Vol. 73, No. 4 (May 1976), pp. 342-52, especially 347-8.

[20] STC 19908.

[21] *A new yeres gyfte* (STC 6087), p. 7.

and here he evidently has in mind the medieval conspectus of society presented in *The Vision of Piers Plowman*. It is a society kept in order – and indeed held together – by its common reverence for God and by the great care with which each estate or degree within the society observes its own boundaries and responsibilities, trusting in God for justice. No one has a right to seek justice outside the channels provided (which, of course, include petition); and no one should seek to rise from his own estate to another one. 'Firste walk in thy vocation/ And do not seke thy lotte to chaunge.'[22]

Crowley starts with the bottom of society – the beggar – and his attitude here is essentially that of the late Middle Ages, when begging was seen as a quite normal activity not merely for the infirm but for such persons as lower clerics on the move. Crowley does go so far as to ask the beggar to reflect whether he has not 'mispent the gyftes thou didst receive' from God, but there is nothing like the supposed 'Protestant work ethic' of admonishing the beggar to go find himself a paying job. On the contrary, the admonition (or 'lesson' as Crowley phrases it) for the beggar is to accept his lot and rely patiently on the other estates' fulfilling their manifest duty of relieving his necessities. When alms are refused him, he is not to complain but to depend on God's eventually changing the heart of the man who spurned him. And, even if he dies in the street, he may comfort himself with the parable of Lazarus and the rich man in the world to come. At the very worst, he is assured that if 'thou dost walke upright/ In thy calling,' he will be 'more precious in Goddes sight/ Then them that be ryche beyond measure.'[23]

The yeoman is told that it is his worthy vocation to labour efficiently on the land, but is warned in very strong language that if he tries to expand his holdings so as to rise to a gentleman's status, he will only incur 'Gods ire/ And shewe thy selfe no christian.'[24] The merchant is similarly told that his function is to provide the country with needed commodities at a fair price, and that he should beware of trying to acquire land and to marry his daughter into the gentry.[25] The essential thing, Crowley seems to believe, is for each part of society to have a clear and respected identity.

Crowley does not, however, define all twelve 'estates' or patterns of life along purely traditional lines. The Protestant reformer is very evident in his 'lessons' for 'the lewed [unlearned] priest,' the 'scholar' (i.e., the young student in the university), and 'the learned man' (i.e., the senior cleric). The first is told that his great need is to acquire knowledge

---

[22] *The voyce of the last trumpet*, 1549 (STC 6894) sig. A 2ʳ.

[23] *Ibid.*, A 2ᵛ, A 3ʳ. (A more 'modern' view, in which two mendiants are satirized as charlatans, appears under 'Beggars' in Crowley's *One and thyrte epigrammes*.)

[24] *Ibid.*, A 5ᵛ.

[25] *Ibid.*, C 2ᵛ–4ᵛ.

of the Scriptures if he is to serve God and the people effectively; the other two are in effect told that the highest use of learning is to further the Reformation.

Crowley's next piece of social criticism bears the descriptive title, *One and thyrtye epigrammes, wherein are bryefly treated so many abuses that may and oughte to be put away*. ('Epigram' here means merely a short piece of verse on a single subject, and there are actually 33 of them.) Crowley is no less sharp in his satire than in *The voyce of the last trumpet*, but the device of simply moving from one arbitrarily chosen topic to another (as from 'almes houses' to 'the colier of Croydon' to 'double beneficed men' to 'obstinate papists') enables him to be lighter and less formal in his approach. The first example tells how a merchant returned from a stay abroad to find that a rich man's elaborate home now occupied the site where an alms house had once stood.[26] The anecdote about the coal merchant of Croydon not only recounts the wealth he gained by driving up the price, but specifies the amount of the recent rise in fuel prices.[27] The general subject is returned to under 'Forestallers' and 'Usuars', again with some specific figures.[28] A number of the items are concerned only with manners, writing about 'common lyars' or about 'nice wyves' and their face-painting in much the same way as other social satirists.[29]

Two more verse tracts of Crowley's appeared under his imprint in 1551, the second of these, *Philargyrie*, unsigned but generally accepted as Crowley's work. The first one, *Pleasure and payne, heaven and hell: remember these foure and all will be well*, again insists that landowners must see themselves as 'but stuards of the land;'[30] otherwise Christ will say to them at the last judgment, 'Ye robde, ye spoylde, / Ye bought, ye solde / My flocke and me.'[31] Crowley insists further that repentance must include reparation, whatever the cost: 'Let the pore man / Have and enjoye / The house he had by Copyehold / For hym, his wyfe / And Jacke, his boye / To kepe them from / Hunger and colde. / And though the lease therof be solde, / Bye it agayne, / though it be dere.'[32] Strange as the twentieth-century reader may find this attempt to deal with the effects of social change by reversing each of the individual processes leading to them, Crowley and his contemporaries would probably have seen such an attempted return to a simpler secular society as not so different from the widespread Protestant effort to return the church to its primitive purity. The root of the problem was to be found in human

---

[26] *One and thyrte epigrammes*, 1550 (STC 6088), A 8ʳ.
[27] *Ibid.*, B 6ᵛ.
[28] *Ibid.*, C8, E8.
[29] *Ibid.*, C 1ᵛ; D 8ʳ.
[30] *Pleasure and pain*, 1551 (STC 6090), C 8ʳ; see also B 2ʳ.
[31] *Ibid.*, B 3ʳ, with a printer's pointing finger placed opposite the words.
[32] *Ibid.*, C 7ᵛ.

greed and the ultimate solution in overcoming that.

Philargyrie of Greate Britayne is Crowley's most elaborate attack on human greed: a well developed satirical narrative about the malevolent British giant who must be fed with gold in ever increasing quantities.[33] He is at first supplied by Hypocrisie (Crowley's figure for the Roman church) from such rich shrines as Walsingham; later on, Hypocrisie's property is seized by Philaute (a figure for some of the Reformers) for his own purposes. Philaute at first tries to fob off Philargyrie with lead and stone, but in response to insistent demands for gold, tries to squeeze more and more wealth from the poor till the King finally decides to intervene.

Crowley's prose tract, *The waye to wealth, wherein is plainly taught a most present remedy for sedicion*, has roughly the same subject matter as most of those in verse, but differs in approach and tone. Dated February 7, 1550, it is obviously aimed at catching the mood of public uncertainty left by the Cornwall and Norfolk risings in the summer of 1549. Crowley opens by emphasizing his own opposition to rebellion of any kind, but then imagines how a poor man might explain sedition as caused by his continuing exploitation by the unscrupulous rich, leaving the poor no recourse but violence.[34] Later, in an evident reference to Ket's rising in Norfolk, he denounces 'the peassant knaves' who rebelled, but asserts that the landlords had been guilty of illegal practices also, and reminds them of how God punished Pharaoh and Nebuchadnezzar.[35] In between, partly on the basis of the Cornish rising which had been touched off by resentment at changes in the church service, Crowley denounces various clerical misdeeds and argues at some length that an effective preaching clergy makes for an orderly populace and could perhaps have prevented the risings.[36]

Crowley, of course, was by no means alone among contemporary clerics in his concern over England's social conditions. Hugh Latimer, the greatest preacher of the age, was known particularly for his rebuking of corruption in high places and his concern with the condition of the lower orders; also, as was pointed out years ago, there was a tradition of such preaching coming down from the late Middle Ages.[37] Other leading members of the Edwardian church, notably John Hooper and John Knox, were forthright in their denunciations of the diversion of church property from education and relief of the needy to court favourites and local magnates. Further names for mention include

[33] 1551 (STC 6089.5).

[34] *The way to wealth* (STC 6096), A 3^r.

[35] Ibid., B 3^v-6^r.

[36] Ibid., A 8^r-B 1^v.

[37] Helen C. White, *Social Criticism in Popular Religious Literature in the Sixteenth Century* (New York 1944), Chap. III.

Thomas Lever, some of whose printed sermons parallel Crowley's tracts, and John Bradford, the future martyr, who was perhaps the most brilliant of the younger clerics. Of these figures, only Lever was to be found among the clerics of Elizabeth's church.

Still another portion of Crowley's Edwardian writing is concerned with attacking Roman Catholic doctrine, an activity which evidently attracted him at all periods of his life. Two works of this sort are attributed to the year 1548. *The confutation of the xiii articles whereunto Nicolas Shaxton subscribed* (STC 6083) is a detailed refutation of the sermon preached, by way of recantation, at Anne Askew's burning, by the apostate Protestant bishop. *The confutation of the mishapen answer to the ballade called the abuse of the blessed sacrament* (STC 6082) debates transubstantiation with the lay Roman Catholic writer, Miles Hogarde, whose 'ballade' now survives only in Crowley's extensive quotations.

3

Of Crowley's activities in England after his ordination by Ridley in the autumn of 1551 there is no record, and of his exile years under Mary there is very little known. Though he presumably formed or reinforced ties with other exiles who were later to be termed 'puritans' in Elizabeth's church, the surviving references suggest that he played no important role in exile activities. He first appears in Frankfurt in the fall of 1555 as a 'student', appears again on a tax list in 1556, and in June 1557 is recorded as living in very crowded quarters with his wife and child.[38] On three occasions during 1557 his signature appears among a number of others endorsing 'the new discipline' which was aimed at limiting the pastoral authority of Robert Horne over the English congregation in Frankfurt.[39]

Back in England by early 1559 with a family to support, he evidently turned his ties with the printing trade to good account. By April 5 he had in print his revision of *An epitome of chronicles . . . continued to the reigne of Quene Elizabeth* (STC 15217.5). This world history, originally produced by Thomas Lanquet, had been previously updated to Edward's reign by Thomas Cooper, a Magdalen College contemporary of Crowley's who as Bishop of Winchester in the 1580s was to write against the Marprelate tracts. Cooper at this time regarded the Lanquet *Cronicle* as his own property and quickly brought out an update of his own, sharply attacking Crowley's version in a foreword.[40] The differences between the two accounts of Edward's and Mary's reigns shed light on Crowley's attitudes. Protector Somerset appears more favourably in Crowley's

[38] C.H. Garrett, *The Marian Exiles* (Cambridge 1938), p. 138.
[39] *The troubles begonne at Frankfort*, Edward Arber, ed. (London, 1905), pp. 154, 202, 209.
[40] *Coopers chronicle*, 1560 (STC 15218), sig. A 1ᵛ.

Woodcut from Robert Crowley's *Confutation of xiii articles* (1548) aimed at the apostate Protestant bishop, Nicholas Shaxton, here shown preaching at the burning of Anne Askew in 1546. The woodcut appears again in the 1563 edition of Foxe's *Actes and Monuments* (p. 666) and in subsequent editions.

account, as is not surprising, since his *Pleasure and Pain* had been dedicated to the wife of Sir Rafe Fane, one of Somerset's closest adherents. The contrast in treatment of the Marian years, however, is very sharp. Cooper, more in accord with earlier parts of the *Cronicle*, devotes much attention to continental events and on the English scene deals only with important figures. Crowley's account focuses almost entirely on England and gives much space to the burning of Protestants from all levels of society – a not insignificant preview of the Marian sections of John Foxe's 1563 classic, since it mentions over 200 martyrs by surname and gives circumstantial detail about most of them. Some of this emphasis on the Marian martyrs is attributable to the publishing trade's special interest in the subject during early 1559,[41] but it is also attributable to Crowley's probably sharing with his friend Foxe the desire to provide Protestant substitutes for Roman Catholic saints.

As cleric, Crowley also seems to have turned his talents and his connections to good account. He was much in demand as a popular preacher: the diarist Henry Machyn mentions eight sermons of his during the years 1559-63, including three from the prestigious pulpit of Paul's Cross.[42] He was shortly installed in the important London living of St. Giles Cripplegate, and his earlier strictures against clerical pluralism did not inhibit him from holding various other livings simultaneously.[43] During the early years of Elizabeth's reign he was certainly to be counted one of the church's leading radicals. In a list of 28 names presented to the future Earl of Leicester sometime between 1561 and 1564 as 'godly preachers who have forsaken Antichrist and all his Romish rags,' Crowley appears along with Miles Coverdale, William Whittingham, Lawrence Humphrey, Thomas Sampson, John Foxe, Thomas Lever and Anthony Gilby.[44]

4

As the Puritans' conflict with the hierarchy sharpened on the issue of ecclesiastical vestments, Crowley became devoted to a new cause. When stricter rules were laid down for the clergy's adherence to the traditional modes of dress, his name appears on an appeal in March 1565 to the Ecclesiastical Commissioners for exemption from the new regulations,

[41] Two relatively minor printers were fined in the first half of 1559 for publishing on the burnings without a license, *A Transcript of the Register of the Company of Stationers of London, 1554-1650*, Edward Arber, ed., 5 vols. (London and Birmingham 1875-94), I, pp. 101.

[42] *Diary*, J.G. Nichols, ed. (London 1848), pp. 215, 229, 269-70, 278, 291, 295-96, 311.

[43] The DNB lists a number of these.

[44] Patrick Collinson, *The Elizabethan Puritan Movement* (London 1967), p. 48, citing Magdalene College, Cambridge, Pepysian MS. 'Papers of State', II, p. 701.

and shortly before Easter of 1566 he led about a third of London's beneficed clergy in a confrontation with Archbishop Parker on the issue. Crowley's statement of their position, *A briefe discourse against the outwarde apparell and ministering garments of the popishe church*, has been characterized by Patrick Collinson as 'the earliest puritan manifesto.'[45]

The London confrontation was only part of the larger conflict, but Parker agreed with Bishop Cox of Ely that 'if London were reformed, all the realm would soon follow.'[46] It was Parker, rather than Bishop Grindal of London, who took the lead in the Easter-time encounters, and his letters to Sir William Cecil give the best single picture of them. Parker planned his moves with some care, conscious of the varied difficulties in his position. He was under orders from the Queen to enforce conformity, yet denied her public support and, as he admitted in the same letter to Cecil, those rejecting the decreed dress included some of the best ministers in London. Without them, it would be almost impossible to provide normal Easter services. Something over 100 parish ministers were summoned to a meeting on March 26 at Lambeth Palace, where they were read the orders on clerical apparel – simultaneously modelled, according to one account, by Robert Cole, the rector of St. Mary-le-Bow, who had originally objected to the prescribed garments but later conformed.[47] With no discussion permitted, the ministers were given the choice of either signing a promise to conform or being suspended from their livings for three months with formal deprivation to follow if they had still not conformed. Parker anticipated that 'many will forsake their livings and live at printing [an evident reference to Crowley], teaching children, or otherwise as they can.' In the event, 37 did refuse to sign, but Parker was more successful than he anticipated at getting Easter-time services provided by his own chaplains and other substitutes, though there was sporadic violence in some parishes over a period of weeks.[48]

The most dramatic clash occurred on April 2, when Crowley, a deputy alderman of Cripplegate ward and other like-minded laymen physically prevented access to St. Giles Cripplegate by choir-boys in surplices who were seeking to participate in a funeral service there. The Lord Mayor complained about the disturbance to Parker, who summoned Crowley before him two days later. Crowley defended his

[45] *Ibid.*, pp. 74, 77.

[46] Parker, *Correspondence*, J. Bruce and T.T. Perowne, eds, (Cambridge 1853), p. 270, writing to Cecil on March 26. For the vestiarian controversy as a whole see Collinson, *op. cit.*, pp. 71-97, and M.M. Knappen, *Tudor Puritanism* (Chicago 1965), pp. 187-216.

[47] John Strype, *Grindal* (Oxford 1821), pp. 144-45. Cole, incidentally, had a separatist past, as a onetime Freewiller; see chapter 3, appendix above.

[48] *Correspondence*, pp. 268, 277-79; see also John Stow, *Memoranda*, printed in *Three 15th Century Chronicles*, J. Gairdner, ed. (London 1880), pp. 138-40.

action as arising from his responsibilities as pastor of St. Giles, from which post, he maintained, he could be removed only 'by order of law.' He would 'be committed to prison' rather than 'suffer such a wolf [i.e., the pope's influence] to come to his flock.' Parker ignored this direct challenge and simply put Crowley under house arrest and bound over the deputy alderman to keep the peace.[49] The conflict then became a slower one of attrition, with each side arguing its case in the press.

Crowley's *Discourse against the outwarde apparell* makes clear at the outset that he is speaking for a group of ministers (each of whom is said in John Stow's *Memoranda* to have given his 'advyce in writinge') but the work is in Crowley's controversial vein and has a verse introduction reminiscent of his earlier tracts in doggerel. Crowley, well aware of the hierarchy's contention that ecclesiastical vestments are 'indifferent' matters, not ordained by Scripture but left by God for the church to decide, takes his stand rather on St. Paul's general admonition to follow courses 'edifying' to Christ's church, and argues from this that the present English church must therefore remove 'the popishe apparell' and other vestiges of superstition and idolatry. Otherwise, 'the simple Christian' will be discouraged and left uncertain of what Protestantism stands for, while the 'papists' of the old regime, now only half converted, will be encouraged to think they need go no further. Recognizing that an adamant stand on clerical garb might put the ministers in defiance of a royal command, Crowley insists that they would not thereby 'give example of disobedience' because 'we do humblye submit our selves to suffer . . . whatsoever punishments man's lawes do appoint.'[50] The tract concludes with a prayer.

Crowley's work was answered, either by Parker's pen or at his instigation, with *A brief examination for the tyme of a certaine declaration lately put in print in the name of certaine ministers of London* (STC 10387). This stated the hierarchy's case in some detail and printed statements by Martin Bucer and Peter Martyr which had helped persuade a reluctant John Hooper to wear the appointed vestments in Edward's reign. A lengthy point-by-point reply followed in *An answere for the tyme to the examination put in print without the authors name, pretending to mayntayn the apparell prescribed* (STC 10388), itself anonymous but readily attributable to Crowley. Three much shorter tracts also appeared, two of them by supporters of the boycott stationed outside of London, William Whittingham, and Anthony Gilby. These did not argue the case in such detail but exhorted the brethren to stand firm in this time of trial, citing

[49] *Correspondence*, pp. 275-79; see also J.J. Baddeley, *The Aldermen of Cripplegate Ward, 1276-1900* (London 1900), pp. 110-11.

[50] *Discourse against the outwarde apparell*, 1566 (STC 6081), sig. B 3[r].

various Biblical characters who had similarly stood firm.[51] In London, at least, the conflict was recognized as a test of clerical endurance.

Despite his defiant words, Crowley, like nearly all the other beneficed London clergy, eventually conformed. Parker succeeded with his plan of applying gradual economic pressure, separating the dissidents by committing them to the custody of various bishops in the country, and publishing various communications indicating that English clergy were being more rigid on the vestments issue than the eminent Swiss divines whom they looked to as mentors. (Particularly effective was the letter Bishop Grindal received from Henry Bullinger and quickly published, since Bullinger had originally been written to for support by Lawrence Humphrey and Thomas Sampson, the chief Oxford opponents of the prescribed vestments.)[52] Crowley's own course cannot be plotted with any precision, but it ended with him re-established as vicar of St. Giles Cripplegate some years later and eventually buried with honour in its chancel. He was in the Bishop of Ely's custody apparently from June of 1566 till sometime after October 27, when the Privy Council asked Parker (possibly at his own suggestion, possibly after a nudge from someone at court) to relieve the Bishop of Ely of this duty and make some other arrangement (unspecified) about Crowley.[53] Three years later in 1569 he is described as living in retirement in Southwark and engaged in writing, 'having more leisure by Gods providence now than at any time since his return out of Germany.'[54]

5

Publishing earlier works and writing new ones indeed seem to have been Crowley's chief occupation during these years. The first of them, a work of detailed theological controversy, identifies Crowley on the title-page as vicar of St. Giles Cripplegate and carries the date of October 14, 1566 but announces in its preface 'To the Reader' that it was actually finished in the previous March. One of the two editions bearing the same date shows Crowley attempting to draw on court connections with an additional preface dedicating the work to Lady Anne Heneage. Lady Anne was a daughter of Sir Nicholas Poyntz, in whose household Crowley had once been tutor, and was now the wife of Sir Thomas

---

[51] The three tracts are listed by the *STC* as *To my faythfull brethren now afflycted*, (STC 10089); *To my lovynge brethren that is troublyd* (STC 10090); *To the reader. To my faythfull brethren we give thanks to God for your constancie* (STC 10091). Also listed are a second 1566 edition of Crowley's *Discourse against the outwarde apparell* (STC 6079), possibly printed in Emden, and a London edition of 1578 (STC 6080).

[52] *Zurich Letters*, H. Robinson, ed. (Cambridge 1846), I, pp. 214-25, 253-55.

[53] Parker, *Correspondence*, p. 285; *A.P.C.*, VII, p. 215.

[34] Strype, *Annals of the Reformation* (Oxford 1824), I, ii, p. 303.

Heneage, vice-chamberlain of the court and a favourite of the Queen's. The tract itself, *An apologie or defence of those English writers & preachers which Cerberus . . . chargeth with false doctrine* (STC 6076-6077), was well designed to exhibit Crowley's own orthodoxy. Its principal target was the radical Protestant, John Champneys, who in Edward VI's reign had been forced to recant his publication, *The harvest is at hand*, and now stood accused of unsoundness on predestination, a subject which was also traditionally in dispute between Protestants and Roman Catholics.

The following year Crowley put into print his 1546 work, *The opening of the wordes of the prophet Joell*, followed in 1569 by *A setting open of the subtyle sophistrie of T. Watson* (STC 6093). The latter undertakes a detailed refutation of one of the leading theologians of Mary's reign, who had expounded the Roman Catholic doctrine of the Eucharist in two sermons before the Queen in early 1554, and had printed the sermons to help the lower clergy in doctrinal disputes with Protestants. Anti-Catholic controversy such as this was to occupy an increasing amount of Crowley's attention during the later years of his life, not only in printed tracts (of which he issued four in the 1580s), but also orally as one of the church representatives appointed to debate Roman Catholic clerics in their prisons.[55]

By the 1570s Crowley was clearly back in the mainstream of London's church and civic life. In September 1574 he delivered the sermon at the Guildhall on the occasion of the election of the new Lord Mayor – the only one of his sermons to survive in print. In 1575 he served on a commission to seek relief for those imprisoned for debt in London prisons.[56] In 1578 came his admission to the Stationers Company, which in due course invited him to give one of its election sermons and which voted his widow a small pension. A deposition in legal proceedings at the time shows him giving spiritual comfort at the deathbed of a former Lord Mayor, along with John Foxe and Dean Nowell of St. Pauls.[57] A more striking tribute came in the Privy Council's letter of March 13, 1579 to the Bishop of London, asking him to get Foxe, Crowley and a third man to reason with three persons being sent up by the Bishop of Gloucester because they 'will not conform them

[55] *An answer to six reasons that T. Pownde requiers*, 1581 (STC 6075); *A briefe discourse concerning those foure usuall notes whereby Christes catholique church is knowne*, 1581 (STC 6081); *Fryar John Frauncis of Nigeon in France*, 1586 (STC 6091); *A deliberate answere made to a rash offer*, 1588 (STC 6084). On his oral disputations, see Strype, *Parker* (Oxford 1821), I. p. 436; *Aylmer* (Oxford 1821), pp. 30-31; *Whitgift* (Oxford 1822), I, p. 198.

[56] Crowley, *A sermon made in the chapel at the Gylde Hall*, 1575 (STC 6092). For his commission post see Eccles, 'William Wager and His Plays', *English Language Notes*, Vol. 18, p. 259, citing *Calendar of Patent Rolls, 1572-1575* (London 1973), p. 566.

[57] Eccles, *op. cit.*, p. 27, and William H. Ingram, *A London Life in the Brazen Age: Francis Langley, 1548-1603* (Cambridge, Mass. 1978), pp. 32-34, citing PRO C. 24/134/16.

selves to orders in Religion but kepe conventicles aparte.'[58] A similar indication of how markedly Crowley's standing with the church establishment changed after 1566 is found in the last year of his life when his name appears on a list of eight clerics, any one of whom was authorized by the Archbishop of Canterbury to license books for printing.[59]

Within the printing trade itself Crowley seems to have had a continuing reputation as a skilled hand at contributing a useful preface or refurbishing an old text. The latter talent is well illustrated in his 1582 updating of Francis Seager's *The schoole of vertue and booke of good nourture for children*, published originally about 1550 and reissued at intervals thereafter as a set of verse admonitions about proper behaviour at table, in school and so on. The 1582 edition not only added various prayers and table-graces by Crowley but also opened the text with a 13-line acrostic of his name. This last feature was to prove remarkably permanent through some half a dozen subsequent editions; one in 1677 added prayers for 'King Charles' but still retained the acrostic of Crowley's name.[60]

Two or three of Crowley's prefaces and endorsements are instructive on his attitudes in the 1570s and 1580s. His preface to Richard Rice's *An invective against vices, c.* 1575 (STC 20973), is in the vein conventionally associated with Puritanism – admonitions to follow the spirit and reject the promptings of the flesh, gambling being particularly mentioned. The 1579 pamphlet, *Wharton's dream* (STC 25295), to which Crowley contributed simply an endorsement along with John Foxe and some half a dozen others, is a denunciation of 'userers, extortioners, leasemongers and such others,' and by its verse form as well as its content is reminiscent of some of Crowley's Edwardian writings. A third and more sophisticated work, Thomas Lovell's *A dialogue between custom and veritie concerning the use and abuse of dancing and minstrelsie*, is dedicated to Crowley and has a short preface by him. The tract illustrates how Protestant clerics of the last decades of the century, in contrast to John Bale and others of Crowley's youth, had become suspicious of the popular arts. Lovell, though writing the *Dialogue* itself in verse, speaks in his prose preface of the whole realm being 'infected' with a 'poysonable plague of the devilish abuse of daunsing and disordered ministrelsie,' announces that 'they which pollute the holy Saboth shall surely dye,' and

[58] *A.P.C.*, XI, p. 74.
[59] The list, issued only ten days before Crowley's death, also contains clerics whose licensing authority is more limited than his. W.W. Greg and E. Boswell, eds., *Records of the Court of the Stationers' Company, 1576-1602* (London 1930), pp. 28-29.
[60] The 1951 *Short-Title Catalogue of Books Printed in English, 1641-1700*, lists no edition later than *c.* 1660 (S-2171), but the 1677 edition is to be found in the British Library (C 118. a1).

seeks to associate Crowley with his position, as 'one for his olde age beeing found in the way of rightenousnes.'[61] Crowley, in a rather bland two pages, pays tribute to Lovell's learning and orthodoxy and his 'suppressing (yea, rather rooting out) of vice and advancing of vertue,' but keeps his distance to some degree and pays indirect tribute to his own writing past by commending Lovell for writing in verse 'that thereby the mindes of wanton persons might be moved to hear that which otherwise they would never regard.'[62]

The record on the last few years of Crowley's life contains two very human touches. One of these appears in Crowley's 1586 anti-Catholic pamphlet, *Fryer John Frauncis of Nigeon in France*. The friar in question is a young English convert to Rome, originally named Samuel Degnam, the son of a onetime maid servant of Crowley's whose education Crowley had in large part paid for. The new friar has recently written at length to his mother and father, proudly recounting his adventures with the secret Roman Catholic network which had smuggled him out of London to safe houses in Sussex and Hampshire and, after a few weeks, to France. He then describes his life in English religious communities on the continent, and finally undertakes by argument to win his parents over to his new faith. Crowley's strong personal emotions get in the way of the ordered controversial writing to be found in his other anti-Catholic tracts, but the outbursts of indignation at times bring him closer to what may be his essential attitudes. He of course makes much of the new friar's lack of due love and respect for his parents, derides the superstitious veneration of relics in which John Frauncis is now involved, and denounces his proving false to his earlier education. But much of Crowley's outrage is on nationalistic grounds: he taxes the young man with disobedience to his prince and, in a prefatory letter addressed to the 'gentlemen' with 'Romysh hartes' who arranged the escape, he tells them that the friar is now attached to 'a sworne enemy to the Crowne and Commonwealth of this, his and your native Country.'[63]

A final glimpse of Crowley appears in his will, made the day before his death on June 18, 1588 and reflecting in some of its provisions both his economic status and his fondness for his professional library. Two charitable bequests are made contingent on there being more than 120 pounds remaining for his wife after all debts have been paid, and provisions are made for the library to be appraised and his successor at St. Giles (who was to be Launcelot Andrewes) given 40 days to purchase it from the executors.[64]

---

[61] *Dialogue between cutsom and veritie*, 1581 (STC 16860), sigs. A 7ʳ, A 3ᵛ, B 1ʳ.
[62] *Ibid.*, B 3ʳ.
[63] *Fryar John Frauncis*, sig. ★2ᵛ.
[64] The will, transcribed in Illston, *op. cit.*, Appendix I, asks the dean and canons of St. Paul's and the Stationers' Company each to appoint an appraiser of the library, but the outcome is unknown.

6

What is to be said in review of Crowley's career? Certainly he lived a varied life, having an imagination attracted to new approaches and a degree of energy which encouraged him to try them out. He cherished his own notions as to where the church's emphases should fall. Not till his final decades was he really at peace with the establishment, and by then he probably seemed a turncoat to some of his old associates in the vestiarian controversy. He would himself perhaps have described his conduct in that affair as a committed churchman's eventual realization that half a loaf was better than no bread. Crowley was articulate on a wide range of subjects – but on this, as on his holding a plurality of church livings, he has left no written apologia. In various respects (as, for example, his efforts to use whatever court connections fortune has given him) he seems little different from his contemporaries. In his career as a whole there is more continuity than is evident at first glance.

One persistent strand is the social gospel of his Edwardian days, when he tried so hard to arouse England's conscience about the treatment of the poor. In Elizabeth's reign he did not return to this effort in his former wholesale way, but neither did he repudiate it. In 1567 he published *The opening of the wordes of the prophet Joell* for the first time and in 1573 republished his *One and thyrtye epigrammes* under a slightly altered title.[65] Avarice, which in his Edwardian tracts sometimes appears as the main source of human ills, came in for special denunciation in the Guildhall sermon printed in 1575 and in his endorsing of John Wharton's pamphlet against usury in the same year. He also engaged in smaller social welfare efforts like that for ameliorating the plight of imprisoned debtors.

A second preoccupation of Crowley's Edwardian career, however, is scarcely to be found in his Elizabethan years. This is the concern for the fourteenth-century foundations of English Protestantism which is seen mainly in his publishing activities. He, like other Elizabethan Protestants, remained sensitive to Roman Catholic jibes about the existence of their church before Luther – as suggested by the reprinting of Crowley's edition of *Piers Plowman* once again in 1561. But from 1563 onwards John Foxe's widely circulated *Actes and Monuments* provided far more comprehensive assurance for most Elizabethans about the deep roots of English Protestantism. Though the Martin Marprelate controversy in 1589 occasioned the reprinting of one of the Edwardian Piers tracts, and Elizabethan editions of Chaucer's works continued to include the *Plowman's Tale*, the poem of *Piers Plowman* was not reprinted

[65] *33 epigrams verye notably describing the abuses of our tyme*, J. Awdely, 1573 (STC 6088.7).

again till the nineteenth century.[66]

Another strong characteristic in Crowley, accounting in part for his eventually conforming on ecclesiastical dress, was his respect for law and orderly procedures. His earliest publication, *An Informacion and petition*, angry though it is against the exploiters of the poor, calls for redress only through man's legal processes and the fear of God's law. *The way to wealth*, a year or two later, suggests that those who rebelled with Ket in Norfolk had been oppressed beyond endurance, but insists that it does not condone their taking the law into their own hands. Even more indicative is Crowley's behaviour in the vestiarian conflict. His refusal to admit the surpliced choir-boys to St. Giles Cripplegate he justified by his responsibility for the spiritual care of a congregation which had been legally entrusted to him. In the *Discourse against the outwarde apparrell*, as noted earlier, he argues that, though conscience may at some point compel the clergy to ignore a royal command, this will not mean disloyalty to the monarch, since they stand ready to accept the penalty involved.

At no point in his conflict with the hierarchy does Crowley seem to have been tempted, like Miles Coverdale before him, to go preach in separatist meetings in the City,[67] or, like Robert Browne later on, to seek reformation-without-tarrying by means of a separatist congregation of his own. His Guildhall sermon cites religious separatism as one of the things which would automatically rule out a candidate for Lord Mayor. A letter by Sir William More addressed a few years later to 'Mr Crowley' reinforces the implication in the Privy Council's letter of March 13, 1579, that he had acquired a certain reputation for coping effectively with separatists. Sir William, who in his long career as Surrey magistrate and member of Parliament was an assiduous defender of the Church of England against both Roman Catholics and sectaries, had been named by the Privy Council as one of two laymen in the diocese of Winchester to assist the Bishop in enforcing the royal proclamation of October 3, 1580, against the Family of Love. From More's letter to Crowley it would appear that Crowley had been one of the clerics called for by the procedure to interrogate suspected Familists, and that he had given a clean bill of health to one Allen. Writing as to a sympathetic correspondent, More explains why he believes both Crowley and the

---

[66] *O read me, for I am of great antiquitie, I plaine Piers . . . I am the gransier of Martin mareprelitte*, 1589? (STC 19903a.5). Besides its retention in the 1561, 1598 and 1602 editions of Chaucer's works (STC 5075, 5077, 5080), the *Plowman's Tale* was reprinted separately a few years into the seventeenth century with a virulently anti-Catholic title page: *The plough-mans tale, shewing by the doctrine and lives of the Romish clergie that the Pope is anti-christ and they his ministers. Written by Sir Geffrey Chaucer, knight . . .* 1606 (STC 1501).

[67] See H. Gareth Owen, 'A Nursery of Elizabethan Non-conformity', *J.E.H.*, XVII (1966), pp. 65-76.

Bishop were deceived in this case, citing Allen's long record as an important Familist leader and More's own recent experience in catching Allen with Familist books in his possession.[68] Crowley does indeed seem to have been outwitted by Allen, but his reputation as a firm anti-separatist continued and even apparently outlived him, for 18 years after his death his name was invoked for support by an ex-separatist in denouncing those who follow 'fantasticall preachers' instead of the ancient fathers of the church.[69]

Another strain in Crowley is English nationalism. This grew stronger as he grew older; formal efforts against Roman apologists bulk larger in his activities in the years after the 1570 papal bull dethroning Elizabeth and the rising concern over the Jesuit missionary priests. There are times, indeed, when Crowley almost identifies England and Protestantism in his denunciation of the young Friar John Frauncis who has forsaken both. But the strain is there in his earliest publication also, when Parliament is reminded that the exploited poor are both fellow Christians and fellow countrymen. His publication of *Piers Plowman* and of the Prologue to the Wycliffite Bible shows him eager, like his friend Foxe, to set forth the English origins of the Reformation. There is also the over-concentration on recent English events in his updating of Lanquet's world history. A touch of nationalism may even be present in his pronounced anti-separatist attitude, for the Tudor separatist tended to be a man who ignored civic commitments to concentrate on his individual spiritual problems.

At all points in his life, from his own conversion on, Crowley saw Roman Catholic doctrine and modes of worship as things which must be strongly controverted, and this strain in him goes far to explain the transition from his earlier concern for the condition of England's poor to his no less ardent concern later about the vestments of the English clergy. The Edwardian poor, as he saw them, suffered not only from corrupt and rapacious landlords but also from corrupt and rapacious priests, the latter not merely cheating on material things like funeral charges but providing superstitious ceremonies instead of spiritual guidance. A new and different clergy – a preaching clergy – was needed, particularly for 'the simple Christian' unable to read the Scriptures for himself. How the new clergy was perceived by the great mass of Englishmen was of crucial importance, and for many an Englishman the clergy's 'outwarde

[68] *A.P.C.*, XII, pp. 232-33, 250, 317-18; Folger Library MS. L. b. 51. More's letter is dated only 26 September; internal evidence limits the year to one between 1576 and 1583; the Privy Council correspondence indicates 1581 to be the most likely. The Council's action of January 25, 1581, in commending to the Bishop of Winchester John Knewstub, an acknowledged specialist on Familism, further supports More's complaint that Allen had managed to deceive Crowley.

[69] Peter Fairlambe, *The recantation of a Brownist or a reformed Puritan*, 1606 (STC 10668), B 2 ᵛ.

apparell' was one of the main things he had to go by. If opposing Roman Catholic faith and practice was important, then insulating English churches from Roman influence was likewise important. 'Keeping the wolf from his flock' was no casual metaphor for Crowley.

On the need for purging the English church of the physical appurtenances of Roman Catholicism Crowley's position was indeed little different from that of the more influential John Foxe. Foxe, in the long tribute to Edward VI which in the 1570 and subsequent editions of *Actes and Monuments* precedes his account of the reign, praises him for following the example of the reforming boy-king Josiah in ancient Judah, who 'plucked down the hill altars, cut down the groves, and destroyed all monuments of idolatry in the temple.' In the accompanying woodcut the two lower scenes show King Edward handing the Bible to the prelates, and a church interior with a minister preaching and a communion table situated in the body of the church. But the whole upper part of the cut is devoted to images being pulled down and burned and to a number of 'papists' leaving England with their 'trinkets' and elaborate attire for a ship labelled 'the Romish church.'[70]

To the twentieth-century eye, the swing from espousing the social gospel to espousing modified freedom of dress for Protestant clergymen still seems a considerable one – so considerable that it is tempting to attribute it mainly to personal idiosyncrasy in Crowley. But to do this one must ignore the closely parallel case of Thomas Lever, who printed his social gospel sermons in both 1550 and 1572,[71] and who likewise stood with Crowley in the vestiarian controversy; one must also ignore the fact that the two men were by no means alone in their efforts, either in the late 1540s or in the mid-1560s. The weight of evidence suggests rather that some wider change occurred between the two eras in what deeply stirred a Protestant conscience.

[70] See frontispiece and n. 2 above.

[71] *A fruitfull sermon made in Poules churche*, 1550 (STC 15543); *A sermon preached before the Kynges Majestie*, 1550 (STC 15547); *A sermon preached at Pauls Cross*, 1550 (STC 15546); *Three fruitful sermons made by T. Lever [in] 1550. Now newlie perused*, 1572 (STC 15551).

Chapter 9

Sidelights on Foxe's Account of the
Marian Martyrs

1

No single characteristic of John Foxes's *Actes and Monuments* can adequately account for its impact on his own generation and those immediately following, when it was the normal companion of the Bible in private homes, in cathedrals and in parish churches. Professor Collinson has recently shown how the work gave Englishmen a conspectus of their whole religious history, so written as to brush aside many minor caveats,[1] while mention has been made earlier in this volume of Foxe's providing Protestants with an answer to the Roman Catholic taunt, 'Where was your church before Luther?'. The present discussion, focusing on two aspects of *Actes and Monuments'* final books (X, XI and XII), suggests still another reason for its contemporary success.

Exaggerating somewhat, one might say that Foxe anticipates twentieth-century historical methods to further a characteristically sixteenth-century end. In his use of archival material and eye-witness accounts, at least, he resembles the modern historian more than most Tudor chroniclers. J.F. Mozley has noted various examples of Foxe's careful checking of his contemporary sources and of his willingness to make later additions in the light of new evidence.[2] In the long sections on Mary's reign Foxe has evidently realized the persuasive force exerted by a mass of factual detail which remained largely subject to independent checking, since the events had occurred during the lifetimes of many of his readers. This concern for meticulous accuracy about the recent martyrs is seen in the time he took in preparing the work – markedly longer than Foxe himself had originally expected or the time thought necessary by Thomas Brice and Robert Crowley, two other men who

[1] Patrick Collinson, 'Truth and Legend: the Veracity of John Foxe's Book of Martyrs,' *Clio's Mirror: Historiography in Britain and the Netherlands*, A.G. Duke and C.A. Tamse, eds. (Zutphen 1985), pp. 31 ff.

[2] J.F. Mozley, *John Foxe and His Book* (London 1940), p. 159. *Actes and Monuments*, first appearing in March 1563, was revised by Foxe in the other editions (1570, 1576 and 1583) appearing in his lifetime.

wrote in praise of the Marian martyrs with somewhat different aims in view.

A second aspect of this part of *Actes and Monuments*, however, shows Foxe in a very different light. On the narrow subject of religious separatists, he no longer appears as an author eager to acquire new information, check it carefully and set it forth fully. Instead, he appears as at best reticent about separatists and sometimes ready to suppress facts.

2

The process whereby the work came to be completed has long been available in its main outlines in Mozley's book on the subject. He has shown how Foxe left England in 1554 with the book as a whole already mapped out in his mind and a substantial part written, but soon realized that the wholesale burnings which started in February 1555 would require a large additional section. It has remained somewhat unclear, however, why this addition should have so greatly postponed the completion of the larger work, since publicizing the story of the current martyrs was naturally of interest to the other Protestant exiles also, and efforts to collect all possible information were to a degree centralized under Edmund Grindal in the English group at Strasbourg.

The surviving letters between Foxe and Grindal on this subject are instructive. Though the first-hand accounts and other documents smuggled out of England were impressive both in nature and quantity, they were still what would now be termed 'raw intelligence' – what Grindal referred to as 'a somewhat rude quantity of matter', providing 'material for constructing a noble edifice', but needing far more extensive treatment than anticipated to present it effectively in context. Writing to Foxe about Foxe's great project in June 1556, he confessed to having thought a year previously

> that before this time we should have had the history of the Martyrs written in our own language, and, if not printed, at least prepared for the press; so that the history might be published nearly at the same time both in English and Latin, the latter being done by your assistance.[3]

Further correspondence explored hopes of speeding up the processing of the intelligence from England and expediting publication, but Grindal, writing a final letter to Foxe on 19 December 1558, as he was hurrying back to England on the news of Mary's death, regretfully concluded:

> As to the history of the Martyrs [i.e., the English version], Sampson and I think it will be best that it should be delayed for a time, until we can procure from England more certain and more copious intelligence.[4]

[3] Edmund Grindal, *Remains*, W. Nicholson, ed. (Cambridge 1843), p. 226. A later letter by Foxe, *ibid.*, p. 231, refers to 'a great farrago of these papers.'
[4] *Ibid.*, pp. 237-38.

He promised to send what he could of this new information to Foxe, who was remaining in Basel to complete the Latin version. It is significant, however, that this work, *Rerum in Ecclesia gestarum, quae postremis et particulosis his temporibus evenerunt*, published with the dedication date of 1 September 1559, attempted no connected account of persecutions in England after Cranmer's burning in March 1556, but merely presented a list of some 151 persons who died at various times and places in the remainder of Mary's reign.

Others were less cautious than Grindal and Foxe about early publication. Some version of the detailed data published by Foxe in September 1559 may even have been circulating in England by mid-1556, for the Roman Catholic propagandist, Miles Hogarde, who is generally reliable in his references to opponents' pamphlets, mentions 'your boke of your stinking martyrs' as one of the ten Protestant tracts which he attacks in the second edition of *The displaying of the Protestantes*. Five of the ten works are definitely identifiable from copies still extant; the other four are probably identifiable as either surviving works or those whose existence is attested by other sources also.[5] In any event, during the early months of Elizabeth's reign the Marian burnings were evidently perceived in the English book trade as a rather lucrative topic – one even producing a degree of competitive ill feeling. Brice's *Compendious register in metre*, which was published sometime in the first half of 1559,[6] consists of some 78 six-line stanzas like the following, arranged chronologically with month and day marginally noted and each stanza having an almost invariable final line:

> When worthy Wattes, with constant cry,
> Continued in the flaming fire;
> When Simon, Hawkes, and John Ardlie
> Did taste the tyrant's raging ire;
> When Chamberlaine was put to death;
> We wished for our Elizabeth.

A list of fines levied over a year's time by the Stationers' Company for various infractions of its rules records Brice's printer, Rychard Adams, as fined five shillings for 'pryntinge *The Regester of all that ware burned*' without a licence. Another printer, Owen Rogers, was also fined for

---

[5] *The displaying of the Protestantes*, July 1556 (STC 13558), fol. 118 ᵛ. I am indebted for the Hogarde reference to Edward J. Baskerville, who allowed me to consult a still unpublished addition to his *A Chronological Bibliography of Propaganda and Polemic Published in English between 1553 and 1558* (Philadelphia 1979).

[6] Thomas Brice, *A compendious register in metre conteining the names and sufferings of the membres of Jesus Christ* (STC 3726). It is dedicated to the Marquess of Northampton, whose title was not restored till 13 January 1559; the action taken against its printer by the Stationers' Company (see n. 7 below) is recorded on a list running from 10 July 1558 to 10 July 1559.

printing a book, now lost, which was likewise identified only as '*The Regester of all them that were burned*'.[7]

The roll of Marian martyrs was somewhat differently presented in Robert Crowley's edition, dated 5 April 1559, of the *Epitome of cronicles*, which Thomas Lanquet had carried from the beginning of the world to the birth of Christ and Thomas Cooper through the early years of Edward VI's reign,[8] and which Crowley now brought down to Elizabeth's accession. But where Crowley's predecessors had paid considerable attention to Europe-wide affairs, his own focus was almost entirely on English events and particularly on the burning of Protestants in Mary's reign. A fairly typical Crowley item reads:

> The xxii of December [1557] were burned in Smithfield John Rowghe, preacher of the congregation of Christ, which in those daingerous dayes had kept themselves in secret . . . [and also] one Margaret Jeames.[9]

The commercial jealousy with which the work was regarded appears in the short preface to a further continuation of this chronicle published in 1560 by Thomas Cooper, who then retitled it *Coopers Chronicle*.[10] The preface records Cooper's anger that

> certain persons, for lukers sake, contrarie to honestye, had caused my chronicle to be prynted without my knowledge . . . Wherein as I sawe some thynges of myne left out, and many thynges of others annexed, so did I finde almost five hundred faultes and errours eyther of the prynter or eles of hym that undertook the correctyon.

He does not specify what any of the changes in text or alleged errors are, but in his own treatment of Mary's reign he restores much of the emphasis on Europe-wide political affairs and omits practically all the burnings except those of prominent clerics. There is a concluding jab at the 'certayne persons utterly unlearned' who are responsible for the erring publication, but only the printers are attacked by name – perhaps because Cooper, who was later to become bishop of Winchester and figure in the Martin Marprelate controversy, had been a fellow member of Magdalen College, Oxford, with Crowley around 1540.

The interest here, however, is in comparing the way the Marian martyrs are presented in both these 1559 publications with Foxe's presentation later. Both Brice and Crowley went immediately to press with the information then available and their books include few details, whereas Foxe prints or otherwise uses official documents about the martyrs in scores of cases and occasionally mentions this practice

[7] *Transcript of the Registers of the Company of Stationers, 1554-1640*, E. Arber., ed., 5 vols. (London and Birmingham 1875-94), I, p. 101.

[8] T. Lanquest, *Epitome of cronicles*, T. Cooper, ed., 1549 (STC 15217).

[9] *Epitome of cronicles*, R. Crowley, ed., 1559 (STC 15217.5), fol. 308.

[10] T. Cooper, *Coopers Chronicle*, 1560 (STC 15518).

explicitly.[11] Even when such documentation is lacking, the amount of circumstantial detail can make his version the more convincing on a point where he differs from Brice or Crowley. The further information he has collected about the burning of the minister John Rough, for example, makes it evident that Crowley, in mentioning the woman burned with Rough, has substituted her husband's Christian name for her surname of Mearing.[12]

A more extensive comparison of Foxe's account of the martyrs with that of the other two writers can be derived from the Index of Martyrs in the nineteenth-century Pratt edition, which is based on Foxe's last revision of the *Actes and Monuments* in 1583. In this, the Marian martyrs total some 287, whereas Brice lists some 235 by surname and Crowley 227 – both of them also mentioning other instances where surnames are not supplied. Neither these numbers, of course, nor those in the paragraph following can be regarded as absolutely firm. The Index of Martyrs, for example, omits entirely the cleric William Tyms, whose trial, burning and prison letters receive considerable attention in the text.[13] But as orders of magnitude, giving a rough measure of Foxe's deeper penetration of the subject, the figures are of some interest.

Rough comparisons are also possible between Foxe and the other two as to their citations of date and place of death for the same person. (Variant spellings of names are, of course, too common in mid-sixteenth-century records to bother with.) Of Brice's 235 persons, a mere 106 – slightly under half – agree with Foxe's data on date and place of death; of Crowley's 227, some 114 – almost exactly half – agree with Foxe's There are 18 instances where Brice and Crowley do not agree with Foxe on these points but do agree with each other. For the final six months of Mary's reign, the data in *Actes and Monuments* are appreciably firmer than those in either Brice or Crowley, but especially so in comparison with Crowley. It may be that Crowley, who was recorded at Frankfurt in the autumn of 1555 and again in June 1557,[14] had only recently returned to England in April 1559 and was working entirely from information previously collected in exile circles. Brice, noted by the *Dictionary of National Biography* as having been engaged early in Mary's reign in smuggling Protestant literature into England, may have had better intelligence connections within the country.

One reasonable inference from these comparisons is support for Grindal's judgement in urging postponement of publishing on the Marian martyrs till the material could be checked against information in England. An allied inference is that results justified Foxe's insistence on

---

[11] *E.g., A. & M.*, III, p. 580; VII, p. 340.
[12] *A. & M.*, VIII, pp. 450-51, 455, 459.
[13] *A. & M.*, VIII, pp. 107-21.
[14] C.H. Garrett, *The Marian Exiles* (Cambridge 1938), p. 138.

subjecting his 'raw intelligence' to many months of checking and painstaking further research among other resources.

3

The fullness of information provided on the Protestant resistance as a whole serves to emphasize Foxe's refusal to mention any separatist role in that resistance. One can read through his whole account without learning that a number of the martyrs and other opponents of Mary's religious policy had played active parts in separatist groups earlier.

It is to be expected that Foxe would want to present the Protestant cause in as favourable a light as possible. Any historian is influenced by the context in which he writes, and Foxe did not pretend to be detached from the events he recorded. His larger concern embraced Protestantism Europe-wide, but his immediate aim was fostering a disciplined Protestant England, its people united like those on a ship in stormy seas. *Actes and Monuments* was the means of communicating this vision to his countrymen; individual parts of the work were to be included or omitted according to their usefulness – on balance – in conveying the larger message. Incidents of physical violence against Roman Catholic priests provide one case in point. We know that Foxe was personally opposed to his contemporaries' readiness to use physical violence to influence religious belief, but he did not shrink from recording Protestant efforts to kill Catholic priests when such incidents were inextricably involved in the subsequent sentencing of Protestant martyrs.[15]

Yet whenever religious separatists are involved, Foxe becomes very evasive. He sets forth at considerable length the beliefs and practices of the Lollards – not, of course, as the separatists of their day but simply as worthy precursors of later English Protestantism. The reader is allowed to assume that their aspirations found complete fulfilment in the national church of Edward VI's reign, though there are official records well into Mary's reign which refer to Lollards as people somehow different from orthodox Protestants.[16] Foxe may, of course, have been ignorant of these and various other references to separatist activity which recent research has brought to light, but the appearance of separatist, or ex-separatist, names among those he celebrates is too extensive for one to believe that he was ignorant of all such cases.

[15] For the 'tumult' of August 1553 at Paul's Cross, where John Bradford saved the life of the Roman Catholic preacher, see *A. & M.*, VII, pp. 44-45; for the martyrdom of William Flower, who had stabbed an officiating priest, VII, pp. 63-76.

[16] A.G. Dickens, *Lollards and Protestants in the Diocese of York* (Oxford 1959), pp. 38, 230-31, 250, notes among other things a prosecution for 'Lollardy' in 1555. See also a generally sophisticated set of visitation articles designed to ferret out covert Protestantism in London, *Interrogatories . . . by the kyng and quenes commissioners . . . inquiring . . . of all such things as now be . . . amysee*, 1558 (STC 10117), Item 14.

Four of those on his register of martyrs had been active previously in the group known as Freewillers. The trial and burning of two of them, Humphrey Middleton and Nicholas Shetterton, at Canterbury in mid-1555 receive considerable attention in Foxe's text, and Shetterton's prison letters are printed at some length.[17] Shetterton's letters from the Protestant cleric, John Bradford, indicate that he had returned to orthodoxy well before his burning, as indeed Middleton and a third Freewiller, George Brodebridge, may have done also; but Thomas Avington, who is listed by Foxe as a martyr at Lewes in June 1555, had signed a Freewiller confession of faith less than six months previously.[18] Foxe, in fact, often avoids referring even to former Freewillers and to close relations with them on the part of orthodox Protestants. Thus the name of Robert Cole, a cleric with a Freewiller past, appears in the 1563 edition of *Actes and Monuments* as one of those assisting in the conduct of the principal London underground congregation, but is removed from the list of pastors in later editions. In the case of another ex-Freewiller, Thomas Upcher, Foxe prints the affectionate and exuberant letter he received from the orthodox Protestant prisoner, John Careless, but suppresses Upcher's name and gives only his initials.[19] Another of the letters of Careless (also surviving in the 'Letters of the Martyrs' collection at Emmanuel College, Cambridge) Foxe has suppressed entirely. This one argues against the doctrine held by John Jacksonne, another signer of the Freewiller confession of January 30, 1555, but addresses him warmly as 'my deare brother' and sends good wishes to 'the reste of youre companye.'[20]

One could cite additional instances where Foxe slides over a possible separatist past in one of his martyrs,[21] but his persistent attitude is already sufficiently established. This attitude is the more surprising in that it was not apparently shared by some of his distinguished contemporaries. John Bradford, the outstanding figure among the orthodox Protestants in the King's Bench prison, started by regarding some of the Freewiller prisoners as a greater menace to the faith than 'the papists' and wrote Cranmer and Ridley to this effect, but a few months later (having found that a number of the Freewillers could be converted by argument) he took a kindlier view of them and wrote to a former Freewiller that it might not

[17] *A. & M.*, VII, pp. 306-18, and Biographical Register of Freewillers, chapter 3 above.

[18] Bradford II, pp. 133-34; *A. & M.*, VIII, p. 151; Register of Freewillers, chapter 3 above.

[19] *A. & M.*, VIII, p. 559 and Appendix, Document VII; Register of Freewillers, chapter 3 above; *A. & M.*, VIII, pp. 189-91 and Emmanuel College MS 260, 108, fols. 213-14.

[20] *Ibid.*, fol. 239. I am indebted for a transcript of this letter to Dr. John Fines, who is engaged in a study of the Protestant prison experience. He tells me that markings on the letter leave no doubt that Foxe had seen it.

[21] *E.g., A. & M.*, VIII, pp. 321-25, 468-82.

be necessary to 'agree on all points'.[22] Cranmer and Ridley had from the beginning of the King's Bench controversy taken a less alarmed view than Bradford's of the Freewillers.[23] Miles Coverdale, who had been Bishop of Exeter in the Edwardian church, actually preached secretly to occasional separatist meetings in early Elizabethan London.[24] Foxe's personal opinion of the Freewillers may have been not unlike that ultimately held by Bradford, whom he obviously admired and spoke of as one who strongly opposed heresy.[25]

But as a publicist Foxe was certainly aware that religious separatists disturbed many of his fellow countrymen and could be a propaganda vulnerability for the English church in its contest with Rome. The 1563 edition of *Actes and Monuments* prints at length the account by John Careless of how his Roman Catholic interrogator embarrassed and upset him by pointed questions about Henry Hart and other Protestant separatists, but Foxe greatly condensed this account in later editions, dropping all the material about separatists.[26] He was probably aware also of the effective propaganda use made of the separatist preacher, 'Father Brown' in Miles Hogarde's tract, *The Displaying of the Protestantes*.[27]

Foxe saw it as important for his contemporaries to know how the national church of Edward and Elizabeth had roots going back through English history to the primitive church, and to know also how the true church had been defended in their own lifetimes by men and women who were not afraid to face the persecuting officials of the Roman Antichrist. But no good end was to be served by telling them about Protestant Englishmen who rejected the national church. Despite the marked individuality of his own opinions, Foxe understood how to appeal to his countrymen and what their reponses were likely to be – as the history of *Actes and Monuments* was to prove.

[22] Bradford II, pp. 169–71, 215–16, 180–81, 194–98.

[23] *Ibid*, pp. 172–73.

[24] H, Gareth Owen, 'A Nursery of Elizabethan Nonconformity', *J.E.H.*, XVII (1966), pp. 65–76.

[25] *A. & M.*, VII, pp. 143–44.

[26] *A. & M.*, VIII, pp. 163–70, reprinting pp. 1529–34 of the 1563 edition. The 1570 edition's account occupies pp. 2001–02 there.

[27] Hogarde, *Displaying* (STC 13558), fols. 124–25^v. For an Elizabethan Puritan accusation that the Marian regime had deliberately encouraged Protestant sectaries as a way of combatting the orthodox Protestant underground, see chapter 7, section 5 above.

Chapter 10

Elizabethan Familists and English Separatism

1

Two related questions arise concerning the small religious sect calling itself the Family of Love and professing allegiance to the continental mystic, Hendrik Niclas. Why did it attract so much public attention in the England of the late 1570s? Why did the Elizabethan establishment become, for a time, so disturbed about it? A rough indicator of the attention is found in the *Short-Title Catalogue of Books Printed in English, 1475-1640*, where the individual entries for Niclas and other Familist writers outnumber all other separatists before 1600, including such men as Robert Browne and Henry Barrow. (In another comparison, they outnumber the entries under Martin Marprelate also.)[1] The establishment's concern was evinced in several ways. The Family was written or preached against by three members of the bench of bishops, besides lesser clerics;[2] matters relating to it were discussed by the Privy Council on 13 different occasions between June 1575 and January 1581;[3] and on October 3, 1580 it was the exclusive target of a royal proclamation.[4]

Until the past decade or two, the attention aroused by the Familists in Elizabethan England has not been much reflected in the writings of modern historians. Those interested in the Family itself have dealt largely with its continental developments. They have described the sect

---

[1] Totalling printed entries for pre-1600 publications in the 1926 edition of the *Short-Title Catalogue*, one finds 15 items credited to Hendrik Niclas and 4 to other Familist writers, as compared with 2 for Henry Hart, 2 for Robert Browne, 2 for Robert Harrison, 9 for Henry Barrow, and 3 for John Greenwood. Similar numbered listings under Martin Marprelate total 13. For those writers listed in the revised Vol. II of the STC (London 1976) the absolute numbers increase somewhat but the proportions are not much changed.

[2] Archbishop Sandys of York in his 'Seventh Sermon', *Sermons*, J. Ayre, ed. (Cambridge 1841), p. 130; statements by Bishops Cox of Ely and Young of Rochester in the prefatory material of William Wilkinson, *A confutation of certaine articles delivered unto the Family of Love*, 1579 (STC 25665).

[3] *A.P.C.*, VIII, p. 338; IX, p. 94; X, pp. 332, 344; XI, pp. 138, 139, 362, 386, 444, 445; XII, pp. 231-33, 250, 269, 317-18. The register has 19 separate entries referring to Familists, some occurring in the same meeting.

[4] *Tudor Procl.*, II, pp. 474-75.

Niclas founded at Emden in 1540, with its emphasis on personal religious experience, spiritual rebirth and the close fellowship of the faithful and they have traced its growth in the Low Countries and contiguous areas. They have noted, of course, that it spread to England and that most of Niclas' works appear in English translations, but what really interests them is the Family on the continent. This focus of interest is understandable. English Familists were predominantly artisans and small traders, not all of them even literate; while in the Low Countries the Family of Love attracted the secret adherence or sympathetic interest of such figures as Christopher Plantin, the Antwerp printer; Abraham Ortelius, the geographer; and even the Spanish Biblical scholar, Benito Arias Montano.[5] Writers on Tudor religious history, for their part, have tended to view the Familists as an imported group that does not quite fit into the English picture.[6]

[5] F. Nippold, 'Heinrich Niclaes und das Haus der Liebe', *Zeitschrift für die historische Theologie*, XXXII (1862), pp. 323-562, remains the most extensive work. The modern authority is H. de la Fontaine Verwey, 'De Gescriften van Hendrik Niclaes,' *Het Boek*, XXVI (1942), pp. 161-211 (with comprehensive bibilography 189-207); 'Trois Heresiarchs dans les Pays-Bas du XVIᵉ Siecle', *Bibliothèque d'Humanisme et Renaissance*, XVI (1954), pp. 312-20; 'The Family of Love', *Quaerendo*, VI (1976), pp. 219-71. See also Jan van Dorsten, *Thomas Basson 1555-1613, English Printer at Leiden* (Leiden 1961), pp. 61-69; *The Radical Arts: First Decade of an Elizabethan Renaissance* (Leiden 1970), pp. 27-39; 'Garter Knights and Familists', *Journal of European Studies*, IV (1974), pp. 178-88; Leon Voet, *The Golden Compasses: A History of the Officina Plantiana at Antwerp*, 2 vols. (New York 1969-72), I, pp. 22-30; B. Rekers, *Benito Arias Montano* (London 1972), pp. 70-104; Wallace Kirsop, 'The Family of Love in France', *Journal of Religious Studies*, II (1964-65), pp. 103-18.
[6] Separatists are excluded by the terms of reference from Patrick Collinson, *The Elizabethan Puritan Movement* (London 1967) and M.M. Knappen, *Tudor Puritanism* (Chicago 1939), but in fact the Familists are mentioned occasionally in each. I.B. Horst, *The Radical Brethren: Anabaptism and the English Reformation to 1558* (Nieukoop 1972) extends the terminal date of the study to discuss Familists briefly. Champlin Burrage, *The Early English Dissenters in the Light of Recent Research, 1500-1641* (Cambridge 1912) gives only glancing attention to the Familists; George H. Williams, *The Radical Reformation* (London 1962) devotes two pages to the English Familists; B.R. White, *The English Separatist Tradition from the Marian Martyrs to the Pilgrim Fathers* (Oxford 1971) does not mention them at all. The recent specialized studies of the English Familists include Felicity Heal, 'The Family of Love and the Diocese of Ely', *Studies in Church History, IX, Schism, Heresy and Religious Protest*, D. Baker ed., (Cambridge 1972), pp. 213-22; Jean Dietz Moss, 'The Family of Love and English Critics', *The Sixteenth Century Journal*, VI (1975), pp. 35-52; 'Variations on a Theme: the Family of Love in Renaissance England', *Renaissance Quarterly*, XXXI (1978), pp. 186-95; J. Hitchcock, 'A Confession of the Family of Love,' *B.I.H.R.*, XLIII (1970), pp. 85-86; Moss, 'Additional Light on the Family of Love', *B.I.H.R.* XLVII (1974), pp. 163-65; Julia C. Ebel, 'The Family of Love: Sources of Their History in England', *Huntington Library Quarterly*, XXX (1966-67), pp. 331-43. Quaker scholars, investigating various forerunners of mid-seventeenth century Friends, produced two of the earliest studies of Familism in English: A.C. Thomas, 'The Family of Love: a Study in Church History', *Haverford College Studies*, XII (1893), pp. 1-46, and Rufus M. Jones *Studies in Mystical Religion* (London 1909), pp. 428-48; but this interest has not been much pursued by more recent historians of Quakerism.

In seeking to explain the positive appeal the Familists held for some of Elizabeth's subjects, it is useful to look first at characteristics Familists shared with other separatist groups, from the Lollards in the fifteenth century on through the Freewillers and other sectaries of early Protestantism to such well known sects as the Baptists and Quakers of the seventeenth century. The shared characteristics varied in prominence from group to group, but the elements of continuity are discernible in the increased emphasis all placed on interior religion, in the way all appealed to the authority of the Bible and were permeated by its imagery, in a strain of anticlericalism, and in the importance all gave to the self-selected gathering of true believers. These were matters more of practice and attitude than of explicit statement and formulated doctrine. Thus, Familists did not profess absolute separation of the faithful for private worship; they simply practised it while professing conformity to the Church of England – as Familists in the Roman Catholic countries professed conformity to Rome.

It will be argued that one important advantage Familists had over any earlier separatist group in England was the way their continental connection enabled them to make effective use of the printing press, and that this circumstances was likewise a factor in raising government fears.

2

The main facts of the Family's development on the continent and activity in Elizabethan England can be readily summarized. Its founder, Henrik Niclas, born probably in Munster in 1502, was a mercer by occupation, and moved about considerably in a lifetime lasting until 1580. He was resident in Amsterdam for some years in the 1530s, in Emden from about 1540 to 1560, and in Cologne for a time in the late 1570s. From childhood on, he believed himself to be in direct communication with God, and around 1540 he moved to set up the Family of Love as a separate sect to express his convictions about inner religious experience and its transforming power. His many tracts were written originally in Low German and usually signed simply 'H.N.' – the initials often being taken to mean also Homo Novus. On paper, at least, the Family was tightly centralized by an elaborate organization of elders of differing status, ranked under Niclas. It actively sought converts and H.N.'s tracts were translated into Latin, French, High German and English. Around 1573, the Family suffered a serious split when one of Niclas' disciples, known variously as Barrefelt or Hiël, repudiated his authority and set up a rival sect. English Familists, however, seem to have remained loyal to Niclas.

Though Dutch circles in London during the 1560s showed some signs of interest in Niclas and other continental religious radicals, the development of the Family in England appears to have been unconnected with these resident Dutch groups. The earliest dated document clearly referring to the English Family comes on May 28, 1561, when two disgruntled members of its Guildford congregation made a series of 66 individually attested statements about it before the Surrey magistrate, William More.[7] These depositions not only describe in detail the group meeting secretly near Guildford, but mention other such groups in half a dozen additional counties and refer to group practices as far back as 'the beginning of Queen Mary's reign.' The members are described as 'all unlearned, saving only that some of them read English,' and in fact one of the deponents signed the document only with his mark.[8]

Awareness that some of their members could not read apparently did not inhibit the Familists' resort to the printing press. It is not known whether, like the Lollards, they had arrangements for reading aloud to illiterate members, but it is clear that in 1574 an influx of Familists' tracts in English began. These, under some 20 different titles, were varied in nature (including a number of 'songs' and one play), mostly undated and all without city of origin; bibiibliographers now attribute them to Nicholas Bomberg of Cologne.[9]

Translation into English (from 'Base-almayne') is attributed to Christopher Vitel, a woodworker by trade who showed unusual ability as a local leader; the Familists' antagonists referred to him as unquestioned head of the Family in England.[10] In 1575 appeared the first indication of government pressure on the Familists: a broadside printing the recantation at Paul's Cross of Robert Sharpe and four other Familists,[11] and a printed 'confession' issued by the Familists protesting their general religious orthodoxy and harmlessness.[12] The five names attached to the recantation, like most of those mentioned in the 1561

[7] More, who inherited Loseley Hall near Guildford in 1549 and was knighted in 1576, sat in nearly all Elizabeth's Parliaments and showed a special interest in keeping both Roman Catholic recusancy and Protestant separatism in check.

[8] Folger Library (Washington) Loseley MS, L.B. 98. The Familists' clerical antagonist, John Rogers, in *A displaying of an horrible secte of grosse and wicked heretiques naming themselves the Familie of Love*, 1578 (STC 21181), 1579 (STC 21182), printed 53 of the items as an appended 'confession' sigs. I^v-K^v 3; St.G.K. Hyland, *A Century of Persecution Under Tudor and Stuart Sovereigns* (London 1920), pp. 103-12, printed more, but not all, of the 66 statements. The depositions do not use either the word 'confession' or 'Familist' at any point, and the latter omission reasonably raised the question of whether the Guildford congregation was indeed Familist. In paragraph 64, however (not printed by Rogers and not understood by Hyland), there is a clear reference to Niclas as top leader of the group. See J.W. Martin, 'Elizabethan Familists and other Separatists in the Guildford Area', *B.I.H.R.*, LI (1978), pp. 90-93.

[9] Thus in the revised STC; the 1926 edition carried many Familist items as '[Amsterdam?]'.

[10] Rogers, *Displaying* (1579) ed.), sig. D8^r; *Wilkinson, Confutation of Articles*, fol. 46^r. See also Chap. 11 below.

[11] *The confession of Robert Sharpe at Paules Cross, the xii of June 1575* (STC 22328).

[12] *A brief rehersall of the beleef of the goodwilling in England which are named the Familie of Love*, 1575 (STC 10681.5)

deposition, sound like native English names, and the chronicler John Stow referred to them as 'Englishmen' in contrast to the 'Dutch' Anabaptists whose recantation at Paul's Cross he had described a few weeks before.[13]

In 1577, the tracts attacking the Familists began to appear. Their three most persistent antagonists – John Rogers, John Knewstub, and William Wilkinson – all indicate detailed knowledge of Familist writings, and Rogers gives the titles of a number of works he says he has read.[14] Familists also provoked some general curiosity in educated English circles,[15] and entered the public consciousness to the extent that references to them were used for rhetorical purposes in books having nothing to do with Familism directly.[16]

From September 1578 on, the government seemed increasingly concerned, and through 1580 the Privy Council periodically discussed such problems as yeomen of the Queen's guard suspected of being Familists and measures needed for suppressing Familist activity in regions as far apart as Devon and Norfolk. The suppressive royal proclamation of October 3, 1580 indicates how the Familists were then perceived by the government, the tone suggesting a rising anxiety over their progress. Familists, it said, made 'privy assemblies of divers simple unlearned people' and deceived them by using 'a monstrous new kind of speech never found in the Scripture nor in ancient father or writer of Christ's church.' They printed abroad certain 'heretical and seditious books' (four titles are given), which they 'secretly brought over into the realm.' Furthermore, Familists held it a principle 'that they may, before any magistrate ecclesiastical or temporal, or any other person not being

---

[13] *Chronicle*, 1580 (STC 23333) p. 1184.

[14] Rogers, *Displaying*, 1579 ed., containing *Certaine letters sent from the same Family maintayning their opinions;* also *An answere unto a wicked & infamous libel made by Christopher Vitel, one of the chiefe English elders of the pretended Family of Love*, 1579 (STC 21180); Knewstub, *A confutation of monstrous heresies taught by H.N.*, 1579 (STC 15050); Wilkinson, *Confutation of articles*. Stephen Bateman's 1577 tract, *The golden book of the leaden goddes* (STC 1583), gives only brief attention to the Family, but Familists apparently saw its author as a special foe.

[15] A letter of October 14, 1579, from Antwerp by the Huguenot diplomat, Hubert Languet, is in evident response to an earlier query by his friend, Sir Philip Sidney, about the Family's continental antecedents: *Huberti Langueti Epistolae Politicae et Historicae ad Philippum Sidnae* (Leiden 1646), pp. 397-99. I am grateful to Jan van Dorsten of Leiden University for this reference and for helpful discussions about Familists.

[16] See the Jesuit tracts of Robert Parsons, *Brief discourse contayning certayne reasons why Catholiques refuse to goe to church*, 1580 (STC 19394) sig. A 3r; and *A brief censure upon two bookes*, 1581 (STC 19393), sig. E 6, plus such Puritan counter attacks as William Charke, *An answere to a seditious pamphlet*, 1580 (STC 5005), sig. A 1v; Meredith Hanmer, *The Jesuites banner*, 1581 (STC 12746), sig. A 3v; John Fielde, *A caveat for Parsons Howlet*, 1581 (STC 10849), sig. D 1r, D 4r. These books, along with Barnabe Rich, *Adventures of Don Simonides*, 1581, (STC 21002), sig. T 2, are among some of two dozen in which Doris Adler kindly noted Familist references for me.

professed to be of their sect . . . by oath or otherwise deny anything for their advantage' – that is, conform outwardly while still holding their own beliefs inwardly.[17]

A few days after the proclamation, letters were ordered sent to several bishops to see to its implementation.[18] An even higher point of concern seems to have been reached in February 1581, when an anti–Familist bill was sent for consideration by a House of Commons committee that included three members of the Privy Council.[19] Then, at some point between February 1581 and late November 1582, the Council's alarm abated, but the evidence does not indicate just when or why. The parliamentary bill died (the bishops had apparently opposed it on jurisdictional grounds)[20] and the Council register contains no more items about Familists.[21] The drop in the Council's anxiety is evident in the letter dated November 30, with original signatures by five Council members, directing the authorities at Cambridge to release certain now repentant Familists imprisoned in the castle there.[22]

Familists remained a part of the English scene, however, for more than a century,[23] and the establishment continued to view them with disapproval. At the same time, however, Familists in their stereotyped role of 'deluded fanatics' could prove useful for those wishing to make indirect attacks on larger groups – whether Roman Catholics or, more frequently, Puritan elements in the Church of England. Thus Richard Hooker, with Puritan opponents surely in mind, spoke of how the Familists 'imagine that the Scripture everywhere speaketh in favour of that sect,'[24] and James VI in *Basilikon Doron* similarly attacks Familists 'who think themselves only pure.'[25] On a more popular level, the name 'Family of Love' provided an obvious target for the easy sneer ('that lovely family') and for literary satirists deliberately assuming that it

[17] *Tudor Procl.*, II, pp. 474–75.
[18] *A.P.C.*, XII, pp. 232–33.
[19] *Journals of the House of Commons*, I, pp. 127–30.
[20] *Archaeologia*, XXXVI (1855), pp. 113–14. See also John Strype, *Life of Grindal* (Oxford 1821), pp. 283–84; J.E. Neale, *Elizabeth I and Her Parliaments, 1559-1581* (London 1953), pp. 410–11.
[21] Relevant documents are missing: there is the 31 month gap in the register starting in June 1582, and we do not know Lord Burleigh's response to a letter from the Bishop of Exeter on June 6, 1581 (Strype, *Annals of the Reformation* (Oxford 1824), III, ii, pp. 180–81) about a Familist problem the Council had discussed three times in the previous year.
[22] Folger MS X, d. 30(9).
[23] In June 1687, James II received a small delegation of Familists, who described themselves as 'a sort of refin'd Quakers . . . chiefly belonging to the Isle of Ely.' John Evelyn, *Diary*, W. Brady, ed. (London n.d.), p. 644.
[24] *Laws of Ecclestiastical Polity* (Oxford 1887), p. 148.
[25] *Basilikon Doron*, 1603 (STC 14349), sig. B 2ᵛ.

referred to sexual love.[26] Somewhat as 'Brownists' became a term applied to Protestant separatists generally, 'Familists' seems to have been applied increasingly in the seventeenth century to a variety of radicals and libertines.

3

The nature of Familism's appeal should be examined first in the translated works of Niclas, whose publications made up most of the Familist output and in the mid-1570s ran to hundreds of pages. His writings were varied as well as copious, including a play and several kinds of verse, in addition to prayers, pastoral letters, and other more specifically religious genres. He evidently liked to write. But he was never a systematic theologian, avoided on principle the closely argued discourse of clerics, and was very fond of figurative language. He seemed more concerned that his verbal expression be faithful to the insight it sought to record than that it be consistent with a previous statement he had made.

To a twentieth-century reader, H.N.'s writings can be heavy going, repetitious, and often unclear. But they were more attuned to sixteenth-century ears than to ours, much of them being well within the boundaries of the apocalyptic tradition, in which were also to be found such pillars of the Protestant establishment as John Bale and John Foxe.[27] H.N.'s favourite phrases were by no means the same as theirs, but one of his underlying assumptions was the same: namely, that God had special purposes, now moving toward fulfilment, for men of the present generation. But where they saw an impending fulfilment in terms of a reformed Church of England and the overthrow of the pope as

---

[26] See Thomas Middleton's early Jacobean comedy, *The Family of Love*, where two citizens' wives use secret meetings of the sect for rendezvous with their pursuing gallants; also William G. Johnson, 'The Family of Love in Stuart Literature: A Chronology of Name-Crossed Lovers', *Journal of Medieval and Renaissance Studies*, VII (1977), pp. 95-112.

[27] Paul Christianson, *Reformers and Babylon: English Apocalyptic Visions from the Reformation to the Eve of the Civil War* (Toronto 1978), points out that the apocalyptic tradition, which he regards as including millenialism, 'provides a vocabulary' for attacking the Church of England under Charles I, but was generally seen as supporting it in the first half of Elizabeth's reign. Christianson does not discuss Niclas and the Familists, nor does Katherine S. Firth, *The Apocalyptic Tradition in Reformation Britain, 1530-1645* (Oxford 1979). For the apocalyptic tradition and Foxe, see William Haller, *Foxe's Book of Martyrs and The Elect Nation* (London 1963), and Viggo Norskov Olson, *John Foxe and the Elizabethan Church* (Berkeley 1973); for the earlier and radical tradition, see Norman Cohn, *The Pursuit of the Millenium* (London 1957). Lynnewood F. Martin, 'The Family of Love in England: Conforming Millenarians', *Sixteenth Century Journal*, III (1972), pp. 99-108, discusses this aspect of Niclas mainly on the basis of his *Evangelium regni* and without mentioning Bale and Foxe.

Antichrist, Niclas had different purposes in mind. When he spoke of 'the great day of the Lord' or announced that 'God hath opened now in the last tyme a great Door of Grace,' he meant the spiritual regeneration that he would express in other metaphors such as 'illuminated in the Spirit with the heavenlie Truth' or inspired by 'the true Light of the perfect Being.' It is not surprising, however, that he should occasionally be thought to mean an earthly kingdom to be enjoyed by the faithful.[28]

Looking at Niclas' works as a whole, one can distinguish, along with other elements, four persistent strains: an insistence that religion is inner personal experience; a saturation in the language and imagery of the Bible; a scorn for formal theological learning; and an insistence that the religious life must be pursued in small face-to-face groups of the faithful – in, as he would put it, a Family of Love.

The most important of these elements is the first. Religion for him was almost entirely a matter of inner experience that put the believer in direct communication with God. He spoke, for example, of 'how much greater and gloriouser' the 'inward heaven' is than 'the whole outward heaven which compasseth the whole world.'[29] As with other mystics, the inner experience for H.N. was overwhelming and essentially incommunicable. He nevertheless tried to convey it with a variety of terms and figures of speech drawn largely from traditional Christianity, though evidently feeling no obligation to use terms like 'baptism' or 'love' in a traditional way. Hence, one may surmise, some of his attractiveness to the partly educated; hence also the fury he aroused in trained Church of England clerics such as John Knewstub and John Rogers. Knewstub, snorting at H.S.'s prose style of 'riddels and dark speeches,' charged (accurately enough) that H.N. took as many liberties of interpretation with the Bible as he would with Aesop's Fables.[30]

The Niclas phrase that struck so many of his contemporaries as blasphemous was 'godded with God' – by which H.N. apparently meant the attainable culmination of the believer's efforts toward closer union with God. As he put it in *The first exhortation*, God, in an exercise of grace, 'manneth himself according to the inner man with us, and we become likewise with the cleernes of his godlie light . . . godded or made conformable in a good-willing spirit to the upright righteousness with

---

[28] The Wisbech glover's apprentice, Leonard Romsye, asserted in the 'confession' he made about 1580 in repudiating Familism that Familists believed that 'their kyngdome, which they call Davides Kyngdome, is to be erected here uppon earth' (printed by Moss in *Renaissance Quarterly*, XXXI, pp. 190-91). But this literalist interpretation of H.N.'s words was rare among his English followers (Heal, *Studies in Church History*, IX, p. 221) and quite contrary to the statement in the 1561 deposition that the Guildford congregation held strictly to the command in I Peter, 2:13-14, on submission to the secular powers.

[29] *Dicta HN*, (STC 18551), fol. 16ᵛ.

[30] *Confutation of heresies*, fol. 26ʳ; 82ʳ.

A ſhorte Inſtruction of an Howſhold-father,
in the Comunialtie of the Loue of Jeſu Chriſt.

O Yee beloued Childꝛen and thou Famelie of
Loue / reſpect well this good Doctrine and Exhortation
of HN / and take the Inſtructions of theſame, effectuallie to
heart : and vnderſtande, what is requyred of you therwith-all.
Not that yee ſhoulde take vnto you alone the ² Knowledge of
thoſe-ſame / ether exerciſe you onlie in the Knowledge therof.
but to take-heede rightlie vnto the Requiringe of thoſe-ſame /
and ᵇ to ſhew-fourth Obedience therin .

2.   For to receaue onlie the Knowledge of the godlie Teſti-
monies / and not to obey oꝛ accompliſh thoſeſame and their Requiringe : and ſo to knowe and to ſpeake anything / againſt the
Obedience / is verelie ᶜ the Seede of the olde Serpent : and
that is the falſe ᵈ Light which ſeduceth and eſtraungeth the Man
from God and his Trueth / and woꝛketh by hym much Contention and Diſcoꝛde .

3.   And the Diſobedience is ᵉ the Seede of the Woman /
wherethꝛough ſo much Falſhod is com into the Woꝛlde : and

        X 2   which

ª Iaco. 1. d.

ᵇ Mat. 7. 12. e.

Ioan. 15. b.

ᶜ Geneſ. 3.

ᵈ Eſa. 5. b. 59. b

ᵉ Gene. 3.

Woodcut from the introduction to Hendrik Niclas, *The first exhortation*
(1574), a Familist tract sometimes used as the first statement given to a
prospective convert. Organizers of conventicles, from Lollard times on,
tended to see their meetings as teaching sessions also.

hym . . . and that is the upright Christian baptism.'[31] Elsewhere the figure Niclas used was that of the believer's attaining mystical union with God by spiritually repeating Christ's sufferings. In his 'Second Epistle' he had Christ asking a series of rhetorical questions such as, 'Who hath borne the contempt, blasphemy and shame with me? Who hath borne such a death on the cross with me?' and then responding that such a man 'shall understand and know the misterie of the Love.'[32]

The most prominent and probably the most baffling of H.N.'s figures was 'the Love', as it appeared either alone or as part of the title of the sect, or in such frequently used phrases as 'the requiring of the Love', 'in the service of the Love', and 'under the obedience of the Love'. Of this term John Rogers complained to the Familists, with justice, that 'sometimes you would have it taken for God, sometime for Christ, and sometime for your whole doctrine and profession, and sometime for a property or vertue proceeding from God.'[33] For Niclas, it sometimes does seem to refer to the whole inner experience of oneness with God, and phrases like 'the obedience of the Love' seem to mean an adherence to the discipline he considered necessary for achieving this direct communion. But in answer to the question he posed, 'What is now this Love which in her service requireth such obedience?' he could reply only in terms of what this central symbol performed for believers: 'The Love is a very true beeing, out of the which the beleefe doth grow and blowe, and becometh fruitful therthrough to bring foorth the upright righteousnes.'[34]

A second element in H.N.'s writings – almost as prominent as the first – is his immersion in the language and imagery of the Bible. He seemed to be always appealing to a Bible-reading public. 'Yee all which daylie search the Scriptures', he said.[35] Almost any page of his works carries a profusion of marginal references to the Scriptures (and only to the Scriptures, not to early church fathers or other authors) in numbers often exceeding the Biblical citations in the tracts opposing him. His references were not always accurate or apposite, as his opponents repeatedly pointed out,[36] but Niclas evidently felt a real need for them, whether to reassure his readers or himself. Biblical history, paraphrase, and allusion permeate both language and structure in his work. In one of his best known books, *Evangelium regni*, more than half the chapters are devoted to a retelling of Biblical history (as the Bishop of Rochester tartly

---

[31] *The first exhortation* (STC 18557), fol. 11ᵛ-12ʳ.

[32] *Epistolae HN* (STC 18552), pp. 11-12.

[33] *Rogers, Answere to a libel*, sig. 7ʳ. See also H 3ᵛ-4ʳ, and Knewstub, *Confutation of heresies*, 23ʳ-24ᵛ.

[34] *Epistolae HN*, p. 324.

[35] *Evangelium regni* (STC 18556), fol. 9ᵛ.

[36] Knewstub, *Confutation of heresies*, sig. 6ᵛ-7ʳ; Wilkinson, *Confutation of articles*, fol. 23ʳ, 46ᵛ, 48ʳ.

noted).[37] The early chapters of *The first exhortation* discuss the Ten Commandments. The 'Seventeenth Epistle' concerns itself with the Fall. So does H.N.'s play, *Comoedia*, which treats the Fall somewhat in the manner of John Bale's dramas.

Anticlericalism, a third element in H.N.'s writings, is seen in his scorn for 'the Scripture-learned'. The Familist elders were, in a sense, a clergy of H.N.'s own, but he evidently regarded them as generically different from the kind of formally educated cleric who debated with his English followers. Religion for him was not a matter of intellect and knowledge but of attitude and spiritual experience, and a real chasm separated what he termed the 'good-thinking' from the 'good-willing'. In his feeling that knowledge is essentially irrelevant for salvation, he was not far removed from the author of *The Imitation of Christ* and various other figures in Christian history. But Niclas' denunciations of Biblical scholarship have an animus that may be due to his seeing the 'Scripture-learned' as the special foes of the Family.[38]

Finally, like other separatists before and since, H.N. stressed the need for true believers to assemble in face-to-face groups for mutual support. (As with the Lollards, this gathering of the faithful in their own fellowship was not seen as precluding all participation in the rites of the established church.) Niclas apparently felt such a compulsion early in his own religious career; at any rate, he referred in his *Introduction to the glasse of righteousnes* to his search for a dedicated group or 'comunialtie . . . comprehended in the service of the Love.'[39] In this 'Communialtie of the Love' there was even available a kind of heaven-on-earth, where 'all goodwillingones' may 'enter into the rest of the Lord and obtain the everlasting Godlynes.'[40] It is evident that the 'Communialtie of the Love' (the term that appears in H.N.'s texts more often than 'Family of Love') had an important supportive role in the day-to-day life of a Familist; Niclas commended it as the 'hand-reaching of the serviceable Woord of the Holie Spirit of Love. And if anyman chance to fall, so help upp then each other again.'[41] In temptation or other spiritual difficulties the Familist was expected to seek the group's help: 'Let him not cover his sinnes, but let him confesse them before his Elder in the holy understanding.' To rely on one's individual strength was indeed to sin.[42]

---

[37] 'Notes upon *Evangelium regni*' in Wilkinson, *Confutation of articles*, sig. A 2^r.

[38] *Introduction to the glasse of righteousness*, (STC 18558), I, fol. 17^v-18^r; II, 11^v; *Evangelium regni*, 10^v, 60^v. In his play *Comoedia* (STC 18550), the character 'Good-thinking' is described as 'attyred before like an hypocrite and behynde and downe to his feete like a devill.'

[39] *Glasse of righteousness*, I, sig. 8^v.

[40] *Evangelium regni*, 4^{rv}.

[41] *Dicta HN*, 23^r. See also *Epistolae HN*, p. 134.

[42] *Dicta HN*, 26^v-28^r.

Niclas also provided the Family with set prayers for use in temptation and other situations.[43]

4

Whatever elements of novelty the Familist appeal possessed, it would have had, for some Elizabethans, elements of familiarity also. Over several generations the Lollards had provided examples in various parts of the country of English men and women who turned to the vernacular Bible for religious guidance, not to the parish priest and the traditional church, and sought in their own self-run meetings for interpretation of the Bible and for emotional support. As noted earlier in this volume, the middle third of the sixteenth century had seen popular access to the Bible increase in several ways – both for those who could read the Scriptures for themselves and for those who could only listen to them as read out by other laymen 'at the lower end of the church'. Familist propagandists had grounds for assuming in their audience a ready familiarity with the language and imagery of the Bible. Meetings of a conventicle, of course, provided a special environment for the reading of the Bible, one where it was not just a thing to be listened to a single time, as at the services of the parish church, but something to be discussed, quoted, paraphrased and discussed again. Familists could assume, also, that many Englishmen, even if they had not themselves experienced the warmth of fellowship which the popular conventicle provided, were at least aware of the institution and its general nature.

In their attacks on what they saw as clerical pretensions, Familists were appealing to a sentiment that had never been very far beneath the surface of English life. In the 1540s anti-clerical feeling had appeared more openly in attacks on priestly hypocrisy through pamphlets attributed to Piers Plowman, the central figure in William Langland's famous fourteenth-century poem, and by a spurious addition to Chaucer's *Canterbury Tales* called 'The Plowman's Tale'.[44] In 1548 John Champneys in his *The Harvest is at hand* had asserted, in terms quite as strong as H.N.'s attacks on the 'Scripture-learned' clergy, that the traditional clergy tried to set up 'man's imaginings' against the word of God, and that a reverent layman could better read and interpret God's word for himself.[45]

One of the four main elements in H.N.'s message, however, had not previously figured in Tudor popular religion. This was his great emphasis on interior religion, an emphasis not explicit in the Lollards or

[43] *The first exhortation*, 51ᵛ-54ʳ; *Dicta HN*, 27ᵛ.

[44] E.g., *I playne piers which cannot flatter* (STC 19903a), *A godly dyalogue and disputacion between Pyers Plowman and a popysh preest* (STC 19903); Chaucer, *Works*, 1542 (STC 5069).

[45] *Harvest at hand*, (STC 4956), sigs. B 4ᵛ, D 8.

in later English sects before such groups as the Seekers and Quakers in the seventeenth century. There was, of course, an implicit emphasis on interior religion in the Reformation movement generally, in that public ceremonies such as the mass were in various ways downgraded and attention was directed instead to the believer's personal acceptance of the Scriptures. The interest of sixteenth-century England in the *devotio moderna*, with its stress on the inner life, was shown by the popularity of *The Imitation of Christ*.[46] Familism's appeal to that interest was explicit in the title of H.N.'s 'Fifth Epistle: A stirring up of the heart to the imitation and following of Christ in the suffering of his cross.'[47]

5

To say just what in Familism made some Elizabethans its devoted adherents one must, however, draw largely on inference – as indeed one would for an equivalent twentieth-century movement, even with today's relatively rich biographical data and sophisticated interviewing techniques. Information about Niclas' Elizabethan followers comes to us almost entirely through hostile channels: the 'confessions' of ex-Familists or of persons suspected of being Familists, statements made in books attacking the sect (which, however, often quoted its defenders at some length) and actions taken by the government against the Family. The inferences seem trustworthy when one finds persistent characteristics in the life of this sect that were not similarly prominent in other contemporary groups. Three such distinguishing characteristics may be singled out. One was Familists' insistence, in effect, that religion was ultimately a private matter, beyond the bounds of public authority. Another was the sect's special relationship to the printed book. A third was the close fellowship the Family evidently provided. For some Englishmen, it is suggested, each of these things tended to make life seem more attractive inside the Family than outside it.

The right to privacy in their religious views was a concept to which Familists had evidently given some thought. Though almost taken for granted in later centuries as a corollary of interior religion, it was a controversial issue in the sixteenth century. The Familist view did not involve individual freedom of belief in any way that a nineteenth-century liberal would have recognized; the organization that Niclas had decreed was tightly centralized under himself and the elders, and the Guildford congregation was described in 1561 as strictly controlling most members' participation in meetings. But, in contrast to the holder of orthodox Protestant doctrines under the Marian regime, the Familist

[46] The STC lists 20 editions of all or part of this work published in English through 1580.
[47] *Epistolae HN*, p. 65.

was not expected by his group to stand up for his beliefs before a hostile magistrate but was given justifications for yielding the outward conformity demanded.

This in itself was a serious point of friction with the Elizabethan establishment. The charge that Familists denied their true beliefs in a meaningless conformity figured prominently in the royal proclamation and, in a somewhat different form, it was often heard from clerical controversialists, who complained of Familists' refusal to 'confer' or engage in oral debate. Recanting had been fairly common among Lollards placed on trial, and in Elizabethan England, as a modern historian has described, both Roman Catholics and Puritans regularly avoided confrontation with the authorities over proscribed beliefs.[48] But it was not an openly avowed practice and, in a decade when Foxe's *Actes and Monuments* kept green the memory of Cranmer, Ridley, and other Marian martyrs, it could easily be made to seem a kind of treachery.

Familists, obvious underdogs in any public debate, based their practice on a rather different view of 'conference'. For Familists, Cranmer and Ridley were identified as the clerics who had burned Joan of Kent for her religion – an act denounced by Guildford members of the sect[49] – and they evidently saw no sense in a public debate that could end, like that at Oxford in 1554, with the losers being immediately put on trial for heresy and ultimately going to the stake. Understandably, they preferred to enter the propaganda contest on their own terms rather than their opponents' – registering publicly their rejection of hostile criticism, but reserving detailed exposition of their views for those they had some hope of converting. As Niclas put it in the 'Eighth Epistle', it is often 'periolous . . . to speake or wryte of the Woord of Lyfe and of his secret clernes [secret splendour] before everyone that would desyre it. For it is not everymans matter.' Men's capacities differ and 'the secret bread of the Holy Woord doth not oftentymes serve for everymans stomach.'[50] But the hostile Rogers voiced a widespread view when he berated individual Familists who recanted in court but 'still reteine your secrete doctrine.'[51]

Familist apologists did not deny that there had been meaningless recantations but, as quoted by Rogers, asked in effect what was to be expected when 'simple men who can scarce read English' were bullied by the judge on points of doctrine.[52] Public recanting, or equivocating in the face of overwhelming power, was similarly defended by an English

[48] Elliot Rose, *Cases of Conscience: Alternatives open to Recusants and Puritans under Elizabeth and James I* (Cambridge 1975).
[49] Paragraph 57 of the 1561 deposition states the principle and cites the example. See also H.N.'s *Comoedia*, 31[v].
[50] *Epistolae HN*, pp. 160, 163.
[51] *Displaying*, K 4[v].
[52] *Ibid.*, M 6[v]-7[r].

Familist by comparison with the plight of Protestants living in Spain or Italy[53] and, in a Niclas statement that cited the authority of Deuteronomy 22: 25-27, by the analogy of a woman who submits to rape in a situation in which her cries cannot possibly summon help.[54]

The Familist position, in any case, accorded with strong tendencies in the religious life of subsequent centuries. One statement, quoted by Rogers from unidentified English Familists, did indeed put the case for privacy of belief on grounds more reminiscent of the eighteenth century than of the sixteenth: 'Let that which is secrete to God only, whereof no proof can be made nor lawfull witnesse broughte, abide to the coming of the Lord, which shall open all the secretes.'[55]

The printed book – that is, the sect's own books – clearly held an important part in Familist life. It is likely that a book had played some part, directly or indirectly, in recruiting a Familist originally and then in instructing and encouraging him during the various stages of his membership. Familists' books were also a main point of friction with the government: as the 1580 proclamation put it, 'the ground of their sect is maintained' by 'heretical and seditious books . . . printed beyond the seas.'

The proclamation understated, if anything, the way the Familists had realized the potentialities of the printing press. For such a new group, the number and variety of their tracts appearing in English would have been a notable accomplishment even if they had been able to print them all legally in London. Besides the four mentioned in the royal proclamation, John Rogers mentions eight titles as 'bookes of H.N. which I have seene' and adds two more that he has only heard of. Modern research, as reflected in the 1976 edition of the *Short-Title Catalogue*, has added a further six, but there is reason to believe that even the new STC list does not include all the Familist items circulating in England in the 1570s.[56]

The Familists' publications were apparently intended mostly for instructing their members, from neophytes on up, and maintaining their devotion. *Dicta AN: documental sentences* [that is, his instructive judgments] is as formal a work as its title implies; *Evangelium regni*, which was translated into Latin as well as English, presumably for reasons of prestige, is likewise rather formal. The 20 pastoral letters contained in *Epistolae HN* transmit the founder's counsel on various problems of the group or its individual members. *The first exhortation,*

---

[53] *Ibid.*, I 7^v-8^r.

[54] *Dicta HN*, 26^{rv}.

[55] Rogers, *Displaying*, N 1^r.

[56] For Rogers's list, see *Displaying*, A 7-8^r; some items are not readily identifiable now. One, H.N.'s *A figure of the true and spiritual tabernacle*, survives only in a 1655 edition printed by Giles Calvert. Also, a previously unknown Familist broadside in English 'Howle, o weepe, for the daye of the Lorde is at hand' (1575) was recently discovered by Professor K.W. Swart, who kindly made a copy available to me.

which contains much expository material on Familist beliefs, was on at least one occasion the first piece of literature placed in the hands of a prospective convert.[57]

Some of the works also had an appeal to a wider public. *A brief rehersall of the beleef of the goodwilling in Englande* was, as noted earlier, aimed at reassuring non-Familists about the fundamental soundness of the sect's beliefs. Verses like those in *Cantica* (STC 18549) and *All the Letters of the A.B.C. in Ryme* (STC 18548.5), which were translations from H.N.'s longer collections in Low German, could appeal even to an anti-Familist.[58] Familist publications also sought attention by appearing in a variety of formats, ranging from the broadside to an abnormally small size (as in *A brief rehersall*), which would make for easy concealment.

For Familist leaders, the printing press provided a degree of personal security in presenting their views; so, at any rate, one may infer from the way their English adversaries, quoting numerous Familist statements for refutation, seldom indicate that the statements were made orally. In one case, indeed, an opponent complained that the written statement of the Familist case was delivered to him only by 'the common carrier in London'.[59]

A third element in Familist life – the holding of 'privy assemblies of divers simple unlearned people', as the proclamation put it – was of course the central characteristic of all separatist groups. But Familists emphasized more than others the close and intimate nature of their gatherings. The name Niclas gave the sect (whether worded as Communialtie, Household, or Family of Love) was strongly expressive on this point and, as noted earlier, he had also prescribed various ways of giving the group a continuously supportive role in its members' lives. The practice of English Familists was described in two of the so-called 'confessions' – the 1561 depositions by two ex-members of the Guildford congregation, and a statement made about 1580 by Leonard Romsye, formerly of the Wisbech congregation in northern Cambridgeshire.[60]

[57] As the convert Leonard Romsye describes his conversion by his employer in his 'confession' printed by Moss in *Renaissance Quarterly*, XXXI, pp. 190-91.

[58] Sir William More, though hostile to Familism, kept copies of two songs from *Cantica* among his papers, Folger MS. L. b. 589.

[59] Wilkinson, *Confutation of articles*, 1ᵛ. Rogers, *Displaying* I 4ʳ-K 2ʳ, prints a long letter that defends the Family and is signed only 'your unknown friend'.

[60] 'Confession' as applied to Familists covers a variety of first-hand testimonies, all made under some degree of pressure. Some, like Sharpe's at Paul's Cross in 1575 and those of several members of the Queen's guard, are direct abjurations in terms considered appropriate by the authorities; a standard form for this purpose is printed in Edward Cardwell, ed., *Documentary Annals of the Reformed Church of England* (Oxford 1849), I, pp. 447-48. Romsye's 'confession' apparently involved no more pressure than his knowledge of the arrest and interrogation of fellow members of the Wisbech congregation. The motives behind the Guildford deposition are not clear, but seem to have included the bitterness of one deponent, Thomas Chaundler, over the marriage that the sect had arranged for him.

None of the three was a highly placed Familist, but their accounts of Familist meetings agree reasonably well with each other and with H.N.'s prescriptions.

For one thing, it is clear that a Familist congregation was a structured and disciplined group. The Guildford congregation is described as meeting secretly at night (with some frequency, it is implied) and possessing such characteristics of a secret society as passwords, ceremonies of admission, and a hierarchy of membership, with full status not to be attained before age 30. Meetings were strictly supervised by the officers, with the neophytes at one stage of the meeting being separated from the others. The Guildford document describes how group funds were collected and Romsye tells how he was promised that, if he were put in prison for the faith, the group's funds would sustain him there. Romsye also remarks that the Wisbech congregation always kept in mind that it had 'an infinite number' of fellow-believers 'in all countries of Christendome.'

How, in detail, a Familist meeting was conducted is not clear. Both the Family's printed tracts[61] and several references in the Guildford deposition indicate that Bible-reading (and of course expounding the Bible) was part of it. The deponents also referred to ceremonies such as the admission of new members with a kiss, washing of feet, baptism, and the laying on of hands; to the celebration of marriage and the sacraments by the 'bishop' or elders; and to the officers' instructing the more seasoned members in 'doctrine' after the neophytes have been asked to withdraw.

It seems likely, however, that discussions of doctrine were not limited to seasoned members, for statements about Familist beliefs take up the largest part of both these 'confessions' by relatively junior Familists. Most of these reported Familist tenets deal with men's daily conduct. In the Guildford deposition, for example, it is stated that alms are to be given only to members of the sect, and that members must in all circumstances be obedient to the civil power; Romsye's confession notes that clerics of the established church 'can not teache the truth' but that the church's sacraments, though meaningless for Familists, may still be 'receaved for obedience to the Quenes procedinge.'

But the reported beliefs also include more abstract points of theology – as the doctrine of the celestial flesh of Christ in Romsye's confession, and (in the Guildford deposition) denial of the Trinity and the statement that 'there was a worlde before Adam's time.' Many of the reported beliefs are as cloudily phrased as H.N.'s own, and one wonders how long and how tenaciously they were held. Some have the sound of propositions thrown out in argument rather than parts of a permanently held creed.

---

[61] *Epistolae HN*, pp. 212-13; Elidad, *A good and fruitful exhortation unto the Familie of Love* (STC 7573), sig. A 2ᵛ-4ʳ.

What they really show, it is suggested, is that a Familist meeting could include a discussion of all kinds of religious matters giving the members concern.[62] And, it would seem, there was a widespread sense of participation in such discussions, since the illiterate Thomas Chaundler of the Guildford deposition evidently felt quite capable of signing with his mark nearly all of the 66 items – those on points of theology as well as those describing how meetings were run.

6

The nature of the government's concern over the Familists is to be inferred partly from the chronology of the Privy Council's attention to the subject, partly from the wording of the royal proclamation. The Council register first mentioned them on June 13, 1575 – a year or so after the first Familist books in English – and then in a rather low key, as something to be taken care of by the Bishop of London's normal ecclesiastical machinery. The proclamation of October 3, 1580, on the other hand, put considerable emphasis on the menace of foreign-printed books and the need to search out and destroy them. Between the two dates, the vigorously anti-Familist publications of Rogers, Knewstub, and Wilkinson had appeared, and several suspected Familists had been discovered among the yeomen of the Queen's guard.

Nevertheless, a royal proclamation devoted entirely to one small sect does demand explaining. One explanation is suggested by the proclamation's reference to those who 'secretly in corners make privy assemblies of divers simple unlearned people.' Any group of religious separatists would seem somewhat disquieting, since the essentially autonomous nature of the sect put it beyond the varied controls of the ecclesiastical system that linked each parish ultimately to the Queen. A largely lower-class sect added further fears about 'the many-headed monster' and popular uprisings, particularly a sect that raised the spectre of vagabondage also.[63] The hostile William Wilkinson charged, among other things, that the Familists' 'chief Elders' were 'some . . . weavers, some basketmakers, some musitians, some botlemakers and such other lyke which by travailyng from place to place do get their lyvyng.'[64] And, unlike refugee Anabaptists, Familists could not be publicly stigmatized as foreigners; their founder, H.N., is so stigmatized, but they are not. Wilkinson, indeed, refers to them as having generally been

[62] Elidad, *A good exhortation*, A 2ᵛ-A 3ʳ, suggests that H.N. intended this.
[63] I am grateful to Christopher Hill for suggesting this point in commenting on a preliminary draft. See also his essay, 'The Many-Headed Monster in late Tudor and Early Stuart Political Thinking', *From the Renaissance to the Counter-Reformation*, C.H. Carter, ed., (New York 1965), pp. 296-324.
[64] *Confutation of articles*, fol. 30ᵛ.

baptized in the Church of England.[65]

The Familists also seemed more disturbing than most other religious dissidents because of their readiness to conform outwardly. There is an undertone of understandable frustration to the proclamation's complaint that they deny their true beliefs even on oath before magistrates.

The government's concern, both about this point and about the influx of books from the continent, probably reflected its much greater concern about possible Roman Catholic subversion. The influx of Familist books, roughly coinciding with the first missionary priests from the continent, would at least raise the question of how effective England's border controls were.[66] Moreover, the Familists' readiness to conform outwardly may have raised doubts about the government's basic policy toward English Catholics – a policy that required the outward conformity of church attendance but was not too inquisitive about beliefs. If the Familists' conformity was delusive, might not that of the 'church papists' be also? That the government in fact saw a parallel is indicated by Archbishop Sandys' 'Seventh Sermon', which attacks Familists for this kind of 'hypocrisy' in one paragraph and raises the same question about Roman Catholics in the next. Internal evidence would date the preaching of this sermon in mid-1580,[67] when worry about the Familists was rising and the pope had in the spring proffered a dubiously received olive branch: the intimation that, for the time being, English Catholics could disregard the bull of 1570 dethroning Elizabeth.

Why had the government relaxed its attitude toward the Familists by late November 1582? The loss of the Privy Council register for the five months before this prevents our knowing what discussion may have occurred, but there is some reason to believe that the Council had been of two minds about the Familists for some time past. In early 1581, for instance, it had first pushed punitive legislation in the House of Commons and then let the bill die. Possibly the government's position was influenced by the discovery that Familists were less numerous than had been feared. The Bishop of Ely's investigation of Familist groups in Wisbech and other parts of his diocese in late 1580 had resulted in

---

[65] *Ibid.*, fol. 11ᵛ.

[66] As far back as 1566 a royal letter had been sent to the Bishop of London about the danger of Roman Catholic books gaining entrance through the port of London (Cardwell, *Documentary Annals*, I, pp. 332-33), and in a memorandum probably written in Rome around 1575, William Allen had boasted that it was easy to smuggle Roman Catholic tracts into London from the southern Netherlands (Catholic Record Society, *Miscellanea* (Aberdeen 1911), II, pp. 64-65).

[67] Sandys, *Sermons*, p. 130; the dating I owe to Professor R.B. Pugh and Francis Edwards, S.J. Lord Burleigh had characterized the Family as 'papistical' in an incidental remark in his letter to Waslingham of August 8, 1578, *Calendar of State Papers, Foreign, 1578-79*, Butler, ed. (London 1903), p. 126.

interrogations of only some 60 members and sympathizers.[68]In addition, it may be that by November 1582 the government felt confident it had cut off the flow of Familist books from abroad. We can only guess.

7

In concluding, it is pertinent to ask what light the Familists shed on the larger subject of Elizabethan popular religion. In this dark area of sixteenth-century society, which lay so largely beyond the ken and control of the established church, separatist groups competed with evangelistic Puritans of the Church of England, with traditional priests giving routine conformity to the new Protestant order, and in effect with practitioners of both 'white' and 'black' magic. As on other aspects of past societies, we have fairly copious records of the appeals that the competitors addressed to their audiences, and very little directly about the response. By their nature, however, separatists have one advantage as a source in that they were outsider groups dependent for support on how accurately they met popular needs. Unlike a competitor such as the Puritan George Gifford,[69] Familists had no church pulpit to speak from. But they did have a popular appeal – one whose growth is suggested by the contrast between the early 1560s, when Familists were a matter of concern to a Surrey magistrate, and the years around 1580, when they were of concern to the Queen's Privy Council.

Of Familist literature, one may say that it seemed to expect no great interest in precisely formulated doctrine on the part of its audience. It assumed members of the Family to be a spiritual elite (as their opponents were quick to point out) but the doctrine of election was not set forth; transubstantiation was neither attacked nor defended; baptism was sometimes used as a figure of speech, and Familist religious practices were certainly consistent with 'believers' baptism' rather than with infant baptism, but the issue between the two was not argued in print. As has been seen, however, the Familist group at Guildford evidently had a taste for a kind of loose discussion of religious beliefs and their application to daily life. Whether for such discussion or for other kinds of emotional support, the close fellowship of the like-minded was evidently assumed by H.N.'s movement to be a popular need.

As to the role the printed word played for Familism, this seems to have been something more than just the discovery that printing had shortened the odds in any propaganda contest between a dissident religious group

---

[68] Heal, *op. cit.*, pp. 220–21.
[69] See particularly Gifford's *A brief discourse of certaine points of the religion which is among the common sort of christians*, 1581 (STC 11845).

and the establishment.[70] Despite the illiterates among the sect's members, the book had a significant role in the group's own life – suggesting that the appeal of the printed word was not limited to those able to read it for themselves, and that its influence in the lower levels of Elizabethan society may not yet be fully appreciated.

Appendix

Niclas' Alleged Stay in England

Writing in the mid-seventeenth century, the eminent church historian Thomas Fuller asserted that Niclas made a missionary journey to England

> and in the latter end of the reign of King Edward the Sixth joined himself to the Dutch congregation in London, where he seduced a number of artificers and silly women; amongst whom two daughters of one Warwick (to whom he dedicated an epistle) were his principal perverts. Mr Martin Micronius and Mr Nicholas Charineus, then the ministers of the Dutch congregation, zealously confuted his errors; but it seems their antidotes pierced not so deep as his poisons.[71]

Fuller's statement has an immediate plausibility to it in that Niclas did much moving about, voluntarily and involuntarily, during his long life, and many opponents of the Roman Catholic church flocked to England

[70] The Familists seem to have been the first dissident religious group to have made this discovery for England. The Lollards had never controlled a printing press, and Protestant exiles using the press against the Marian regime generally wrote as members of a true national church temporarily ousted from power. The Freewillers in Edward VI's reign had enjoyed a relatively permissive climate for publication: the government saw menace in the meeting they held at Bocking in 1550, but one of the two tracts of their leader, Henry Hart, was issued by a printer (John Oswen) who held a royal monopoly for religious publishing in Wales.

[71] *The Church History of Britain*, J.S. Brewer, ed., 6 vols. (Oxford 1845), IV, pp. 409-10.

during Edward's reign, some by invitation and others simply for refuge.

The one piece of written evidence Fuller refers to is *An epistle sent unto two daughters of Warwick from H.N., the oldest father of the family of love. With a refutation of the errors that are therein by H.A.,* Amsterdam, 1608 (STC 18553). This, read in context, gives useful information about the early history of Familism in England, but it does not support Fuller's assertion about H.N.'s physical presence there. Nor does the testimony of the two Dutch ministers as printed by well informed English opponents of Familism in the 1570s. They quote or cite a dozen pages or so from these and other Dutchmen about H.N.'s doctrines and, more briefly, about his physical characteristics, but cite nothing about his having visited England.[72] Furthermore, ten extensive letters of Micronius to Henry Bullinger, written from London in the latter part of Edward's reign (1549-1553) refer several times to the trouble caused by foreign sectaries and discuss in detail a number of these groups or their views, but with no mention of Niclas or persons who are clearly his followers.[73] We know of Niclas, moreover, that though he had to seek new places of refuge at various times in his life, the years 1540-1560 found him safely established in Emden.

The *Epistle* cited by Fuller is one of those documents which survive only in the successive paragraphs quoted by an opponent for purposes of detailed rebuttal. In this case, the early seventeenth-century separatist leader, Henry Ainsworth, prints 34 numbered paragraphs concluding with H.N.'s signature as 'your unknown friend,' and indicates in his preface that these were originally written to persuade two young followers of Niclas against 'suffering affliction for the ordinances of Christ against the Romish Antichristian doctrines and ceremonies.'[74] Niclas writes as if from some distance to these 'two young daughters of a certayn place named Warwick,' whose names he says he does not know, but whom he wants very much to convince that true religion is inner experience and does not require them to sacrifice their lives in protest against a mere outward ceremony such as the mass. He quotes I Corinthians 13 on the futility of giving one's body to be burned if one still lacks this inner religion.[75] The letter continues with various characteristic H.N. statements, insisting that it is only the workings of the spirit which give meaning to ceremonies such as baptism or to the letter of the Scripture. Cherished Protestant and Roman Catholic beliefs are ridiculed in adjoining paragraphs. The pope, he asserts, is not Antichrist: 'Antichrist is nearer unto us' and is indeed 'the wisdome of the flesh.' As to transubstantiation, it is absurd 'that God should be

[72] Knewstub, *op. cit.*, fols 87r-90v; Rogers, *Displaying*, 1579, sig. A 4r-5v.
[73] *Original Letters*, II, pp. 560, 574, 581.
[74] *Epistle to two daughters*, sig. A 1r.
[75] *Ibid.*, pp. 10, 64, 21 (H.N. paragraphs 1, 34, 4).

appeased with an elementish body,' as if God himself were 'fleshly.'[76]

The *Epistle*, while giving no support to Fuller's statement about Niclas' visit to England, does shed additional light on the early history of Familism there. The paragraphs quoted from H.N. may well be the earliest writing of his to appear in English and certainly show that by Mary's reign he had followers in England who would be guided by his advice (as Ainsworth's preface says the two Warwickshire women finally were). It makes more probable the assumption that Christopher Vitel was already coming under Niclas' influence when he spoke admiringly to Henry Orinel in 1555 about an unnamed man 'who lived. . . beyond the seas.'[77] It gives support also to the deposition made in 1561 that in the second year of Mary's reign Familist policy shifted from opposing the services of the Marian church to passively attending them, but it suggests that English Familists were then not yet under the full discipline of a congregational system and needed a message from Niclas himself on this issue.

[76] *Ibid.*, pp. 55, 61 (H.N. paras. 27, 28).
[77] Wilkinson, *Confutation of articles*, prefatory historical material, sig. AA 4ᵛ.

Additional Note

Since 'Elizabethan Familists and English Separatism' appeared in the 1980 *Journal of British Studies* two important books on Familism have been published:

Jean Dietz Moss, *'Godded with God:' Hendrik Niclaes and His Family of Love* (Philadelphia 1981), dealing mainly with the Family in England.

Alastair Hamilton, *The Family of Love* (Cambridge 1981), dealing mainly with the Family on the continent.

Chapter 11

Christopher Vitel: an Elizabethan Mechanick Preacher

1

'Mechanick Preachers' – as the seventeenth century pejoratively termed self-appointed lay evangelists of the artisan class – are associated mainly with the English Civil War period, which saw such notable examples as the Quaker George Fox and the Baptist John Bunyan. But though the famous figures come from the seventeenth century, authentic examples are to be found in the sixteenth century also. I am interested here in one such figure: Christopher Vitel, the reputed carpenter (or, more precisely, joiner) who was the acknowledged leader of the Family of Love in England during the 1570s.

The basic characteristics of the mechanick preacher are indicated by the term itself. 'Mechanick' emphasizes his coming from a part of society where a man lived by manual labour and was expected in religious matters to be a listener only. The category could include those who had been small farmers or small traders as well as artisans in the strict sense – the shoemaker, for example, to whom George Fox was once apprenticed would have sold shoes also. A tinker or other craftsman who carried his skills with him had obvious advantages over the husbandman or small merchant for part-time or itinerant evangelism. A mechanick preacher needed more than normal energy and force of mind, and his concern with religion – interior religion – was strong indeed. While ignorant of the ancient languages, theology, and other clerical disciplines, he was highly articulate in English and intimately acquainted with the vernacular Bible. To it he turned constantly for personal counsel and as the ultimate external authority in matters religious.

Preaching to others had usually been preceded by a restless search for personal religious certainty. Bunyan has vividly described his fears of hell, Fox his quest for one who would 'speak to his condition,' and the spiritual autobiographies of the seventeenth century record many parallel examples.[1]

---

[1] Bunyan, *Grace Abounding* (Cambridge 1927); Fox, *Journal*, J.L. Nickalls, ed. (Cambridge 1952), pp. 1-39. Not all Quaker and Baptist leaders were mechanick preachers, but most Quakers preachers (men and women) wrote spiritual

The search usually started from dissatisfaction with his own parish church's 'formal worship,' which a future Quaker saw as merely 'to read and sing and to rabble over a prayer;'[2] it then proceeded by various routes – sometimes through other parish churches to seek the guidance of more eloquent and apposite sermons, sometimes through discussions with other young men similarly concerned[3] or through temporary affiliation with one or more radical religious groups.[4] In the mechanick preacher's subsequent career his own immediate group, or conventicle, played an important part. It gave him not only economic help but also the needed emotional support of fellowship – a relationship which Tudor and Stuart governments seem to have recognized in directing their suppressive efforts not just at the radical preachers but at the entire conventicle membership.

2

The Family of Love, which Christopher Vitel led in England, originated on the continent about 1540 and, as described earlier in this volume,[5] continued to regard the founder, Hendrik Niclas (H.N.) as its chief leader. It was an evangelizing sect and England proved to be one of its major spheres of activity, seen largely through the circulation of H.N.'s translated works, printed abroad and smuggled into England in sizable quantities. The Family also aroused vigorous opposition there, both from the government (which issued a suppressive royal proclamation in October 1580) and from clergy of the Church of England. Three clerics – John Rogers, John Knewstub and William Wilkinson – each published detailed rebuttals of the Familist tracts and evidently made determined efforts to investigate Familist leaders.[6] Most of what we know about Vitel comes through them.

autobiographies and many Baptists did, as well as the founder of a rival sect, Lodovick Muggleton (*The Acts of the Witnesses of the spirit*, 1699). See William Y. Tindall, *John Bunyan, Mechanick Preacher* (New York 1934), Chaps. I, II, for a literary survey of the autobiographies, and Luella M. Wright, *The Literary Life of the Early Friends* (New York 1932), pp. 274–81, for a 105-item list of early Quaker autobiographical writings.

[2] Edward Burrough, *A warning from the Lord to the inhabitants of Underbarrow*, in *Memorable Works*, 1672, p. 14.

[3] For example, *Remarkable passages in the life of William Kiffin* (London 1823), pp. 10–12, where the future Baptist minister describes how he and fellow apprentices met for early morning discussion before attending one or another of the London churches.

[4] A minor Quaker preacher said he 'tried almost all persuasions among Protestants', John Gratton, *Journal*, 1720, p. 32.

[5] See chapter 10, section 2 above.

[6] John Rogers, *The displaying of an horrible secte . . . naming themselves the Familie of Love*, 1578 (STC 21181), 1579 (STC 21182), *An answere unto a wicked libel made by Chris. Vitel*, 1579 (STC 21180); John Knewstub, *A confutation of monstrous heresies taught by H.N.*, 1579 (STC 15040); William Wilkinson, *A confutation of certaine articles delivered unto the Family of Love*, 1579 (STC 25665).

Vitel's role in the history of the Family in England is hard to determine precisely. Unlike many of his seventeenth-century counterparts, he left no spiritual autobiography and, by accident or design, he seems to have stayed out of court and other public records. We do not even know the date or place of his birth and death. But the several hundred pages of anti-Familist tracts contain many personal references to him, and also include an aggregate of some 70 pages of direct quotations from Vitel and other Familist leaders. Various factual inferences can be drawn from the way these direct quotations rebut some of the hostile statements about him and let others stand. From the whole there emerges with reasonable coherence a figure fitting the general pattern of the mechanick preacher. Particularly marked is the restless search for personal religious assurance; Vitel's principal opponent, John Rogers, says of him that he 'could never lyke of any publicke doctrine which was taught but had always a desire for singularitye.'[7]

The assertions of Vitel's opponents that his evangelism had not always centered on Familism find some independent corroboration in the earliest firm record of Familist activity in England. This is a set of 66 individually attested depositions describing the sect, made by two disgruntled ex-members before a Surrey magistrate on May 28, 1561; the last five of the 66 items mention a number of Familist leaders, including Niclas, but Vitel's name is not among them.[8] By the late 1570s, however, Vitel's position is unquestioned: Rogers speaks of him as 'the oldest Elder of our English Familye,' and William Wilkinson, another well informed opponent, calls him H.N.'s 'heyre.'[9]

Vitel's occupation of joiner, or practitioner of the lighter kinds of woodworking, is much emphasized by his antagonists – partly for the traditional reasons and partly, it would seem, to give the impression of a man irresponsibly on the move, if not quite a vagabond. (Of the Family as a whole Wilkinson wrote that its 'chief Elders' were 'some . . . weavers, some basketmakers, some musitians, some botlemakers and such other Lyke which by travailyng from place to place do get their lyvyng.'[10]) His surname is variously spelled (the 't' or 'l' being sometimes doubled and a final 's' added): his national origin has been left sufficiently in doubt for some modern historians to have referred to him as a native Dutchman.[11] But his contemporaries, fond as they are of

---

[7] *Answere unto a wicked libel*, sig. L 4[r].

[8] Folger Library (Washington) MS L. b. 98.

[9] Rogers, *Displaying of an horrible secte*, 1579, sig. D 3[v]; Wilkinson, *Confutation of certaine articles*, fol. 46[v].

[10] *Ibid.*, fol. 30[v].

[11] *E.g.*, George H. Williams, *The Radical Reformation* (London 1962), p. 789, and a reference in Margaret Spufford, *Contrasting Cummunities: English Villagers in the Sixteenth and Seventeenth Centuries* (Cambridge 1974), p. 247. Neither cites specific evidence for assuming Vitel to be Dutch born.

stigmatizing him as an unlearned joiner, do not stigmatize him as a foreigner; they charge him, for example, with having brought Familism and other nefarious heresies 'into England . . . out of Delph in Dutchland,' not with having been born there himself.[12] Variants of 'Vitel' appear in contemporary records as an indigenous English surname,[13] and there is at least one mention of the Familist Vitel's having English relatives. Rogers, marshaling evidence that Vitel held Arian views during Queen Mary's reign, cites as a first-hand witness a 'cosin' of Vitel's, 'one Jone Agar, an olde mayde which wayted on those in office for the Cittye [of London] as Mayors and shrieffes.'[14]

Vitel's movement through various religious opinions is described by Rogers in 1579 as going back 'almost this 36 yeares' and continuing 'inconstant' through the last years of Henry VIII's reign and all of Edward VI's till Vitel became 'a playne Arryan' in Mary's reign.[15] An extended statement quoted by another of Vitel's opponents gives a first-hand picture of his evangelistic activities during this phase of his career. The person quoted – one Henry Orinel, husbandman, of the north Cambridgeshire village of Willingham – encountered Vitel in surreptitious Protestant meetings at Colchester in Essex, occurring (as Orinel records it) about Michaelmas 1555. That Vitel was already much attracted by Niclas is indicated by Orinel's remark that Vitel spoke highly of a man 'who lived as he sayd beyond the seas an holy life,' a man whom 'he praysed very much and reported many wonderful thynges of his Angellike behaviour.' But Vitel did not then identify this man nor, in contrast to his behaviour some years later when he sought Orinel out in Cambridgeshire, did he have a group of 'disciples' or try to get Orinel to join him. What stuck chiefly in Orinel's memory of the Colchester meetings were the 'many straunge opinions' which Vitel himself put forth. These included rejection of infant baptism, of the Edwardian Book of Common Prayer, of 'godly' people terming themselves miserable sinners, and of the belief that the pope was Antichrist. What impressed Orinel especially, however, was Vitel's holding the Arian doctrine that 'Christ was not God,' a position he maintained successfully

---

[12] Wilkinson, fol. 4ʳ; Rogers makes almost the same remark in *Answere unto a wicked libel*, sig. K 2ʳ, but earlier in this tract (E 8ᵛ) taxes Vitel with being reputed to be of Dutch ancestry, citing as evidence Vitel's 'falling from one error to another as those countrymen are apt unto.'

[13] The register of a London parish church notes the marriage on November 10, 1580, of a local girl to 'Sylvester Vittle of Gyllingham, son of Richard Vittle, yeoman.' (*Register of St. Peter's Cornhill*, Leveson Gower, ed., Harleian Society (London 1877), p. 232). London port records for September 1568 note a Christopher Vittell as the merchant importing miscellaneous textiles by the ship *Spredegle* out of Antwerp (*The Port and Trade of Elizabethan London*, Brian Dietz, ed. (London 1972), p. 128).

[14] *Answere unto a wicked libel*, sig. L 2ᵛ-L 3ʳ.

[15] *Ibid.*, K 3ʳ.

in extended debate with two orthodox Protestants, to the distress of Orinel and other orthodox listeners.[16]

These views attributed to Vitel can most of them be found in other sixteenth-century religious radicals, as well as in the voluminous writings of Niclas. Niclas, however, tends to give most of them a different emphasis and direction, since his usual purpose is to record as vividly as possible his varied religious insights, not to construct a logically coherent doctrinal system. When Niclas denies that the pope is Antichrist, for example, he is not trying to defend the pope but to attract attention to his assertion that Antichrist is the worldy wisdom within man himself.[17] It was not doctrine in the normal sense which gave power and coherence to Familism but rather H.N.'s personal leadership and the system of individual congregations which he set up. Vitel in 1555 does not himself seem to have reached this understanding of H.N., and in any case the impact he then left on Orinel was that of an Arian heretic.

The Arian phase of Vitel's career evidently came to an end sometime after 1558 with his making a formal recantation at Paul's Cross at the instance of Edmund Grindal, then Bishop of London. The nature and circumstances of this recantation were a subject of some subsequent controversy between Vitel and his clerical antagonists, but both sides seem to agree that it was Arianism, not Familism, that he recanted there; the disputed point is whether, as Vitel maintains, he recanted by voluntary arrangement with Grindal in order to clear his name.[18] The Family's attackers make much of the recantation as a way of emphasizing the previous Arianism and general religious instability of the man who had become Familism's principal English leader.[19] The date of the Paul's Cross recantation is uncertain. Rogers says it was 'in the first yeare' of Elizabeth's reign, 'as by the register of the bishop of London doth manifestly appeare,' but this recantation evidently did not attract the attention accorded the recantation of five Familists at Paul's Cross in June 1575.[20]

His espousal of Familism is described by Vitel himself in terms of complete conversion: 'when the Lord of his goodness had . . . opened mine eyes, then saw I that all people upon earth which were without the

[16] Wilkinson, prefatory historical material. The narrator's name appears there as both 'Orinel' and 'Crinel' but Dr Spufford establishes the former as the correct version (p. 246, n. 34) through her knowledge of Willingham local records.

[17] Niclas, *An epistle sent unto two daughters of Warwick*, 1608 (STC 18553), p. 55.

[18] Quoted in Rogers, *Answere unto a wicked libel*, sig. L 1ᵛ.

[19] Wilkinson, prefatory historical material; Rogers *Displaying of an horrible secte*, 1579, sigs. F 1ʳ, H 2; *Answere unto a wicked libel*, K 2ʳ-3ʳ, L 1ʳ-3ᵛ.

[20] Rogers, *Displaying*, 1579, D 3ʳ. The chroniclers Stow and Holinshed, who recount the 1575 recantation, ignore this one, as does the diarist Henry Machyn; nor is it mentioned in the record of Paul's Cross events by Millar Maclure, *The Paul's Cross Sermons, 1534-1642* (Toronto 1958).

house of love were all wrapped in unbelief . . . stryfe and contention, reviling, blasphemy . . . and condemned all others for hereticks and false Christians.[21] From then on he was sure of his vocation, but the date of this change also is uncertain. As already noted, he had apparently attained no prominence in the English Family by 1561 when the two ex-Familists made their deposition. Further testimony to the same effect is provided by an uncontradicted assertion of Rogers to Vitel relating to the circumstances of Hendrik Niclas' flight from the German city of Emden, an event generally dated in 1560. Vitel's statements on this subject, Rogers tells him, are based only on hearsay because 'at that time you were not acquainted with H.N. nor his doctrine.'[22]

At some time after 1561 and before 1574, when the first Familist tracts appear in English, Vitel presumably spent enough time on the continent to become recognized thereafter as H.N.'s principal representative in England, and to cope with the practical problems of translating, printing, and smuggling into England nearly all of H.N's varied works. These bear no printer's name or place of publication on them, and many are without even a date, but bibliographers now attribute them to the presses of Nicholas Bohmberg in Cologne.[23] Most of the publications appear to be no more than direct translations of H.N's works into English, with Vitel assuming no role but that of conveying an unchanged message to a new public.[24] That he possessed sufficient influence at Niclas' headquarters to get occasional adaptations made in Familist publications is, however, attested by the preface to the tract, *A reproofe spoken . . . against all false Christians* (STC 77) published under the name of Abia Nazaremus and bearing the date 1579. The preface denounces by name three books attacking the Familists in England: Stephen Bateman, *The golden booke of the leaden goddes*, 1577; Rogers, *Displaying of an horrible secte* in its 1578 edition; John Knewstub, *A confutation of monstrous heresies taught by H.N.*, 1579. Rogers' later attacks and that of William Wilkinson were presumably not yet available for denunciation.

One cannot say just how Vitel attained this close relationship with Niclas – in the seeking of which, John Rogers implies, he had much competition from other English admirers of Niclas.[25] Vitel's success is

[21] Quoted in Rogers, *Answere unto a wicked libel*, C 4ᵛ-C 5ʳ. Rogers has already in effect admitted (C 1ʳ) the fact of Vitel's sharp change of religious allegiance.

[22] *Ibid.*, E 7ʳ.

[23] The 1976 edition of the STC makes this conjectural attribution, altering the 1926 edition's similar attribution to Amsterdam. The hostile Stephen Bateman refers to Niclas as 'nowe of Colone' in his preface to the 1578 edition of Rogers' *Displaying*, A 8ᵛ.

[24] One statement quoted by Rogers suggests that Vitel's part was more one of supervising the translating than of personal participation: 'I have geven forth certayn bookes which we translated word for word as near as we could out of the bokes of H.N.' *Answere unto a wicked libel*, D 3ᵛ.

[25] Rogers, *Displaying*, A 3ᵛ.

easier to explain, however, if one assumes that he spent many of the years between 1559 and 1574 on the continent in an occupation giving him ready access to Niclas – that, in fact, he was during these years the textile merchant Christopher Vitell who is referred to in the London port record of 1568.[26] Dealers in textiles were a familiar phenomenon in the towns of the Low Countries (Niclas himself had been one throughout his working life), just as joiners and other itinerant artisans were in rural England. Nor, if we may credit Rogers' account of the Anabaptist David Joris' living unrecognized for eleven years in Basel as a conservative merchant, would Vitel be the only religious radical to adopt successfully a second identity.[27] Such a double identity for Vitel would also help explain how he, unlike many Familists, kept out of reach of the law at the time of the 1580 royal proclamation against the Family.

From 1577 on – when Vitel is first mentioned in a hostile tract[28] – there is no suggestion of any continuing foreign travel, but rather of missionary activities that keep him continually on the move within England. Rogers refers to him in one passage as based for a time in Southwark, but 'trudging about the country' to infect 'simple men with this poysoned doctrine;' elsewhere he remarks that Vitel's wife, 'resident in London,' is reputed not to have seen him for the past two years.[29] There was probably a strain of wariness also in this itinerating zeal, a wariness elsewhere obvious in the Familists' unwillingness – much commented on by their clerical adversaries – to engage in face-to-face debate with those who had the power to denounce and arrest them for heresy. (As Rogers put it in the passage about Vitel cited immediately above, 'In corners does this man creepe and dare not show his head.') Print was a more satisfactory medium for the Familists, offering both wider dissemination for their views and greater safety for their persons, but even in exploiting this their wariness was marked. Wilkinson describes how the Familists' written exposition of their views, earlier requested for printing in *Confutation of certaine articles*, reached him only by their being 'delivered to the common carrier in London.'[30]

The wariness of which Rogers and Wilkinson complained may have been what saved Vitel from arrest when the government adopted an increasingly repressive policy toward the Familists in the fall of 1580. Arrests were made in various parts of England, and some 60 persons interrogated in the diocese of Ely, which had been a centre of Familism as far back as 1561[31] but Vitel was evidently not apprehended. By the late

---

[26] See n. 13 above. I am indebted to A.G. Dickens for this very helpful suggestion.
[27] Rogers, *Displaying*, 1579, A 1^r-3^r.
[28] Bateman, *The golden book* (STC 1583), fol. 33.
[29] *Displaying*, 1579, A 3^r, D 3^v.
[30] In 'Preface to the reader'.
[31] Felicity Heal, 'The Family of Love in the Diocese of Ely', in *Studies in Church History IX: Schism, Heresy and Religious Protest*, D. Baker, ed. (Cambridge 1972), pp. 220-21.

autumn of 1582 the Privy Council's concern over the Familists had abated,[32] and though hostile references to the Family continue, it is no longer a major target as in earlier tracts. Whether by cleverness or by chance, Vitel seems to have escaped any further public note or notoriety; he simply disappears from the historian's view.

The influence Vitel exerted on fellow Elizabethan Familists was probably more constant and substantial than the written record can document directly. The Family itself underwent considerable change between 1561, when it was of concern to a Surrey magistrate, and the years 1575-1580, when it was repeatedly discussed in the Privy Council and made the subject of a royal proclamation. The difference between the two eras in the Family's life came largely from its exploitation of the printing press. We do not know how much of the responsibility for this was Vitel's, but, his share was probably greater than that of anyone else. One of the Family's lesser critics in the 1570s apparently considered Vitel's share comparable to H.N.'s own. Picturing the Familists in 1579 as a disruptive force in English society, the literary physician, John Jones, picks up a common hostile quip about the origin of the sect being divided between David Joris and Hendrik Niclas and adds Vitel's name as the third person responsible. Jones refers to the English Family as a bird 'laide by Davy George of Delf and hatched by Henry Nicholas of Amsterdam, but made fligge [fit to fly] by Christopher Vittel of Southwarke, Joiner.'[33]

Very occasionally, in remarks quoted by the Family's opponents, we get a hint of Vitel's skill as a controversialist. English Familists, as both they and their adversaries realized, had suffered a damaging blow when John Rogers obtained a copy of the very detailed deposition about the sect's beliefs and practices, made by the two disgruntled ex-Familists in 1561, and printed most of it as a 'confession' attached to his *Displaying of an horrible secte* in 1578. Disclosures since 1561 had provided at least partial confirmation for some of the assertions in the 'confession' so that few readers would find credible the insistence of one Familist, as quoted by Rogers, that the deponents 'never were of the Family of Love.'[34] Vitel, as quoted by Rogers on the same subject, shows the shrewd propagandist's sense of what can plausibly be denied and what can not. Vitel does not deny that the deponents were Familists of a sort but portrays them as only peripheral to the movement. He asserts that 'of H.N. his doctrine at that time they knew not' – implying that the

---

[32] It sent a letter on November 30, 1582, to local officials in Cambridge directing the release of certain now repentant Familists, Folger MS X. d. 30(9).

[33] John Jones, *The arte and science of preserving bodie and soule*, 1579 (STC 14724), p. 91. I owe this reference to Familists, along with a number of others, to Doris Adler.

[34] *Displaying*, 1579, sig. L 7ᵛ.

publishing of Niclas' teachings in English had made the 1561 state of the Family largely irrelevant.[35]

3

Comparing Vitel with the mechanick preachers of the seventeenth century, one is struck not only by the similarities of social background, temperament, and personal experience, but also by the differences three-quarters of a century has made in their situation. Both Fox and Bunyan could testify to the danger of imprisonment still faced by the unorthdox lay preacher, but they were not constrained to 'creepe in corners' and avoid oral debate to the extent Vitel was. And, with the breakdown of the established church's suppressive machinery in the early 1640s, conventicles and self-appointed evangelists had so increased in number that Quaker and Baptist preachers were almost as likely to be disputing with each other, or with other sectaries, as with the clergy to the established church. Proportionately more people than before were reading the Bible or tracts about the Bible. The existence of conventicles as small groups largely devoted to reading and expounding the Bible was not dependent entirely on the spread and increased availability of the English Bible – as had been shown by generations of Lollard activity without benefit of printing presses. But, as the history of English Familism had shown between the early 1560s and the late 1570s, the availability of the printed word for stating its case could make a considerable difference in the public attention a group received.

If it was indeed Christopher Vitel who perceived this and applied it to furthering the Familist cause in his time, then he may be partly responsible for the enhanced fortunes of the mechanick preachers – his spiritual kin – who came after him.

---

[35] *Answere unto a wicked libel*, K 1ᵛ.

Chapter 12

The Elizabethan Familists
as Perceived by their Contemporaries

1

The contemporary outsiders' perception of a religious group sheds light both on the group itself and on the society containing it. For a Tudor sect, the outsiders' views should be seen also in the long perspective of the Toleration Act of 1689 when sectaries were granted a limited legal status by their fellow citizens. In Tudor times, whether a group explicitly avowed separation or not (and till Elizabeth's last two decades hardly any separatist groups did) the situation was very different. The establishment then looked with deep suspicion on any self-selected group holding periodic meetings for worship and discussion of their religious concerns without the participation of an authorized cleric of the national church. The separatist, unlike the most radical of the Church of England clerics, was an unpredictable figure, outside the chain of authority which reached from the Queen through the hierarchy to the most remote parish church. He was someone who had set himself to a degree apart from the rest of Tudor society – how far apart, the pages following will try to examine. The sect known as the Family of Love, which in 1580 was the sole target of a royal proclamation, provides a useful case history.

Various questions arise regarding contemporary perceptions of any separatist group. To what extent did the public then – as historians often do now – identify a group of separatists by the specific points of theology they espoused? Did contemporaries make careful distinctions between one group of separatists and another, or did they tend to lump them under some comprehensive name such as 'Anabaptists' or 'Brownists'? (Sir Walter Raleigh, for example, when he spoke to the House of Commons in 1593 of ten or twelve thousand 'Brownists' in England, certainly had others in mind besides Robert Browne's immediate followers,[1] as Sir Andrew Aguecheek in *Twelfth Night* probably does

---

[1] Quoted in J. E. Neale, *Elizabeth I and her Parliaments, 1584-1601* (New York 1953), p. 289. Similarly, Francis Hastings, brother of the third Earl of Huntingdon, addressing the House of Commons in 1601, spoke of 'the Brownists or Family of Love' (without further elaboration) as one of the religious groups of which he disapproved, Claire Cross, *The Puritan Earl* (London 1966), p. 37, quoting from Simon D'Ewes, *Journal*, 1693 ed., p. 682.

when he declares, 'I had as lief be a Brownist as a politician.') How fully
can one explain the strength of the antagonism separatists aroused? Are
there indications of admiration for any aspects of the separatists that
helped bring an eventual change in the severe hostility toward them?

Answers to such questions can to some degree be inferred from the
way various members of Elizabethan society refer to separatist groups –
in the case examined here, to the then new sect called the Family of Love.
These 'Familists' left no lineal descendants much beyond the end of the
seventeenth century and, at least till the last decade or two, have received
little attention from religious historians. They do, however, exemplify
most of the separatist characteristics just mentioned, and they were
prominent enough in the England of the late 1570s to attract the repeated
attention of Elizabeth's Privy Council. Other case histories could be
found in earlier separatist groups such as the Lollards or the Freewillers of
Edward VI's reign (as well as in various later sects), but the Familists'
strikingly successful exploitation of the printing press gained them more
public attention that any other separatists in Elizabeth's reign.

As noted in greater detail earlier in this volume,[2] the Family of Love
was founded by the North German mystic, Hendrik Niclas (often
referred to as H.N.) in Emden about 1540, and on the European
continent attracted a following of intellectuals as at least secret
sympathizers. In England, where its appeal was mainly to the artisan
level of society, the first firm evidence of its activity comes from a 66-
point deposition before a Surrey magistrate, made by two disgruntled
ex-Familists who describe the life of their local congregation and
mention others in half a dozen English counties. Beginning in 1574, over
a dozen of Niclas' tracts, printed in English translation abroad, brought
wider attention to the group – which was known also as the
'Communialty' or 'Household' of Love. In 1575, five Familists made a
forced recantation at Paul's Cross, and between then and 1581 the Privy
Council discussed the sect on 13 different occasions. Niclas' apocalyptic
language attracted a special attention. He was fond of using traditional
Christian terms like 'baptism' in untraditional and inconsistent ways,
and often employed such phrases of his own as 'under the obedience of
the Love' and 'godded with God'. By the latter expression he apparently
meant the attainable culmination of the believer's efforts toward a closer
union with God, but to many of his contemporaries it seemed mere
blasphemy. His doctrinal writings were particularly offensive to Puritan
clerics, three of whom wrote detailed refutations, while one – John
Rogers – carried on an extensive controversy in print with the English
Familists' principal leader, an artisan named Christopher Vitel. Rogers
obtained a copy of the 1561 deposition by the two ex-Familists and
printed the greater part of it as an appendix to his 1578 tract, *The*

[2] See Chapter 10, Section 2, above.

displaying of an horrible secte of grosse and wicked heretiques, strongly implying that the group, among other things, practised communism of goods. The royal proclamation against the Familists was issued on October 3, 1580,[3] and early the next year Parliament for a time considered special legislation against them, but by late November 1582 the furor had evidently died down.

2

The present discussion is not concerned with the religious message which H.N.'s tracts, in hundreds of pages, tried to convey to the English reader. Nor does it deal, except tangentially, with the detailed case against the Family put forward by the three writers who had carefully read and annotated H.N.'s tracts, investigated the sect's associations abroad, and engaged in direct controversy with its leaders in England. The focus here is not on those who had made a study of the sect but on those whose opinion was more casually formed, who had done little more than overhear the specialists contending or possibly had a brief contact with a Familist. My concern here is not with Elizabethan Familism itself but with the public image of it.

As to the government's perceptions of the sect, the register of the Privy Council shows Familists to be a surprisingly frequent preoccupation in the period between June 1575 and January 1581 but does not convey any dominant impression beyond the evident assumption that they were a threat to public order and security. Of the 19 items relating to the sect, five have to do with the suspected Familists in the Queen's guard, another six with complaints about the sect's activity in various counties, three with protests from clergy ousted from their livings for suspected Familism, and the rest with moves to implement the royal proclamation or with similar suppressive measures. It is tantalizing, of course, to have recorded only the actions taken by the Council, not the discussions lying behind the actions.

The royal proclamation of 3 October 1580 does undertake to explain why the sect is dangerous, but since such documents usually had a propaganda dimension, the mention of a Familist characteristic in the text does not necessarily mean it was important in the government's own perception of the Family. Thus, in terming H.N.'s highly figurative language 'a monstrous new kind of speech never found in the Scripture nor in ancient father or writer of Christ's church', the proclamation was probably just making an easy propaganda point. Several other points, however, suggest real alarm over potential security problems raised by the Familists. For one thing, they are perceived as holding 'privy assemblies of divers simple unlearned people'. Another point is their

---

[3] *Tudor Procl.*, II, pp. 474–75.

having printed abroad certain 'heretical and seditious books' (four titles are given) which they 'secretly brought over into the realm'. Finally, Familists are said to believe 'that they may, before any magistrate ecclesiastical or temporal, or any person not being professed to be of their sect . . . by oath or otherwise deny anything for their advantage' – that is, conform to the Church of England outwardly while still holding their own religious convictions inwardly.[4]

All of these accusations had a solid basis in fact: Familists, for example, presented a well-argued case for their insistence that religion was ultimately a private matter beyond the province of public authority. Taken together, the accusations portrayed a group of people who seemed beyond the normal controls of church and state, and hence a potential source of rebellion. The Familists' ability to smuggle in their books from abroad may also have suggested to some members of the government the more serious overseas menace of Roman Catholic tracts and missionary priests; Lord Burghley, at least, had privately referred to the sect as 'papisticall' a year or two before.[5] It is perhaps noteworthy that Familists' belief in yielding outward conformity without reference to their real religious convictions is almost the only belief which the proclamation portrays them as holding. It is charged at one point that Familists believe only their own members 'to be elect and saved', but the 'heretical and seditious' content of the smuggled books is not otherwise indicated.

Turning to the perceptions found in the public at large, one finds that Familists sometimes seem to have aroused simple curiosity. A Latin letter of October 14, 1579, to Sir Philip Sidney from his friend Hubert Languet, the Huguenot diplomat, writing from Antwerp, makes it evident that Sidney has asked him to report what he can discover about the continental origins of this strange sect.[6] The situation has its ironies, in that the stories sent back by Languet about the sect's founder refer not to Niclas but to a notorious Anabaptist, Jan Williams of Roermond,[7] and that neither Languet, in giving Plantin's printing establishment as his Antwerp address for letters, nor Sidney, in writing to Plantin a few years later to order Ortelius's *Theatrum Orbis Terrarum* and several other

---

[4] Familists fall into the category denounced by Calvin as Nicodemists. Niclas had maintained that 'the secret bread of the Holy Woord doth not serve for everymans stomach' (*Epistolae HN* (STC 18552), p. 163) and had defended public recanting in the face of overwhelming power by the analogy of Deuteronomy 22. 25-27's justification of a woman's submitting to rape in a situation where her cries could not possibly summon help, *Dicta HN* (STC 18551), fol. 26.

[5] Incidental remark in his letter of 8th August 1578, to Walsingham, *Calendar of State Papers, Foreign, 1578-79*, Butler, ed. (London 1903), p. 126.

[6] *Huberti Langueti Epistolae Publicae et Historicae ad Philippum Sidneium* (Leiden 1646), pp. 397-99.

[7] H. de la Fontaine Verwey, 'The Family of Love', *Quaerendo*, VI (1976), pp 260-61.

books, shows any awareness of either the printer's or the geographer's having been a secret Familist.[8]

References to Familism in the press, by writers concerned primarily with something else, are about as hostile as those by the three clerics directly attacking the sect, but they occur in a variety of contexts. Familists figure prominently in some sharp pamphlet exchanges starting in 1580 between English Jesuits and a number of clerics of Puritan tendencies in the established church. Robert Parsons, advancing the familiar argument that Roman Catholicism stood for unity and Protestantism for disunity and a mass of sectaries, shows his awareness of both the Puritan clerics' differences with the church hierarchy and their antagonism to separatists by the way he introduces the Family into the argument. There are now in England, Parsons asserts blandly, 'fower known religions . . . distinct both in name, spirite and doctrine . . . the Catholickes, the Protestants, the Puritanes, and the householders of love, besides al other petye sects newly born and yet grovelinge on the ground'. This association of Puritans and Familists, put forward in the dedicatory epistle of a tract justifying Catholics disobeying the recusancy laws, is reiterated in the text proper and again by Parsons in a later controversial tract.[9]

A number of Puritan clerics replied with predictable anger to the Jesuit tracts, insisting that heresies like 'the Anabaptists and Familie of Love' antedate Luther and are to be blamed rather on the Roman church.[10] The authorities in Protestant England have taken strong repressive measures against the Familists, William Charke says, asking why those in Roman Catholic countries 'do so little to the punishment of them'.[11] These clerics and a number of others write from the implicit assumption that Familists threaten the integrity of the church[12] – a view repeated down to the final years of Elizabeth's reign, when a joint tract by John Deacon and

---

[8] Pierpont Morgan Library (New York), MS. M A 409; printed by Carl F. Buehler in *Review of English Studies*, XII (1936), p. 67.

[9] *A brief discours contayning certayne reasons why Catholiques refuse to goe to church*, Douai, 1580 (STC 19394), sig. A 3ʳ; Parsons, *A brief censure upon two bookes written in answere to M. Edmonde Campions offer of disputation*, Douai, 1581 (STC 19393), sig E 6. The 'Epistle Dedicatorie (to Queen Elizabeth), from which the first quotation comes, is formally ascribed to John Howlett, a pseudonym for Parsons; Douai imprints are believed to be covers for surreptitious printing. I am grateful for these Familist references to Doris Adler.

[10] William Fulke, *A briefe confutation of a popish discourse*, 1581 (STC 11421), fol. 13ᵛ; see also Percival Wiburn, *A checke or reproof of M. Howlets untimely screeching*, 1581 (STC 25586), fol. 16ʳ.

[11] *A replie to a censure*, 1581 (STC 5007), sig. P 1ᵛ; see also Charke, *An answere to a seitious pamphlet*, 1580 (STC 5005), A 1ᵛ; Fulke, *A retentive to stay good Christians*, 1580 (STC 11449), p. 125.

[12] See John Field, *A caveat for Parsons Howlet*, 1581 (STC 1044), sig. D 4ʳ; also John Dyos, *A sermon preached at Paules Crosse the 19th of July*, 1579 (STC 7432), fols. 61ʳ, 36ᵛ.

John Walker sees examples of such divisiveness coming 'from the Anabaptists in Europe, from the Donatists in Africke, from the Jesuites in Germanie, in France and elsewhere, from the Familists and Barrowists in England.[13]

Other writers saw the Familists, as the royal proclamation did, more as a threat to national unity. The literary physician John Jones, addressing himself to the governing classes and emphasizing the importance of a well educated orthodox clergy 'that Unitie may be maintayned and Sedition avoyded', not surprisingly sees the Familists as a threat to social concord generally. Mentioning the titles of several Familist books and obviously drawing on statements in the 1561 deposition by ex-Familists printed by John Rogers, Jones speaks of the Familists as 'congregating themselves in one house or other of the Familie, which if he be a disciple they call Rabbi, accompting all things in common otherwise than as the laws of God & our Prince doth warrant, teaching principles ful of sedition, communitie & blasphemie'.[14] Francis Shakelton, in *A blazyng starre or burnyng beacon seene the 10 of October laste* (1580), asserts that comets are signs sent from God, reminds his readers that false prophets are also foretold in the Bible, belabours the Familists as some of these and, without specifically mentioning the royal proclamation of 3rd October, rejoices that the Queen has now taken punitive action against them.[15] Thomas Rogers, who later became chaplain to Archbishop Bancroft, saw Familists as people who endangered the state by their refusal to bear arms – an allegation about their practices which he apparently took from the 1561 deposition printed by John Rogers. In dedicating to the Queen an anthology of Biblical passages, he speaks of the magistrate's duty to defend 'Religion, the Realme and good people' against foreign enemies, and insists that such a 'war is good, let the brainsick Anabaptists & the new fantastical sect, the Familists, imagine what they list.[16]

When writers do mention the theological tenets of Familism, they usually do so as a way of strengthening or illustrating the author's argument on some other topic. Thus, in a book stressing the importance for Christians of remembering the day of judgment, Thomas Rogers denounces the ancient Manichees for disbelieving it entirely and the modern Familists for maintaining it has already come[17] – referring apparently to Niclas's frequent insistence that 'now in the last tyme' the

---

[13] *A summarie answere to Master Darel*, 1601 (STC 6440), pp. 207-08. I am grateful to Jackson C. Boswell for this and the reference from Bishop Cooper noted below.

[14] Jones, *The arte and science of preserving bodie and soule in al health*, 1579 (STC 14724 a), sigs. O 3^r-4^v; S 1^r.

[15] Shakelton, (STC 22272), B 2^r-5^r; B 7^r-8^v.

[16] *A golden chaine taken out of the rich treasuries of the Psalms*, 1579 (STC 21235), sig. A 3^r.

[17] *The general session*, 1581 (STC 21233.3), p. 16.

biblical prophecies are fulfilled in the spiritual regeneration offered by Familism. Familist teachings about human perfectibility and union with God in this life are used by other writers against the Jesuits. John Field, accusing the Roman church of agreeing with various heretical groups on various doctrines, cites as an example 'that monstrous head of the frantike Family of Love, who perverteth all the scripture and glorieth in an essential righteousnes'.[18] Meredith Hanmer, attacking the Society of Jesus for their 'dayley meditations about divine matter', insists that 'heer the societie shaketh hands with the Familie of Love, who say that God is hominified in them and they deified in God'.[19] Shakelton, in his *Blazyng starre*, attributes to the Family the Arian denial that Christ is co-equal with God, mentioning it as one of the justifications for the Queen's outlawing the sect.[20] Stephen Bateman simply includes the Familists at the end of a long compilation about heathen gods and deviant Christian sects; Bishop Cooper casually categorizes them as 'blasphemous'.[21]

In view of the efforts John Rogers made to portray Familists as somehow related to the radical and violent Anabaptists of the continent and also as pro-Roman Catholic in their tendencies, it is rather surprising to find how seldom either of these identifications is explicitly made in other sixteenth-century publications. In the only Familist reference where the Anabaptists' seizure of Munster in 1535 is mentioned, the technique of guilt by association is applied against Roman Catholics as well as against Familists. Meredith Hanmer, in one of his anti-Jesuit tracts, writes: 'The Family of Love have their prophets and disciples. The Anabaptists out of Munster, the heade City of Westphalia, sent abroad (as Sleidan reporteth) in the evening 26 Apostles. And the Pope hath lately, about 40 yeares past, confirmed the sect of Jesuits & sent them abroad, in the evening of the world, with the Anabaptists . . .'[22] Other references are explicit in their charge that Familists at least incline toward Rome.[23] John Field, who apparently sees heresy as adopting different guises in different eras, refers in the preface to one of his translations of French Protestant writers to a recent profusion of 'Anabaptists, Libertines (which are indeed at this day al shrouded and fostered under

[18] *A caveat for Parsons Howlett*, sig. D 1ʳ. See also Field (translator), *Thirteen sermons of Maister John Calvin*, 1579 (STC 4457), preface, A 3ʳ; also Charke, *A replie to a censure*, sig. P 2ʳ; Shakelton, *A blazyng starre*, B 7ᵛ-8ʳ.
[19] *The Jesuites banner*, 1581 (STC 12746), sig a 3ʳ. See also Hanmer, *The great bragge and challenge of M. Champion*, 1581 (STC 12745), A 4ᵛ.
[20] *A blazyng starre* B 7ᵛ-8ʳ.
[21] Bateman, *The golden book of the leaden goddes*, 1577 (STC 1583), fo. I 53ʳ-35ᵛ; Thomas Cooper, *An admonition to the people of England*, 1589 (STC 5683), p. 74. See also Richard Greenham, 'Fifteenth Sermon' in *Works*, 5th ed., 1612 (STC 12318), p. 362; also Bateman, *The doom warning all men to judgement*, 1581 (STC 1582), p. 414.
[22] *The great bragge and challenge*, sig. A 4ʳ.
[23] Charke, *Replie to a censure*, sig. P 1ᵛ; Wiburn, *A checke . . . of M. Howlett*, fo. I. 16ʳ.

the name of the familie of Love . . .'.[24]

Certain other aspects of the Family emphasized by John Rogers, or the royal proclamation, are virtually absent, or treated with surprising lightness, in the references by other writers. Only John Jones mentions Familists as practising economic communism, a statement made in the 1561 deposition printed by John Rogers but not made in other exposés of the sect and finding no real support in H.N.'s writings.[25] Nor are Familists generally perceived as either foreigners or dissemblers, despite the innuendoes attempted in the royal proclamation. More surprising is the scarcity, during Elizabeth's reign, of passages associating 'Family of Love' with sexual love, though the 1561 deposition contains a few low-key suggestions that Familist sexual mores were somewhat unconventional, and there were to be many suggestions to this effect in the Stuart period. The Elizabethan fondness for playing on words resulted in various jabs such as 'that lovely family' or 'family of lust', in much the same vein as the burst of rhetoric about ' a familie of falshode, a familie of pride, a familie of idolatry, a familie of ignorance and folie', in John Dyos's Paul's Cross sermon of 1579.[26]

In one of Barnabe Rich's romances the term Familist is used as a counter-epithet to 'Puritan'. Don Simonides, quarrelling with his friend Antonio, calls him a 'dispiser of beautie and disparager of women . . . an Hereticke and . . . too precise Puritan'; Antonio responds with, 'I take you to be of the Familie of Love. If I be to precise, thou art to pevish [out of one's senses; mad]'.[27] But the literary satirists' deliberate assumption that the Family's 'Love' was to be interpreted as Eros seems to have started with Thomas Middleton's early Jacobean stage comedy, *The Family of Love*, which drew recognizably on portions of the 1561 deposition and portrayed two citizens' wives as using secret night meetings of the sect for assignations with their gallants.[28]

By the last decade of the century still another public image of the Familist had appeared – that of the deluded fanatic, more a nuisance than a danger. In such a role the Familist could provide a useful device for those wishing to make indirect attacks on powerful opponents. Richard Hooker, really aiming at Puritan targets, could speak of how 'Familists

[24] Philip de Mornay, *A notable treatise of the church*, Field, trans., 1579 (STC 18159), sig. A 5ᵛ. See also Field, trans., *Four Sermons of Maister John Calvin*, 1579 (STC 4439), A 4ᵛ; Jones, *The arte and science*, O 4ᵛ.

[25] Jones, *The arte and science*, O 3ᵛ.

[26] Dyos, *A sermon . . . the 19th of July*, (STC 7432), fo. I. 62ʳ.

[27] Barnabe Rich, *The Strange and wonderfull adventures of Don Simonides*, 1581 (STC 21002), sig. T 2ʳ.

[28] See William G. Johnson, 'The Family of Love in Stuart Literature: a Chronology of Name-Crossed Lovers', *Journal of Medieval and Renaissance Studies*, VII (1977), pp. 95-112.

imagine the Scripture everywhere speaketh in favour of that sect'.[29] James VI, writing about statecraft shortly before he succeeded Elizabeth on the English throne, was concerned about religious dissidents (inside and outside the established church) as a divisive force in the nation and as a people who invoked scruples of conscience for thwarting the royal will. He evidently thought it more politic to use the term 'Familist' in denouncing such persons, and he does so comprehensively, ignoring distinctions among the various dissident groups. He speaks of 'that vile sect among the Anabaptists called the Familie of Love,' refers to Robert Browne and John Penry as leaders of it who have tried to evangelize Scotland, and mentions stands taken about the use of the surplice in worship and popish tendencies in bishops – matters with which the historic Familists had never concerned themselves. But he evidently felt he had a recognized public image to refer to – that of people, as he put it, 'agreeing with the general rule of all Anabaptistes in the contempt of the civil Magistrate and in leaning to their own dreams and revelations . . . accounting all men prophane that answeres not to their fantasies . . . making the Scripture to be ruled by their conscience & not their conscience by the Scripture'.[30]

Hints that their fellow Elizabethans found anything about Familists to admire are few, guarded and indirect. The Surrey magistrate, Sir William More, was more disposed than many of his countrymen to see Familists as a menace (as is testified by a letter of his lamenting over-leniency by ecclesiastical authorities toward a Familist missionary), but the fact remains that he preserved in his papers manuscript copies of two songs from the English version of Niclas's *Cantica*, identified as Familist in More's own hand but with a few words of the scribal copies altered to make them less characteristically Familist in tone.[31] The noted Puritan divine, Richard Greenham, generally a denouncer of Familists,[32] and one of the ministers brought in by the Bishop of Ely to reason with imprisoned members of the Wisbech congregation in 1580,[33] has one rather ambivalent passage about Familists which seems to accept implicitly one of their standard complaints against the beneficed clergy. 'In these days', Greenham remarks, 'we attribute so much to ministerial knowledge, and have so little profit by the teaching of the Spirit, and . . . we brag so much of faith and have so little love;' therefore, he continues, 'the Lord for contempt of his truth doth now teach us by deluding spirits

---

[29] *Laws of Ecclesiastical Polity* (Oxford 1887), p. 148.
[30] *Basilikon Doron* (STC 14349), sigs. B 4^v; b 1^r-2^r.
[31] Folger Library MS L. b. 51; Folger MS L. b. 589.
[32] See 'Grave counsels and godly observations', *Works*, 5th ed., 1612 (STC 12318), p. 3; 'Of prophesie and preaching', *Works*, p. 770.
[33] Felicity Heal, 'The Family of Love in the Diocese of Ely', in *Studies in Church History IX: Schism, Heresy and Religious Protest*, D. Baker, ed. (Cambridge 1972), p. 220.

and fantastical devisers and the lying Familie of Love.'[34] The popular success of the Familists, he implies, should show the Puritan clergy that in emphasizing the objective doctrinal side of religion, they have been neglecting its subjective side, the inner spiritual experience which should accompany theologically sound belief.

Laurence Chaderton, the future head of Emmanuel College, preaching at Paul's Cross in 1578, when clerical concern over the Familist threat was rapidly rising, similarly saw the sect's popular appeal as highlighting shortcomings of the Church of England. 'And surely,' he said, 'it is our shameless conversation that terrifieth both the ignorant and wavering Catholicks and the simple sort of the common people, beyng ready to imbrace any religion (as appeareth by these which have imbraced the erroneous doctrine of H.N. and his familie, falsely termed the familie of love) from the true profession of the gospell of Jesus Christ.'[35] Later on, when official fear of the Familist menace had receded, Chaderton became one of those using the Family as an arguing point for a particular interest of his own. In a sermon published the same year as Emmanuel was founded as the great training institution for Puritan divines, he asked why superstition and immoral conduct had persisted so long and 'whence come such swarm of atheists, idolaters and papistes, erroneous and heretical sectaries of the family of love and such like?' – and immediately supplied the answer: 'There are no doctors to teach, nor pastors to exhort.'[36] A page or two later he expatiated on the advantages to the authorities (both secular and religious) of having a nation-wide network of parish ministers through whom they 'might truely knowe, within a short tyme, by name, who and how many enemies there are . . . to religion and the common wealth. How many obstinate, malicious and traiterous Papistes? how many Anabaptists, Libertines? how many of the Family of Love? how many Atheists?'[37]

A still different comment came from Thomas Rogers. Indefatigable in his detailed pursuit of Familist theological errors,[38] he nevertheless conceded that their daily lives were as decorously conducted as one could desire. 'For who, never seeing their bookes,' he asked rhetorically, 'would thinke that to be a Familie of ungodlines & heresies which so

---

[34] *Works*, p. 453. The passage occurs in his long 'Exposition on the 119 Psalm' and, unlike most things in Greenham's collected works, can be accurately dated, there being a marginal notation, '1580 & 1581'.

[35] *An excellent and godly sermon . . . preached at Paules Crosse*, 1578 (STC 4924), C 5^r.

[36] *A fruitful sermon . . . upon 12 chapter of St. Paul to the Romanes*, 1584 (STC 4926), p. 72.

[37] *Ibid.*, p. 73.

[38] In Rogers's work, *The Catholic Doctrine of the Church of England*, published in stages from 1585 on, index references to Familists in the standard 19th century edition, J.S. Perowne, ed. (Cambridge 1854), outweigh all competing entries except 'papist'.

discrete men, sober women, so aunceient fathers, so grave and godlie matrons, doe favour?'[39]

3

What conclusions about the Elizabethan Familists' public image are suggested by these varied references? First, of course, the references support the familiar view that religious separatists as such were generally regarded as subversive of both church and state – a view evident not only in official documents but in books addressed to the sixteenth-century reader generally. The modern reader who is surprised by the intensity of feeling shown against an insignificantly small group may reflect that, in an era when England's population could be assumed to contain no non-Christians, a group that seemed to threaten the integrity of the church would also arouse the feelings involved in xenophobia.

But, while many references to Familists confirm or illustrate the familiar, others have their surprising aspects. James VI might confound Familists with other religious dissenters, but most references to them show more discrimination. Though Familists were evidently regarded as quite as inimicable to orthodox Protestant England as Anabaptists or Roman Catholics were, the efforts of John Rogers to imply that Familists were almost the same as either of these do not seem to have convinced many other writers. Familists were at least conceded an identity of their own. Nor is significant attention given to the trait complained of in the royal proclamation: Familists' willingness to give a deceptive outer conformity when pressed.

These perceptions of the Family by outsiders also provide some hints as to how separatism may have gained public acceptance. Cases cited above show an aspect of Familism (its emphasis on interior religion, for example, or its appeal to uneducated common people) which evokes a little grudging admiration from convinced opponents. These aspects have little to do with Familists' doctrines, however, which seem to have interested other Englishmen only to the extent that such beliefs confirmed already existing unfavourable views of the sect or could be used as arguments against Roman Catholics.

It is surprising also, in mid-Elizabethan England, to find how greatly such a sect's position has come to depend on the printed word as a means of communication. As noted earlier, the Familists themselves were very active in using the press for propaganda, being evidently aware (among other things) of how it could help the individual evangelist keep out of harm's way; taunts about this practice appear sporadically in the long

[39] *The general session*, pp. 23, 24.

tracts of the Family's principal opponents.[40] The more casual views of the sect expressed by outsiders also reflect this situation. Scarcely any of the references examined suggest that it derives from a face-to-face contact with a Familist. (Possible exceptions are some of the quotations from Richard Greenham and Thomas Rogers a few paragraphs above.) On the other hand, a number of these anti-Familist statements seem to have been based on John Rogers' printing of the 1561 deposition, and for one or two of these (notably the assertion that Familist congregations practised economic communism) there is no other known source.

One must end by noting the tentative nature of these conclusions, which are based on dozens, not hundreds, of references and concern only a single sect, a sect in some ways far from typical. The Family's name, its unusual command of printing facilities, and possibly the adventitious circumstance of John Rogers' obtaining and printing the 1561 deposition about the Guildford congregation, all tended to give it special attention. Tending to keep Familists out of the public eye, on the other hand, was their conviction that true religion was so private a matter that they could – under duress – validly conform to the outward observances of the national church. There were no Familists burnt at the stake like the Dutch Anabaptists in 1575 and Francis Kett in 1589, or hanged like Henry Barrow, John Greenwood and John Penry in 1593. Sects by their very nature differ from each other as well as from the established church, but the Familist characteristic drawing heaviest attack in this period was that common to all sects: the simple fact of worshipping apart.

Nevertheless, a number of the statements suggest an underlying assumption that Familists are something that must be lived with, not a cancer that can be excised once and for all. Such an assumption is illustrated in two very different writers who mention the Familists a decade or so later than the well-researched books attacking them in detail and the royal proclamation suppressing them. Thomas Nashe, in the boisterous descriptions of the London scene in *Pierce Peniless his supplication to the devill* (1592), refers to 'adulterous Familists' (and several other contemporary sects) along with impecunious youths parading in fine clothing, rich and threadbare money-lenders, foolish merchants' wives, and similar targets of satire.[41] Earlier, in a 1589 pamphlet replying to some of the *Martin Marprelate* tracts, Nashe had listed 'all the upstart religions in this Lande: the Anabaptists, the Familie of Love, . . . the diversities of Puritans and Martinists . . .'[42] The Puritan cleric George Gifford, in the seventh sermon of a series on the Book of Revelation, sees 'the Anabaptists, Lybertines, Familie of Love and other such monsters'

---

[40] See William Wilkinson, *Confutation of certaine articles*, 1579 (STC 25665), Preface to the reader; John Rogers, *Displaying of an horrible secte*, 1579 (STC 21182), sigs. A 3ʳ, D 3ᵛ.

[41] Nashe, *Works*, R.B. McKerrow, ed., 5 vols. (Oxford 1958), I, p. 171.

[42] *Ibid.*, I, p. 74.

as Satan's instruments in contemporary England, paralleling similar instruments used 'in the Apostles times.' The presence of such sects, he adds in an anti-Catholic jab, cannot be blamed on Protestants' 'preaching of the Gospell' any more than the earlier heresies can be blamed on 'the preaching of the Apostles.'[43]

Such references to the Familists, of course, are still a long way from a perception of England as a religiously pluralistic society, but they are pointed in that direction. A further step may be identified a half-century or so later in John Milton's anti-prelatical tracts. Using 'Familists,' like 'Brownists' and 'Anabaptists,' as a generic term for separatists, he labels prelacy's claim to be defending England against dangerous sects as a 'fraudulent aspersion' and asserts that 'the Primitive Christians in their time were accounted such as are now called Familists and Adamites, or worse.'[44]

[43] George Gifford, *Sermon upon the whole booke of Revelation*, 1596 (STC 11866), p. 80.
[44] *The reason of church government urged against prelaty* (1641), *Works*, Columbia ed. (New York 1931), III, p. 217.

Index